I0812996

IMAGES
of America

MARSHALL

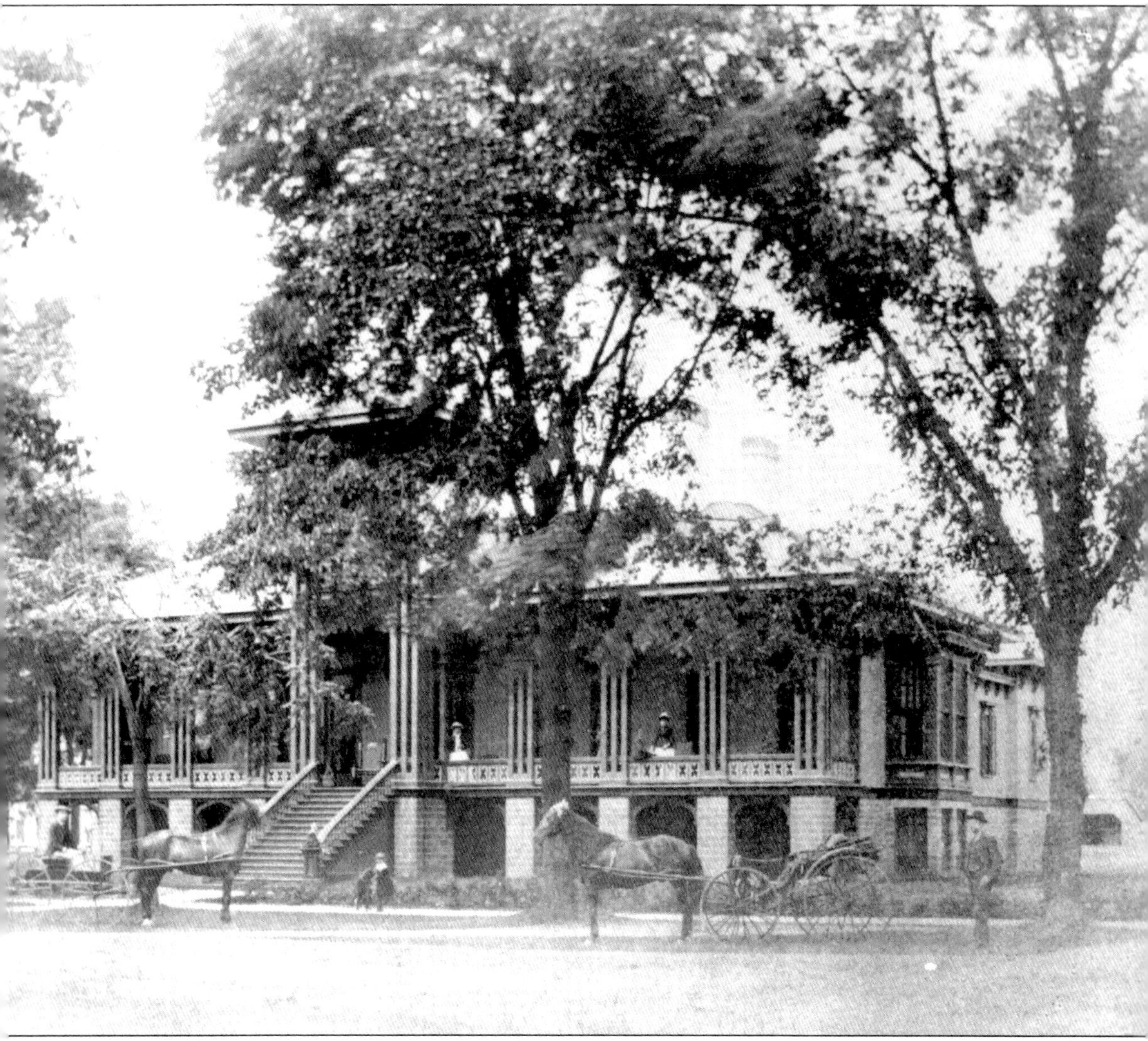

With more than a touch of whimsy and a big dose of tropical fever, Judge Abner Pratt was determined to bring back more than just a few trinkets from the Sandwich Islands (now called Hawaii), where he had served as U.S. counsel in the early 1850s. Returning to Marshall because of his wife's illness, Pratt wanted to create the tropics in this charming Michigan town, which is a recipient of the Dozen Distinctive Destinations award by the National Trust for Historic Preservation. Pratt hired architect William L. Buck to design a home that combined Victorian and tropical features both inside and out using exotic woods shipped from the Sandwich Islands. What they created is the lush Honolulu House, which anchors the city's historic downtown and is run by the Marshall Historical Society. One of many splendid homes in Marshall, it stands at the edge of the downtown welcoming all.

On the cover: As horses gave way to cars, taxis were the way to travel. Here they line up in front of a garage at this Marshall taxi stand. Note the drivers in uniform. (Courtesy of the Marshall Historical Society.)

IMAGES
of America

MARSHALL

Susan Collins and Jane Ammeson
in cooperation with
the Marshall Historical Society

ARCADIA
PUBLISHING

ISBN 978-0-7385-5117-3

Published by Arcadia Publishing
Charleston, South Carolina

Printed in the United States of America

Library of Congress Control Number: 2006939092

For all general information contact Arcadia Publishing at:
Telephone 843-853-2070
Fax 843-853-0044
E-mail sales@arcadiapublishing.com
For customer service and orders:
Toll-Free 1-888-313-2665

Visit us on the Internet at www.arcadiapublishing.com

This book is dedicated to John Collins for making the history of Marshall so much fun for the last 35 years and to Martha Jones for sharing her love of history with me when I was a child.

—Susan Collins

CONTENTS

ACKNOWLEDGMENTS

As with any book about a community, it took a lot of help from many people to make this happen. We would like to thank the citizens of Marshall who so kindly went through their families' and churches' old photograph collections and shared them with us. Among those are Helen Hensick, Ann Weinert, JoAnn Dickey, Howard Butson, Jim Leonard, Tina Hamilton, Becky Davis, Mike Schragg, and Gerry Lehman. We would also like to thank Sue Moore of Schuler's Restaurant and Sarah and Karl Loomis for making available their collection of memorabilia of William Wallace Cook. Debbie Pardoe was very generous with her vast postcard collection, and John Twist brought a treasure trove of his grandfather Harold C. Brooks's photographs.

A large number of photographs included in this book belong to the Marshall Historical Society. Cherie Riser and the board were very nice to allow us to scan them for inclusion. We did rely on the research of the three authors of Marshall histories written in the last 30 years: Dr. Mabel Cooper Skjelver's *Nineteenth Century Homes of Marshall, Michigan*, Robert Lowman and Richard Carver for their *Marshall Public Schools: the First 150 Years*, and Richard Carver's *A History of Marshall.*

If it were not for family to listen to us we would not have had the ability to finish. Peggy Wright listened to the ups and downs with her usual good nature.

INTRODUCTION

An architectural treasure and one of the largest National Historic Landmark Districts in the country, with over 850 buildings in that district, Marshall had its beginnings way back in 1830, as the winter snows were beginning to melt. That was when Sidney Ketchum, a land speculator from Peru, New York, pulled his horse to a stop along the banks of Rice Creek and the Kalamazoo River. Here, Ketchum decided, would be a perfect spot to start a settlement. An admirer of Chief Justice John Marshall of Virginia, Ketchum named his community after him and hoped that Marshall would become the state capital. For a while, that seemed so likely that many prominent professional people—judges, lawyers, doctors, and even two ambassadors—moved here. And Marshall prospered—within seven years of when Michigan had become a state, the population had grown to 1,000. When the vote to move the state capital was finally taken 10 years after that, the city lost out to Lansing, which in 1847 had only eight registered voters. But Marshall rebounded, becoming a major stop on the stagecoach lines that connected Detroit to Chicago and then also a center for the burgeoning railroad industry.

Marshall was a station along the Underground Railroad and a strong antislavery city whose citizens were not afraid to stand up for what they believed to be right. When Kentucky slave chasers tried to capture escaped slave Adam Crosswhite and his family (the couple had five children), who had settled in Marshall, the town's citizens instead arrested the Kentuckians. They aided the Crosswhite family's escape to Canada, an act that could have put their property, freedom, and even their lives in jeopardy. But these valiant people chose instead to help and were convicted of "depriving a man of his rightful property" in a Detroit federal court in 1847. They paid fines of $1,926 (a large amount of money back then) and considered it not a shame or a hardship but a badge of honor. The Crosswhite family returned after the Civil War, and Adam Crosswhite now rests in the town cemetery, just a few hundred feet from several of his rescuers.

Marshall also sent many men off to war, some of whom would never return. They are remembered now at Grand Army of the Republic Meeting Hall, built in 1902 by Marshall Civil War veterans as a meeting place for their organization, the Grand Army of the Republic. The hall now houses a museum dedicated to the city's history and valiant war efforts.

While in Marshall, take time to stroll the historic downtown where architectural styles include Victorian commercial, Greek Revival, and Italianate. Make sure to stop in at the Shops of Marshall House, which once was a stagecoach stop, and the Mole Hole where live music is often performed on the old Barton theater organ (from the Garden Theatre, once across the street) by Scott Smith, who is the store's staff organist. Stop in at Schuler's, a fourth-generation family business and one of the oldest restaurants in Michigan.

Because history is important to Marshall, the Marshall Historical Society offers several wonderful museums, including the Honolulu House, a fanciful home built in 1860. There are more museums here as well, including the American Museum of Magic with three floors of artifacts and props from all the great stage magicians of both the 19th and 20th centuries such as the escape apparatus used by Harry Houdini. But besides that, the museum also features a half million pieces of memorabilia from thousands of lesser-known practitioners of the magical arts. The Marshall Postal Museum, housed in the Greek Revival–style post office built in 1932, is the second largest in the country and contains memorabilia from the early advent of postal history. Features include a storefront post office from the 1890s, a horse-drawn mail buggy dating from 1905, old uniforms, and railroad mail sacks, as well as a restored 1931 Ford Model A one-half-ton mail truck.

The stories of Marshall, its buildings, and its people are stories of triumph over tragedy, hard work, and, overall, a recognition of the city's special heritage that connects the past to the future.

One

Downtown

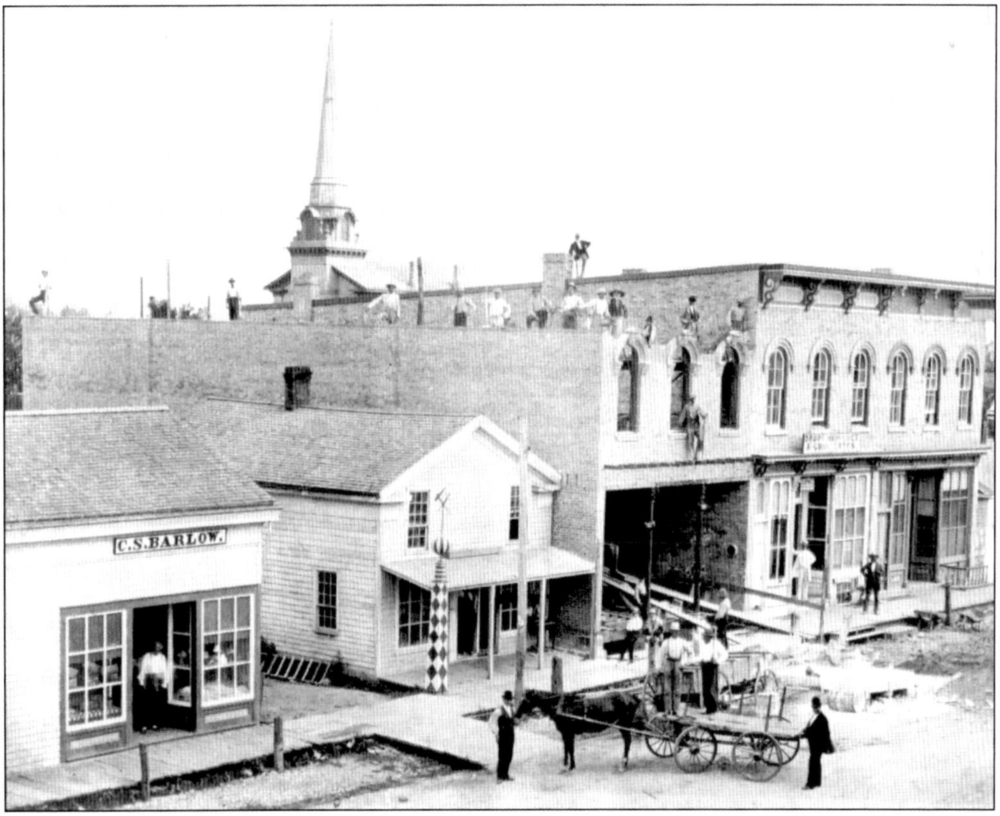

In the beginning, the streets were made of dirt and were either dusty in dry weather or muddy in wet. But still, downtown Marshall thrived, as the city movers and shakers built attractive edifices that survive to this day. According to historian Mabel Cooper Skjelver, the architectural tradition of southern Michigan is based upon the New England and New York heritage of the area's early settlers.

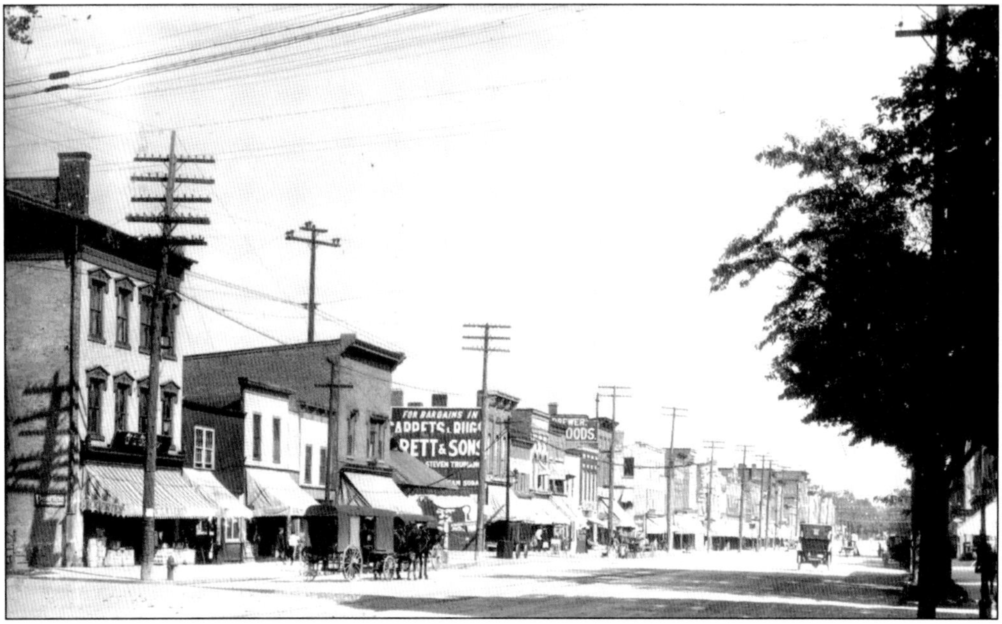

By 1913, around when this photograph was taken, horses and buggies, although still one way to get around, were being replaced by cars. Electricity had also come to Marshall with fancy streetlights (notice that there are no electrical lines in the preceding photograph). This is a view of Michigan Avenue, at the time still called State Street.

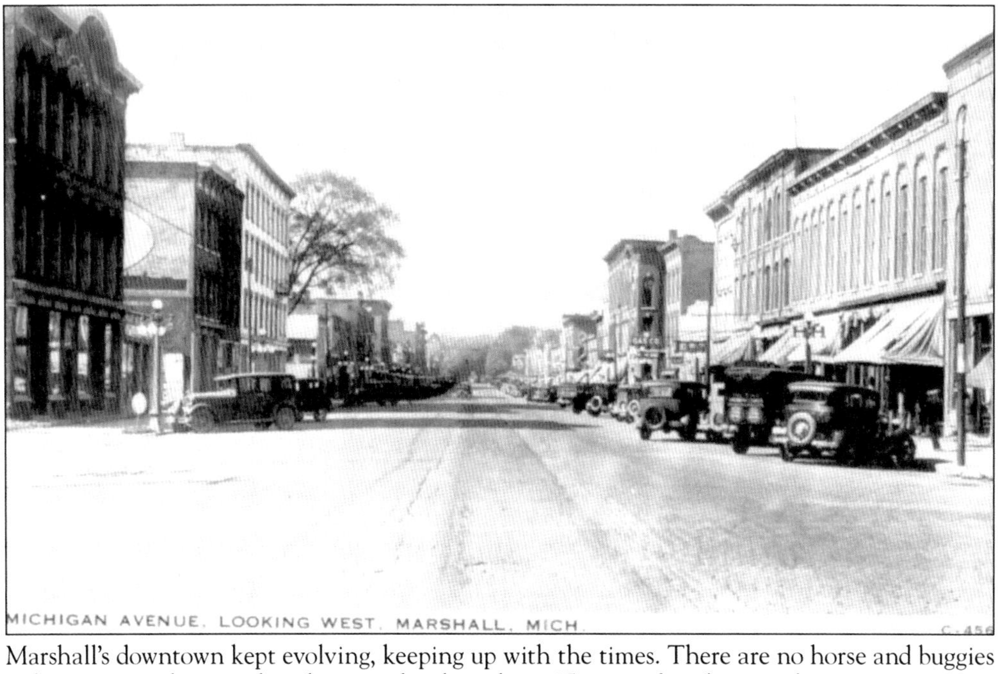

Marshall's downtown kept evolving, keeping up with the times. There are no horse and buggies to be seen anywhere in this photograph taken about 15 years after the one above.

The Cook family owned several stores in downtown Marshall and was an important part of the city's social and commercial life. Here, in this building located at 219 East Michigan Avenue, Col. C. T. Cook opened a store in 1855 in a building that replaced the Exchange Hotel, which burned down in a fire in 1846.

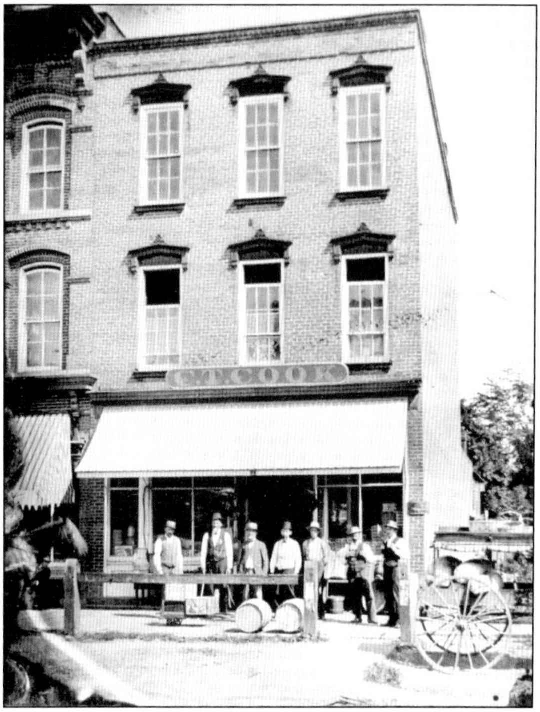

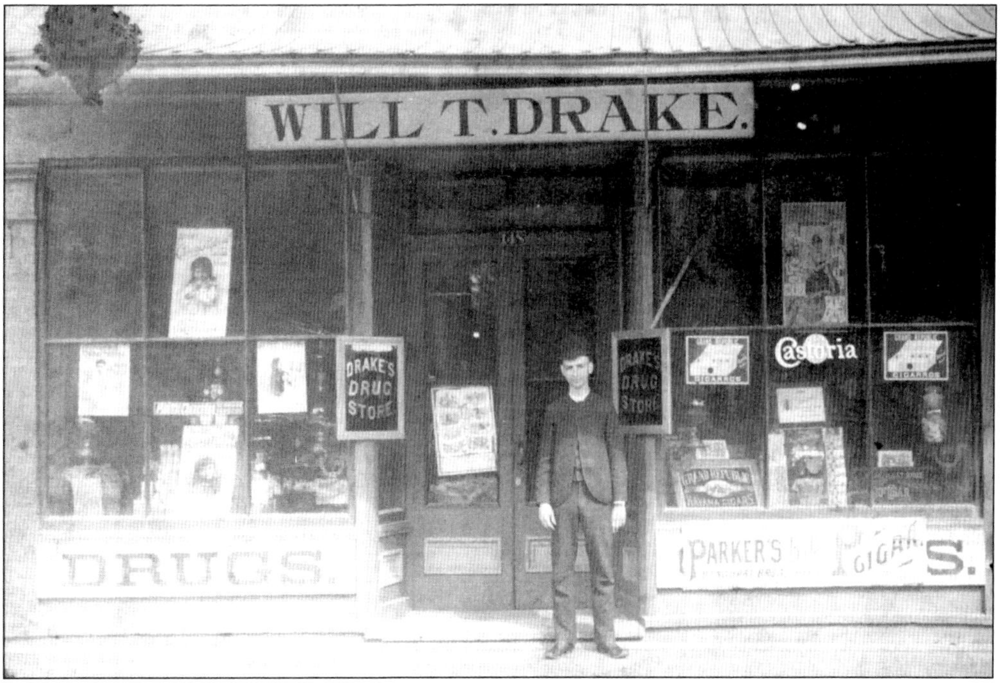

In an old photograph labeled "the Pill Doctor," a man stands in front of a pharmacy. Will T. Drake, most likely pictured here, opened his drugstore at 140 West Michigan Avenue. Drake, besides owning the pharmacy, also took over telephone service, which had been located in an office in another pharmacy. According to *A History of Marshall* by Richard Carver, the cost of a telephone call to Battle Creek in 1883 was 15¢ for five minutes.

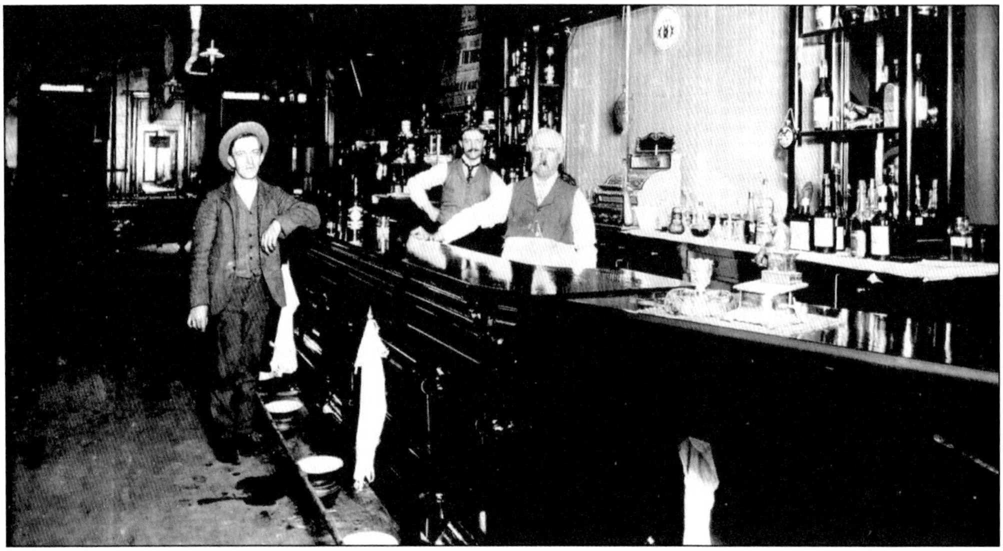

No downtown would be complete without a place to stop for a drink (back in the old days, most saloons served men only). This photograph is labeled "Charlie Noneman Saloon," which, after Noneman bought it in 1883, changed names from the Ben Faust Saloon. Charlie's brothers, Louis and Ernest, also worked there. It is now the site of the American Museum of Magic, located at 107 East Michigan Avenue.

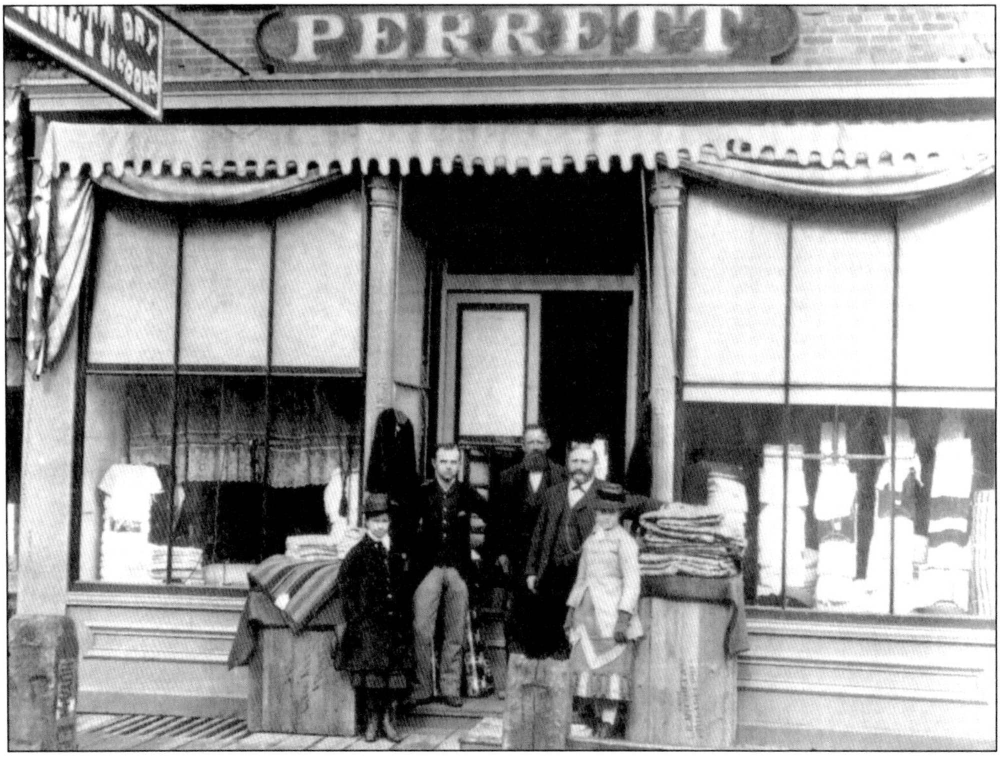

George Perrett and Sons Dry Goods was located at 146 West Michigan Avenue. Perrett bought the business in 1868, and he and his sons ran it until 1918. This photograph is from around the late 1800s.

Another dry good business, this one owned by C. D. and E. G. Brewer, was located at 202 West Michigan Avenue. This photograph, taken in 1870, shows the muddy streets. Boards were laid down to help keep people's feet from getting too dirty.

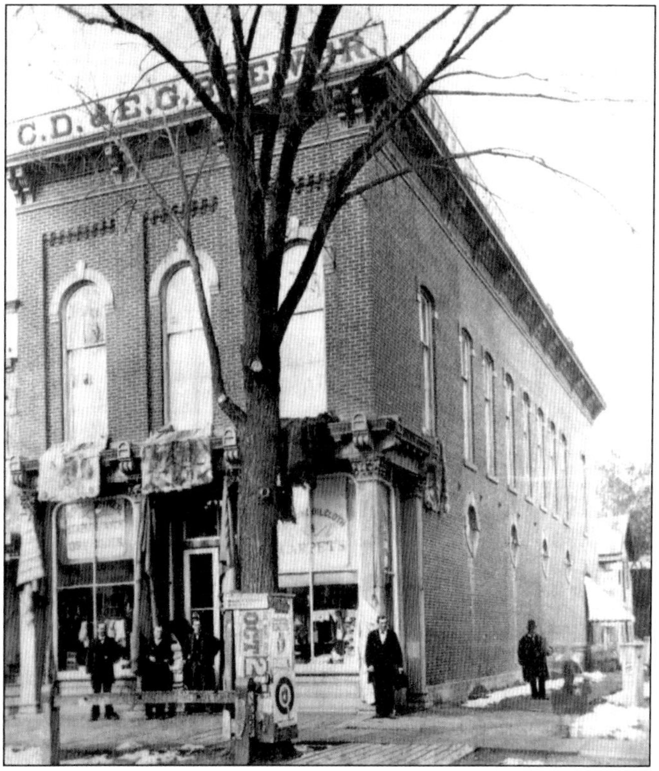

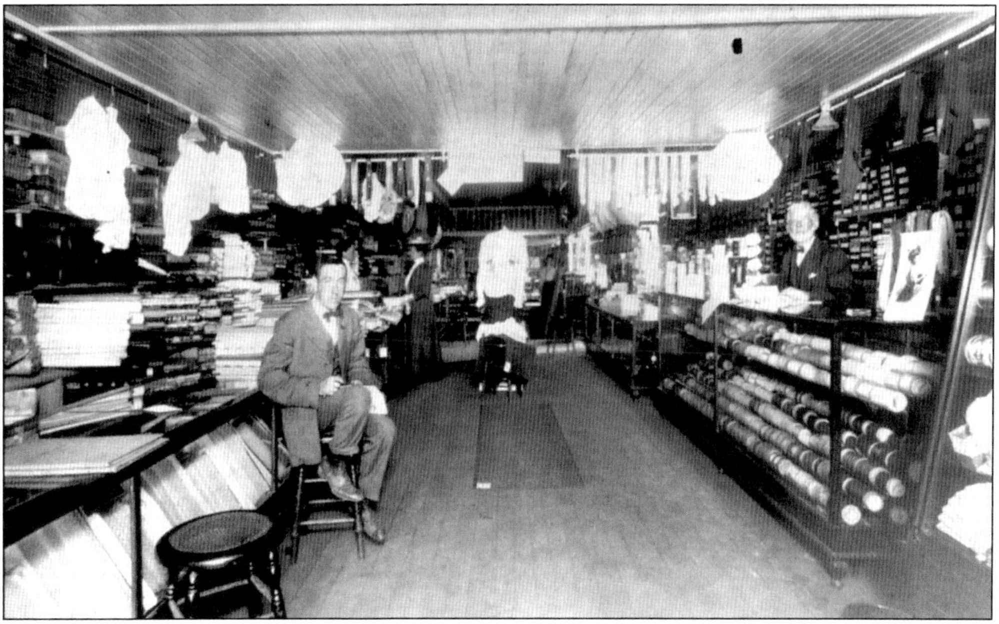

The interior of the Brewer family dry goods store is pictured here. Chauncey M. Brewer started a dry goods business with Charles T. Gorham (both were from New York) in 1836. They moved to this site two years later. When Gorham left the partnership, the store changed names, first to Butler, Brewer and Dusenbury, and then, when Chauncey's sons joined him, it changed again. The Brewer family was involved in this business, for the most part, until 1925.

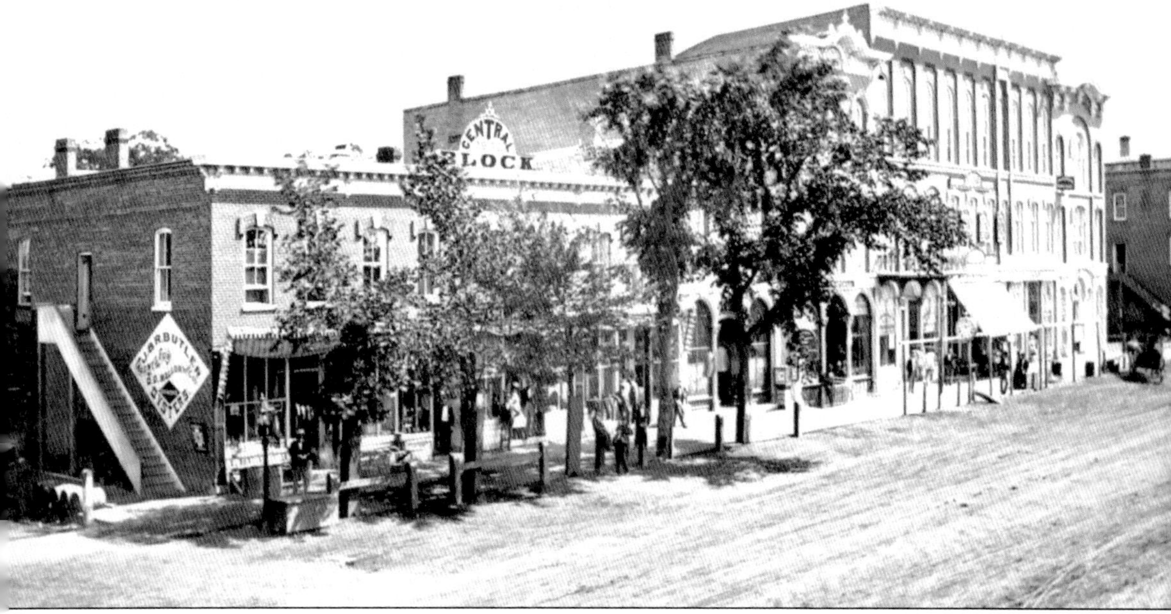

The J. and R. Butler Grocery store was located on the north side of State Street. The street's name would later become Michigan Avenue in 1923 when Marshall, in response to a request to all towns on the route between Detroit and Chicago made by the state, changed the name. Note that the Butlers are advertising the sale of oysters—a food that had to be shipped quickly by railway from the East Coast.

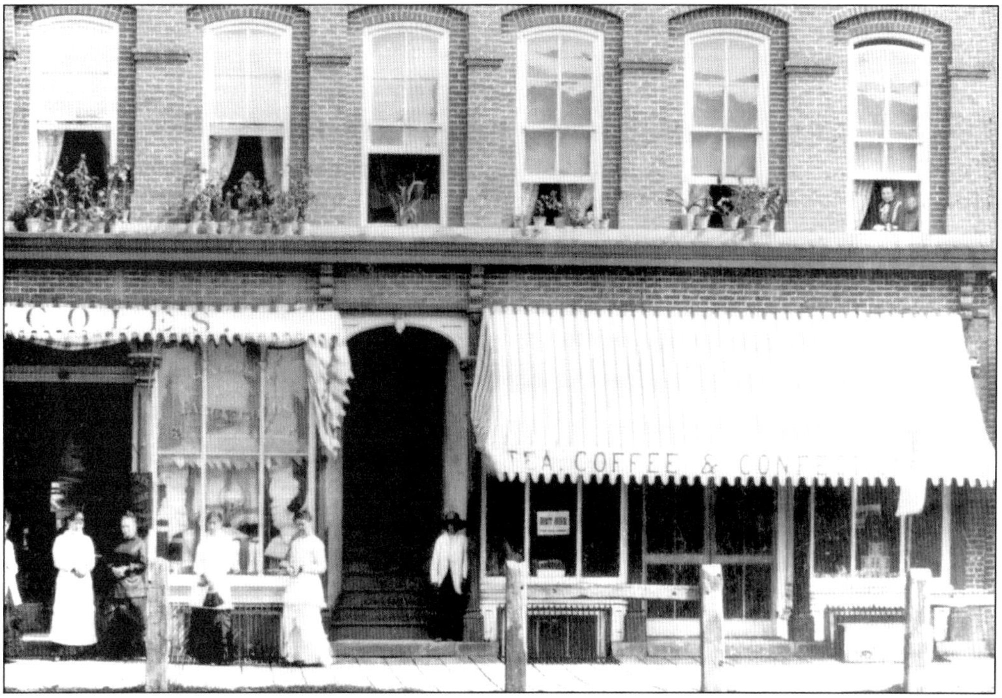

Built in 1863, this building at 305 and 307 East Michigan Avenue housed Sally Cole's Dress Shop (note the women out front in all their finery) and E. W. Potter's East India Tea Company where one could also buy candy and other sweets. On the second floor, people peer out the window, and flowerpots sit on the ledges. This photograph was taken in the 1800s.

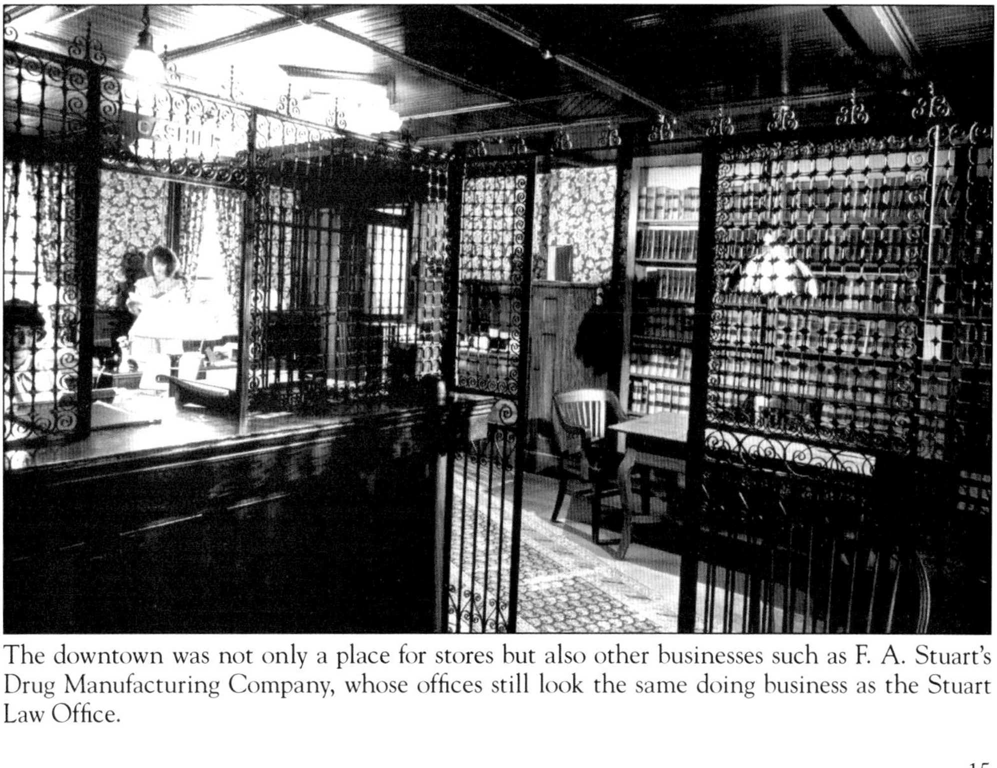

The downtown was not only a place for stores but also other businesses such as F. A. Stuart's Drug Manufacturing Company, whose offices still look the same doing business as the Stuart Law Office.

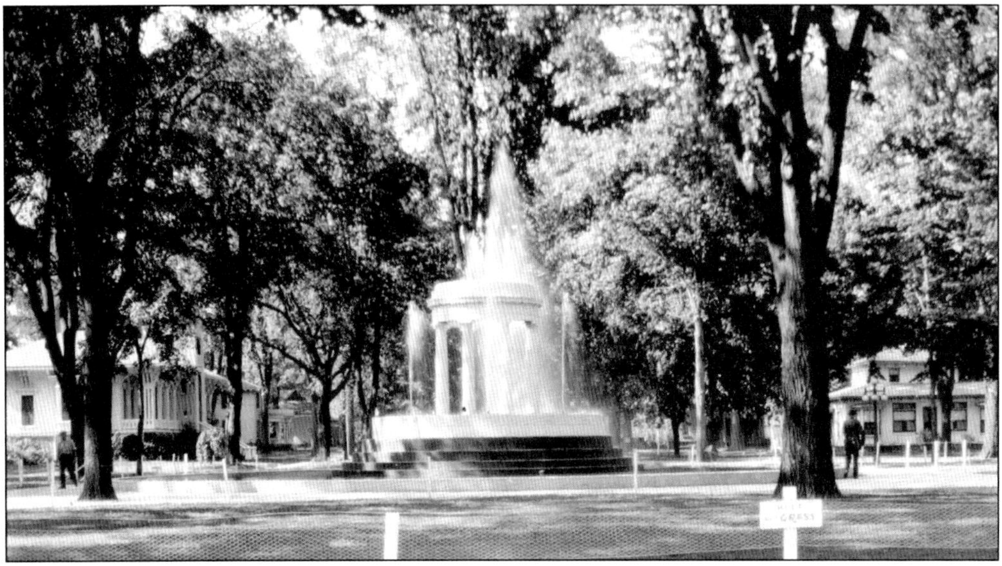

The Brooks Memorial Fountain was dedicated by Harold C. (H. C.) Brooks, one of Marshall's most illustrious citizens, a noted historian, philanthropist, and owner of the Brooks Rupture Appliance Company, to his father, Charles E. Brooks. The fountain, with Greek Doric columns, stands on Fountain Circle. Nearby are the town hall, which at one time was a livery, with its magnificent clock tower, and the internationally renowned Honolulu House, built in 1860 and now open to the public.

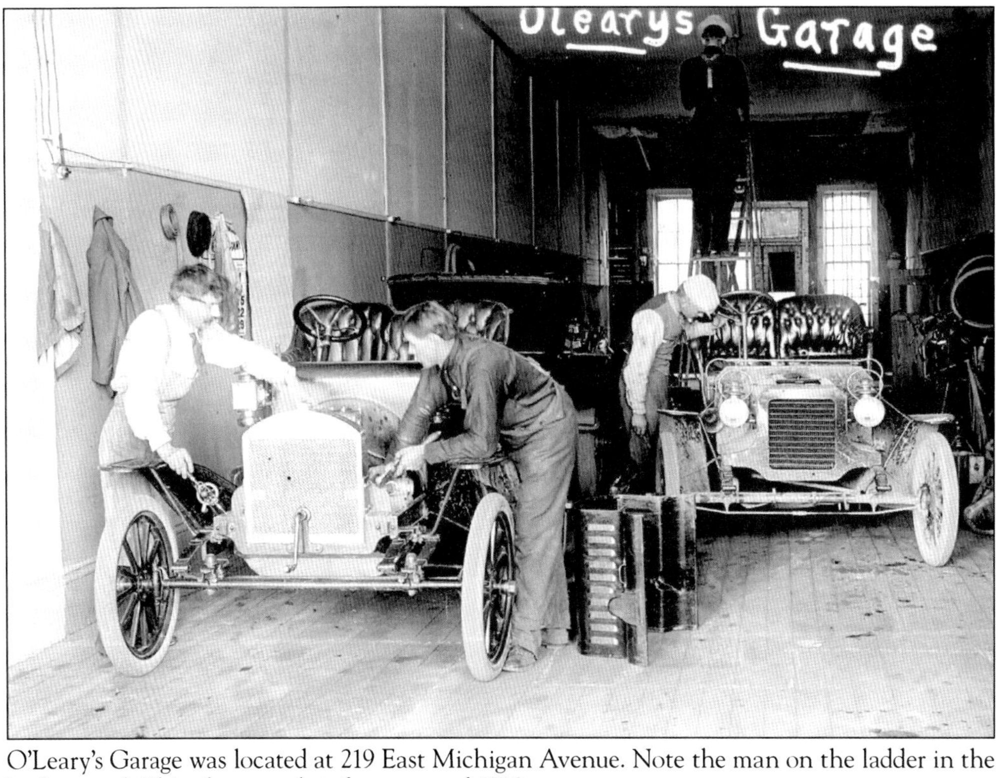

O'Leary's Garage was located at 219 East Michigan Avenue. Note the man on the ladder in the background. This photograph is from around 1910.

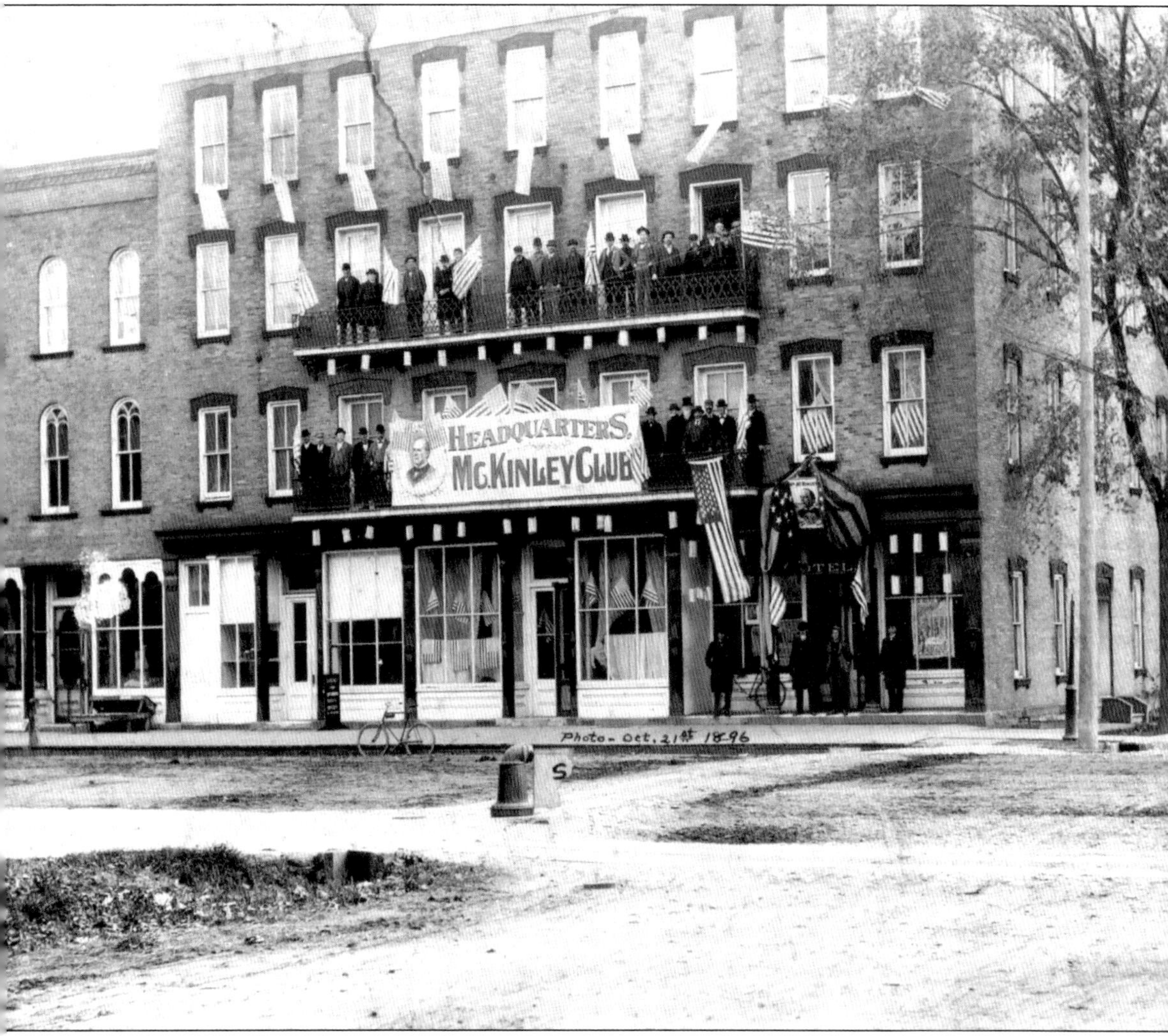

Pres. William McKinley's campaign headquarters in Marshall was located in the Herndon Hotel at 202–206 East Michigan Avenue, the site of the current U.S. post office. This photograph was taken in 1896. Over the years, many important politicians have visited or lived in Marshall, including Pres. William H. Taft, several governors, three ambassadors, and W. D. Boyce, a Chicago farm journal publisher, explorer, and author, and the founder of the American Boy Scouts. His stately 1860 Victorian mansion was built on land once owned by author James Fenimore Cooper. It is now the Rose Hill Inn Bed and Breakfast.

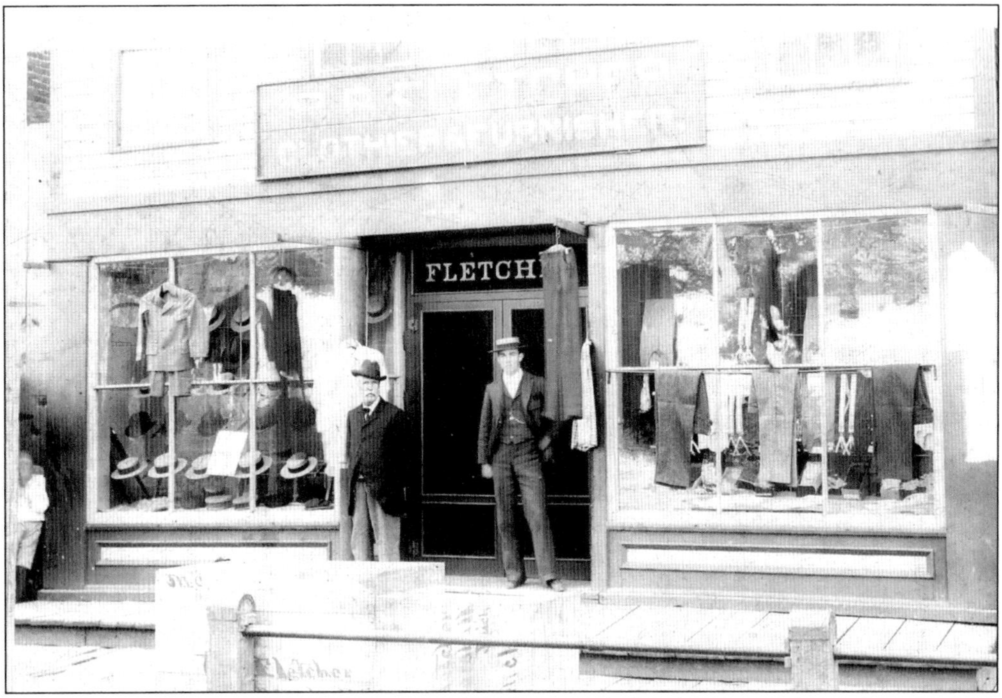

Fletcher Clothier and Furnisher, as seen in this photograph dated 1897, was located at 105 West Michigan Avenue next door to Lee Cheung Laundry.

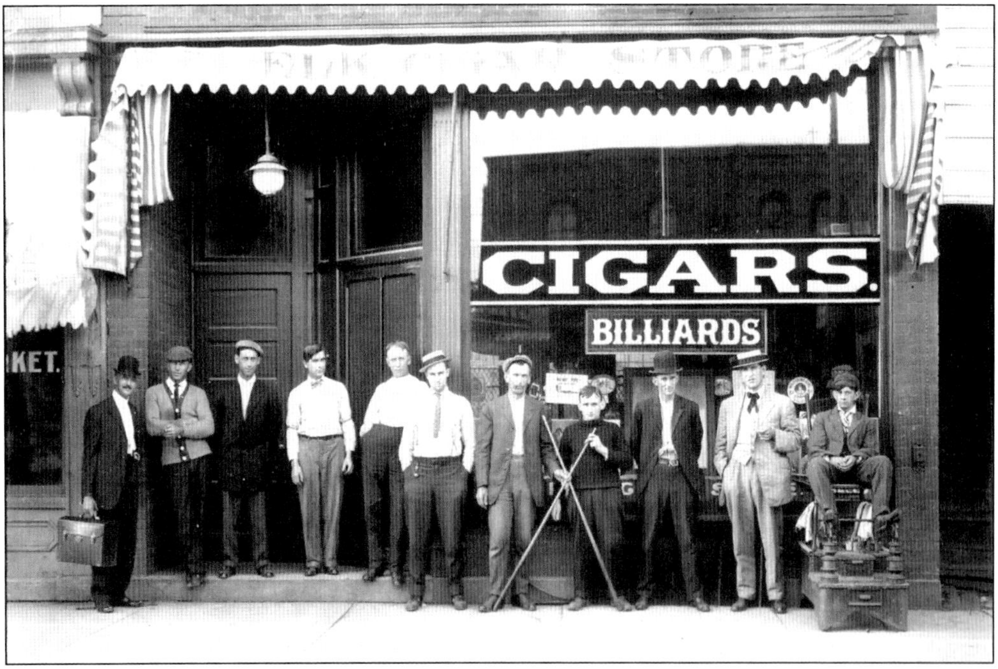

Every town had to have its billiards parlor where men could shoot pool and smoke a cigar, and Marshall was no different. The Elk Cigar Store and Billiard Hall was located at 208 West Michigan Avenue. Third from the left is William S. Murray, sixth from the left is Clyde Jacoby, and second for the right is Doc Haller, rural free delivery carrier.

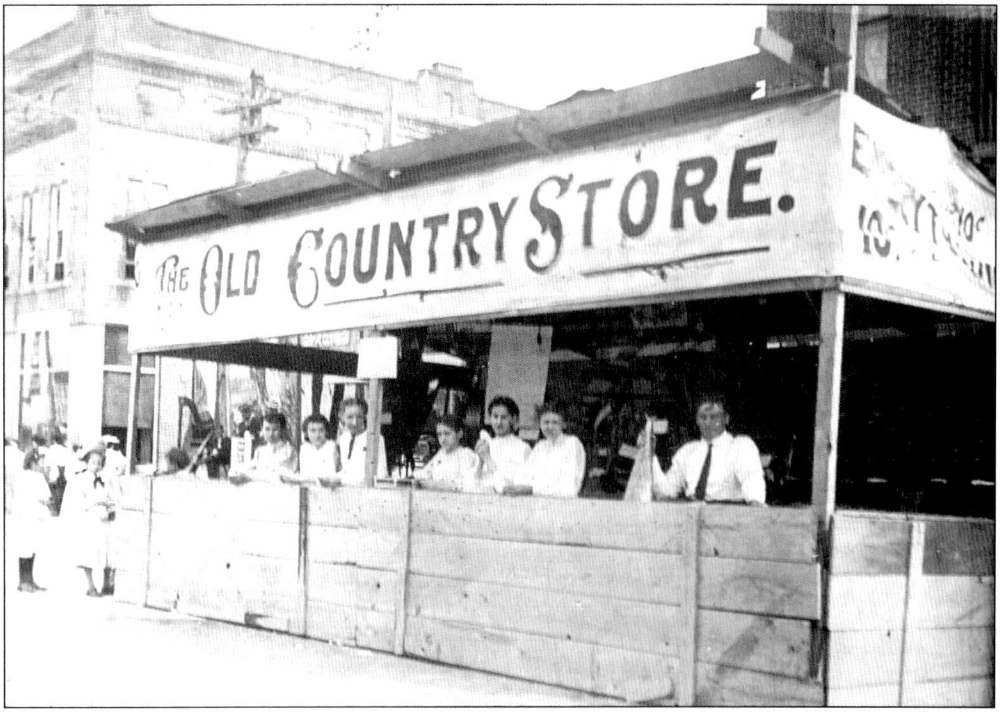

This photograph, labeled "the Old Country Store," shows a ramshackle wood structure set in the middle of Marshall's downtown. Note the young girl in her crisp white dress.

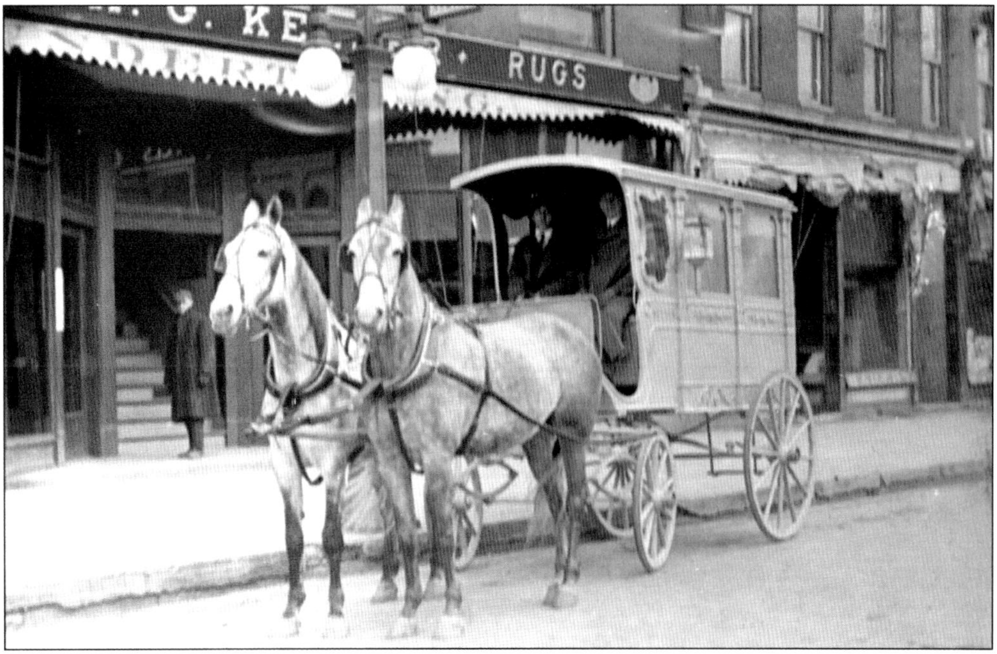

A horse-drawn hearse stands in front of H. G. Kelser Furniture and Undertaking at 110–112 West Michigan Avenue. Although it seems an odd combination now, furniture makers often made coffins, so undertaking became one-stop shopping. Guy Kelser bought the business in 1906 from F. B. Snyder. This photograph was taken between 1914 and 1921.

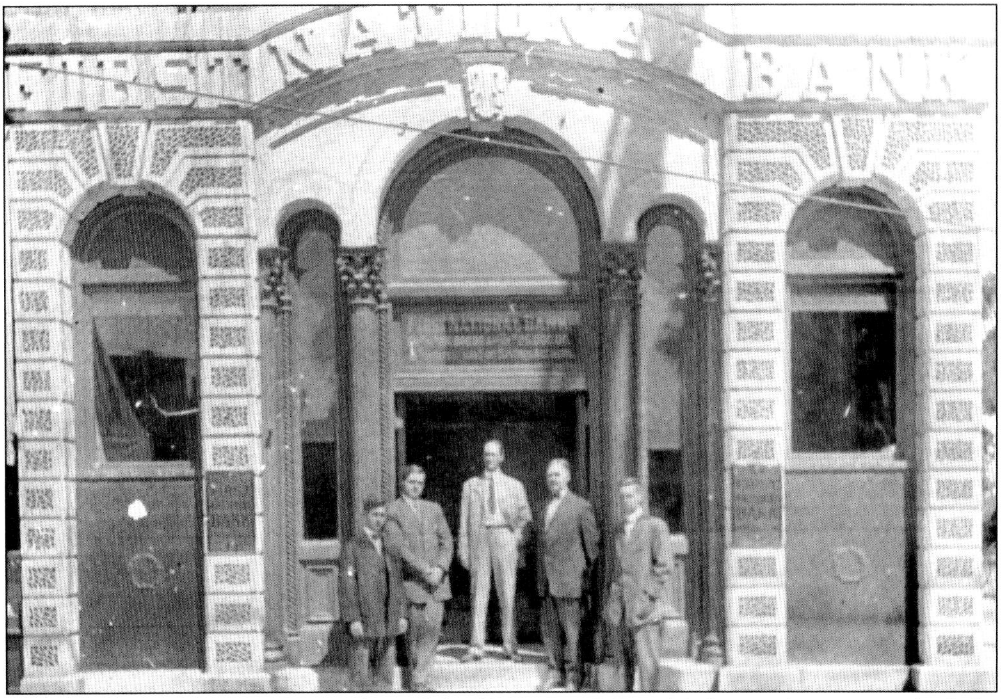

The exterior of the First National Bank building at 117 East Michigan Avenue was built by Charles Gorham in 1868. The bank itself dates back even further to 1865, when the First National Bank of Marshall was chartered.

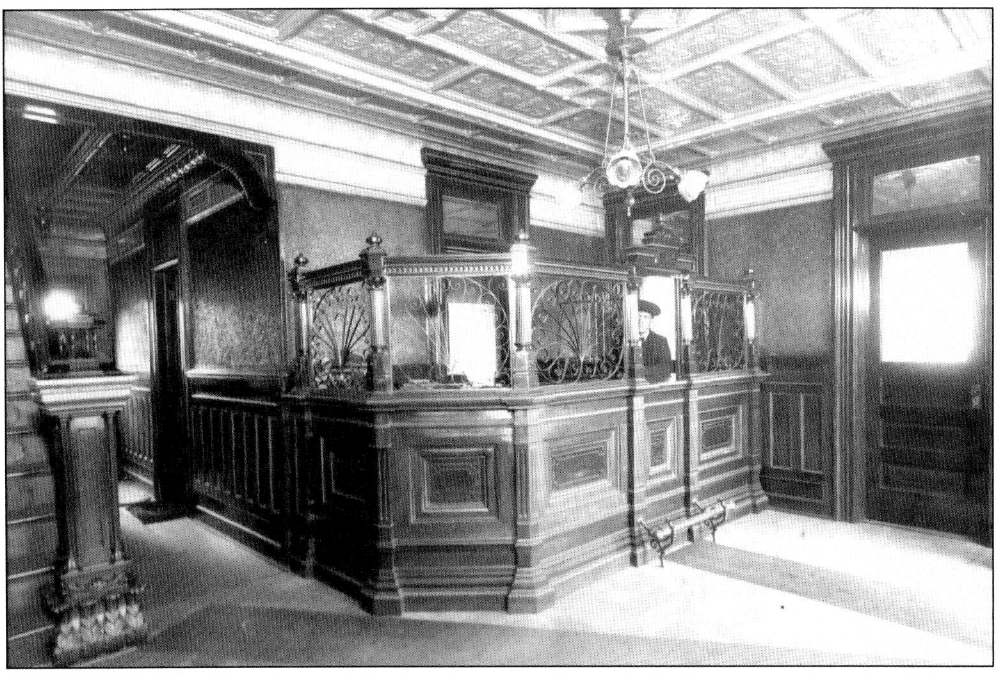

The interior of the First National Bank is shown in the early 20th century. Note the elaborate metal grills separating the tellers from the public, the magnificent chandelier, the pressed tin ceiling, and the burnished wood staircase.

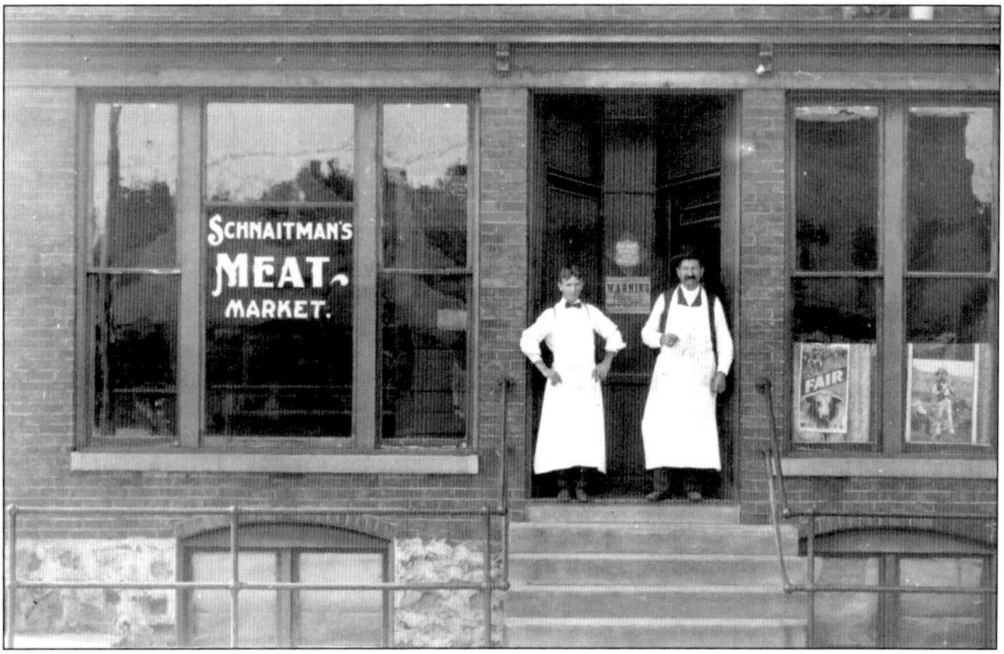

Schnaitman's Meat Market was located at 221 West Michigan Avenue. Fred Schnaitman ran a restaurant here after erecting the building in 1901, but it soon became a meat market operated by J. F Schnaitman. Members of the family would operate a meat market at this location, with a three-year hiatus from 1911 to 1914, until 1957. The meat market also had a smokehouse in the rear.

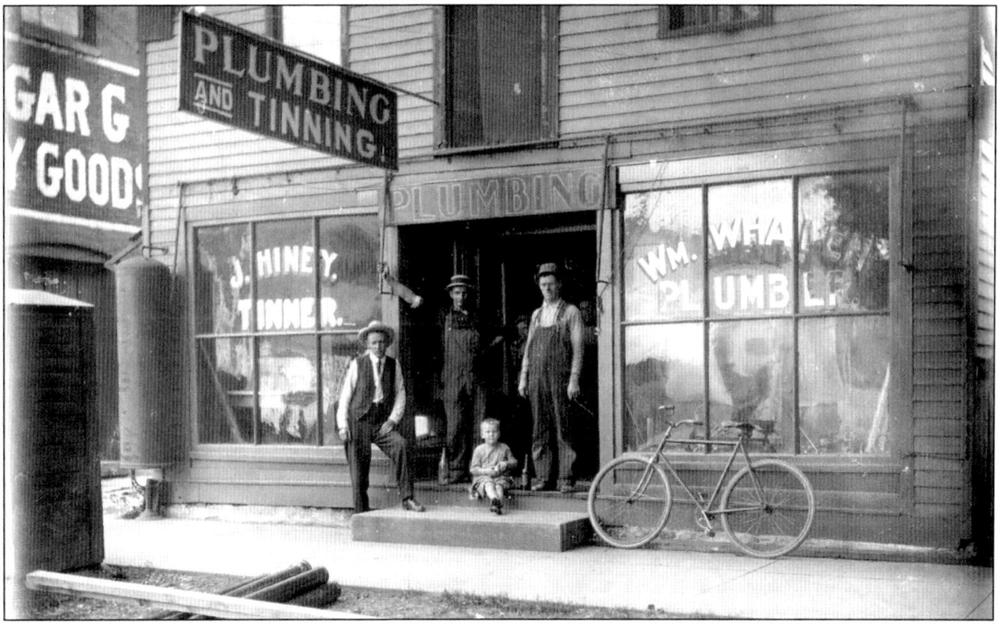

Jocko Hiney is shown with his father, Andrew, and brother Frank at their 105 North Eagle Street store. The Hineys were tinners, and they also, according to the back of this c. 1900 photograph, built the sidewalk in front of their store. The other man in the photograph is thought to be Bill Whalen, a plumber.

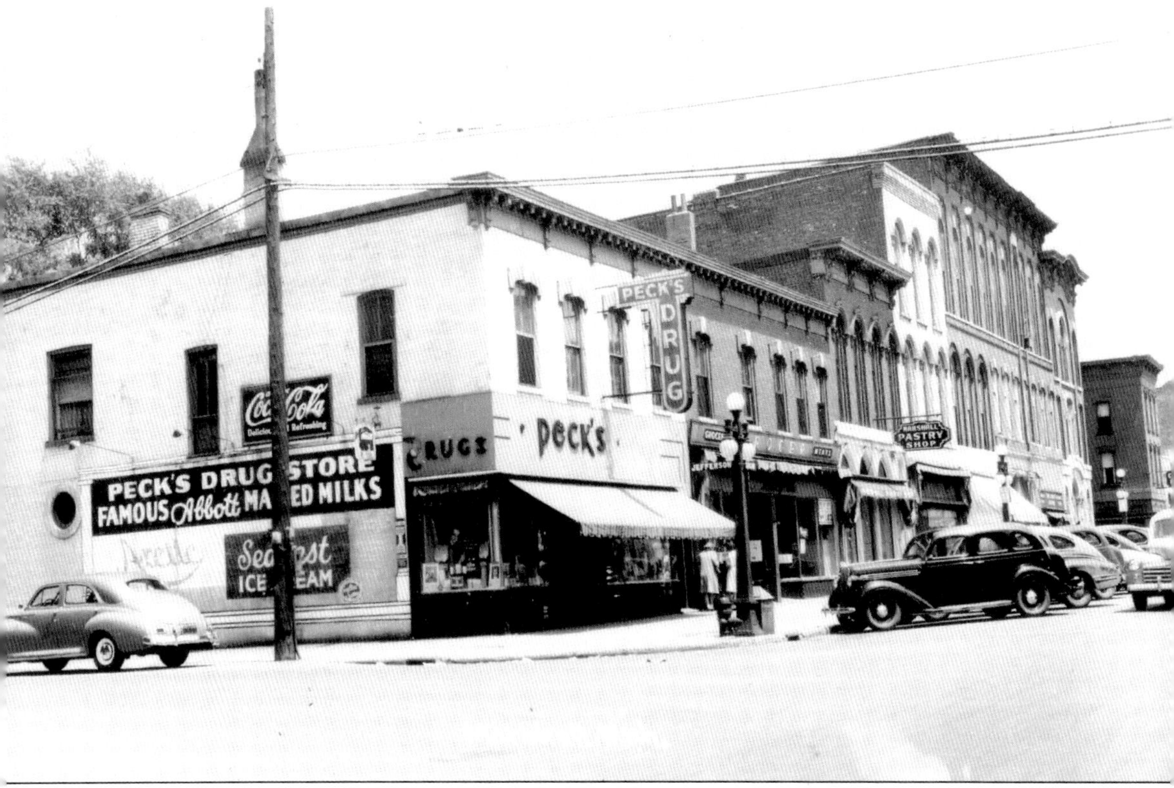

Peck's Drug Store was famous for its Abbott's Malteds, a drink similar to a milk shake. Now All the Write Wrappings (a handmade-card store) and Calhoun Travel are located in this historic building on Michigan Avenue.

Two

Historic Marshall Homes

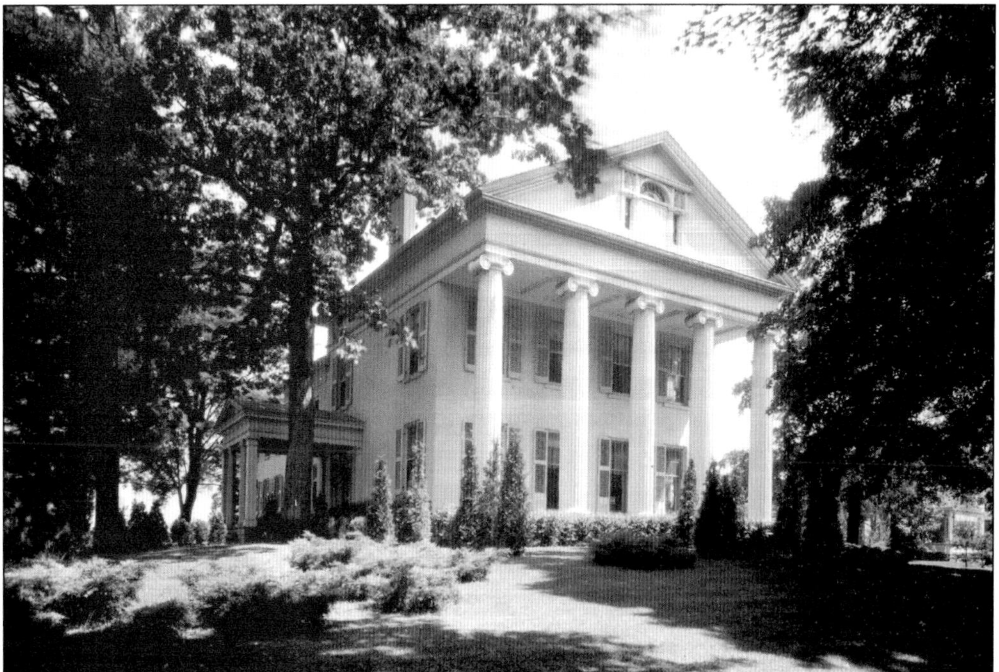

Marshall is most famous for its historic homes. Over 850 of them are included in one of the largest National Historic Landmark Districts in the country. The Marshall Historic Home Tour is the oldest in the Midwest, having its beginning in 1964. Harold C. Brooks bought the Fitch Gorham house. He then hired noted landscape architect Jens Jensen to define the exterior of the property and its rear gardens. Jensen's whole concept was to make things look natural. The five-column Greek Revival architecture was rare.

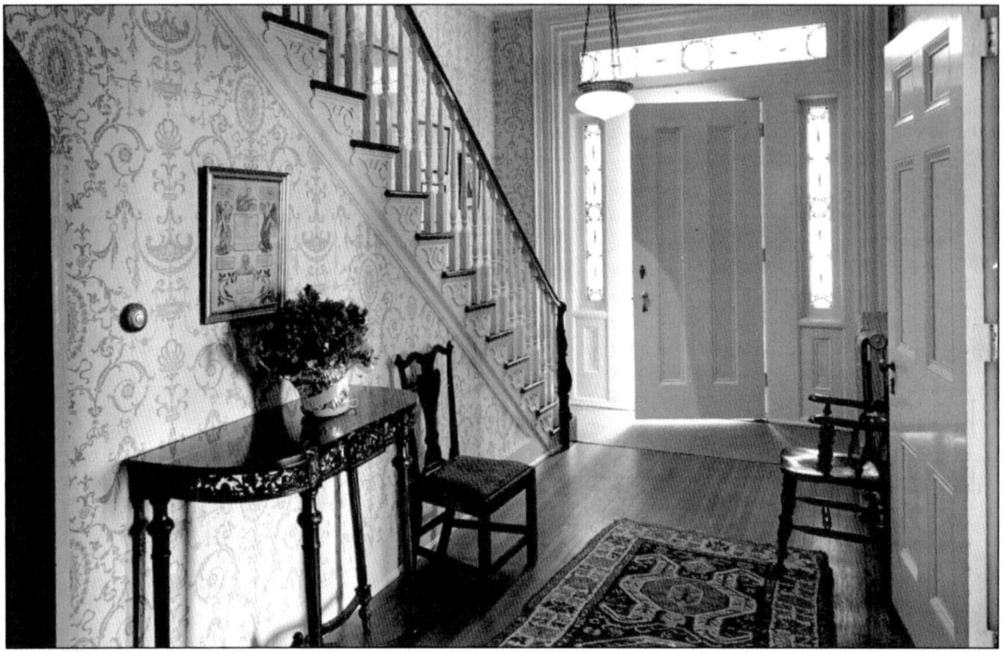

Harold C. and Gladys Brooks not only restored the exterior of the house on North Kalamazoo Avenue, they also collected antique furniture to finish the interior. The house is unusual in that the central hall runs all the way through the house parallel to the double parlor and the front porch, thus creating two front doors. While Harold C. Brooks was "Mr. Outside," his brother, Louis, was "Mr. Inside" and was one of the leading authorities in the country on 18th-century American chairs.

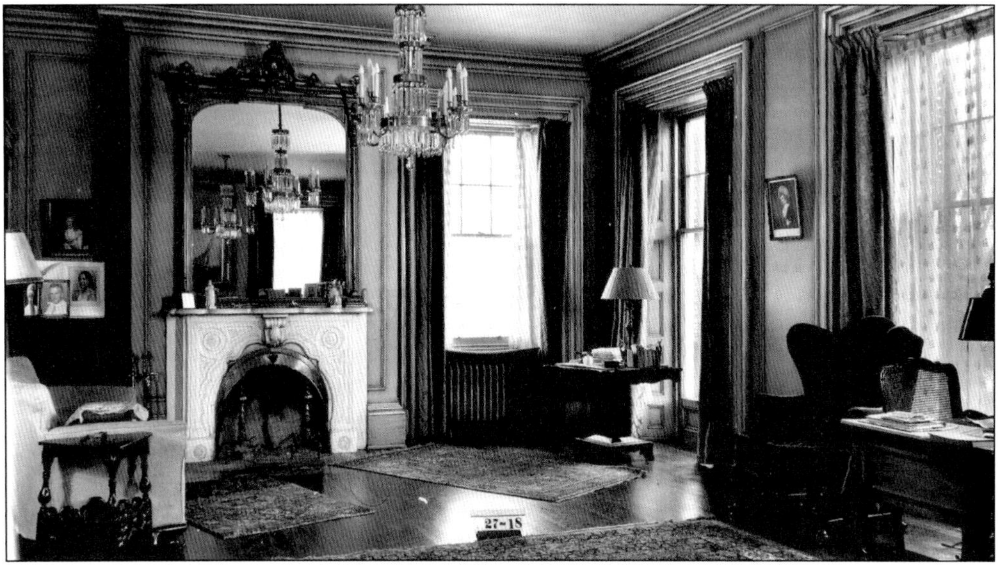

This view shows one end of the double parlor that extended along the front of the house. The four large windows facing south provided a large amount of natural light, also giving access to the front porch with its five columns. Both H. C.'s and Louis's homes had a double parlor with a fireplace at either end of the room. It is doubtful that the white marble fireplaces were original, but they certainly added a great deal of grandeur to the rooms.

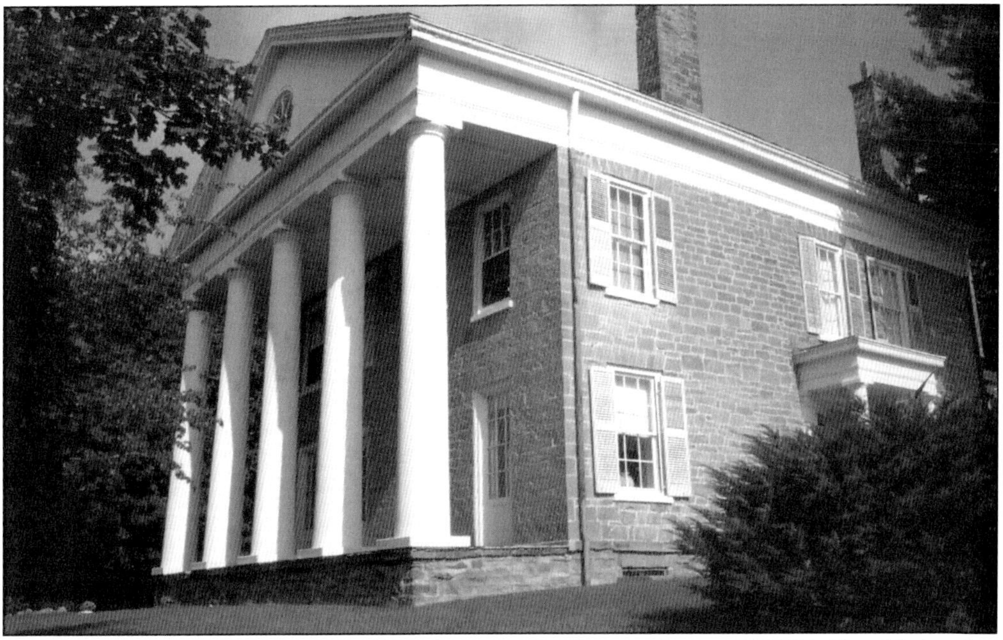

Harold C. Brooks bought Stone Hall in the 1920s for the grand sum of $2,700. Harold's brother Louis Brooks offered to buy it from him but said that he would not pay him a penny more than Harold C.'s purchase price. Louis then put almost $500,000 pre-Depression-era dollars into the restoration of the house. The carriage house for this house is the only two-story Marshall sandstone one in Marshall.

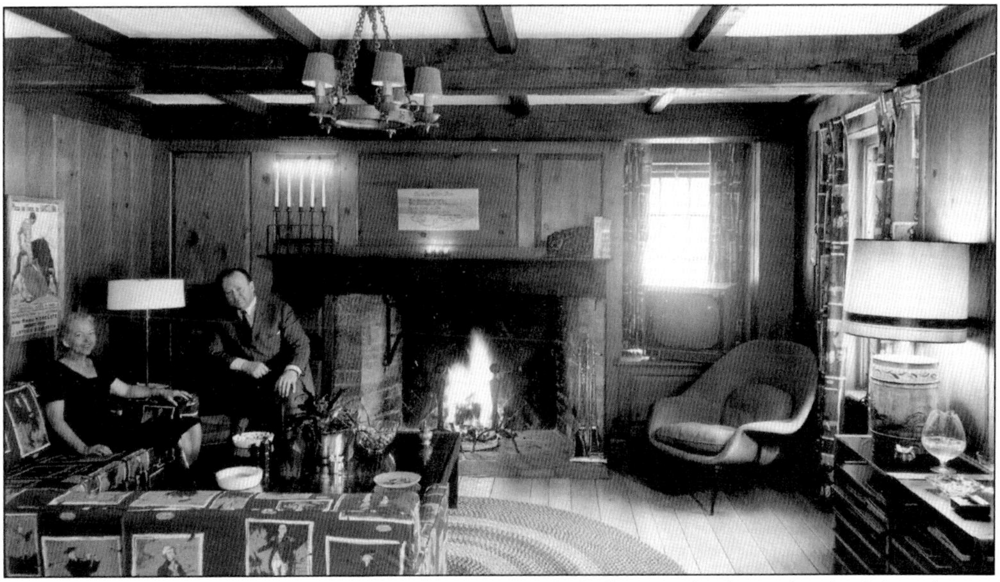

Ellie and Mickey Finn loved to entertain in the rathskellar on the lower level of their home, Stone Hall, in the late 1940s. The house has four floors going from this room through the two formal floors all the way to the 40-foot-by-60-foot ballroom on the top level of the house. It was quite a project when the grand piano was moved from the ballroom. The oval window over the porch had to be taken apart to allow the crane access to the piano before it could be lowered to the ground some 50 feet below.

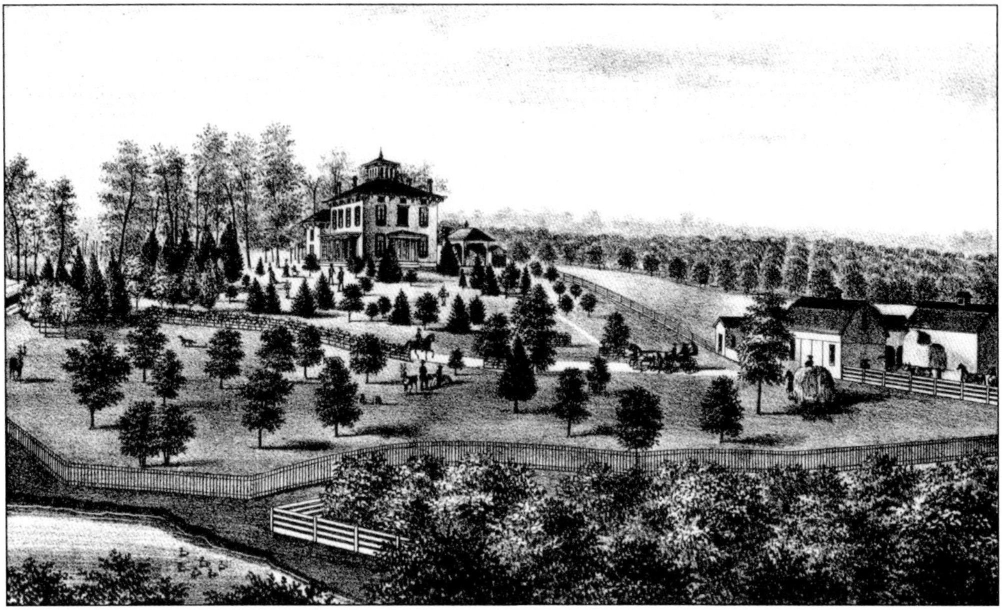

Chauncey M. Brewer built this house in 1858 at the north end of Eagle Street. The name for the house has been Oakhill at least since 1877 when this picture appeared in *History of Calhoun County, 1830–1877*. Brewer surrounded it with acres of orchards and several assorted outbuildings. The entrance was placed on the east side in the anticipation of Eagle Street continuing on north with the growth of Marshall. The porch was extended around the south side of the house sometime after 1895.

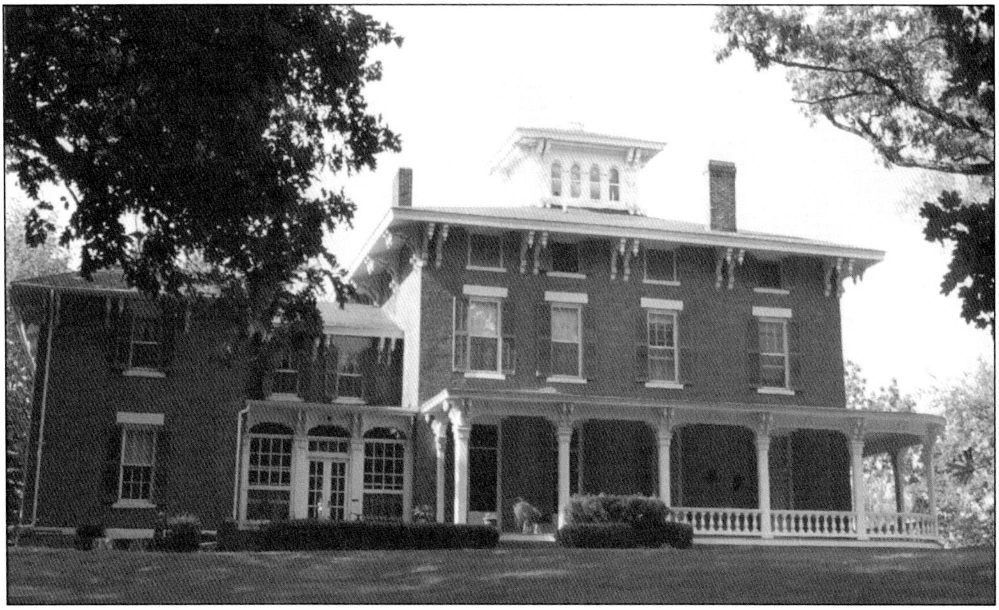

Brewer came to Marshall in 1836 from Oneonta, Otsego County, New York, to open a general store with Charles T. Gorham. They built their store on the northwest corner of Kalamazoo Avenue and State Street (now Michigan Avenue). That store was later moved near the Michigan Central Railroad depot and became known as Marshall House. In 1838, they bought land on the corner of Eagle and State Streets, where they erected the first brick store.

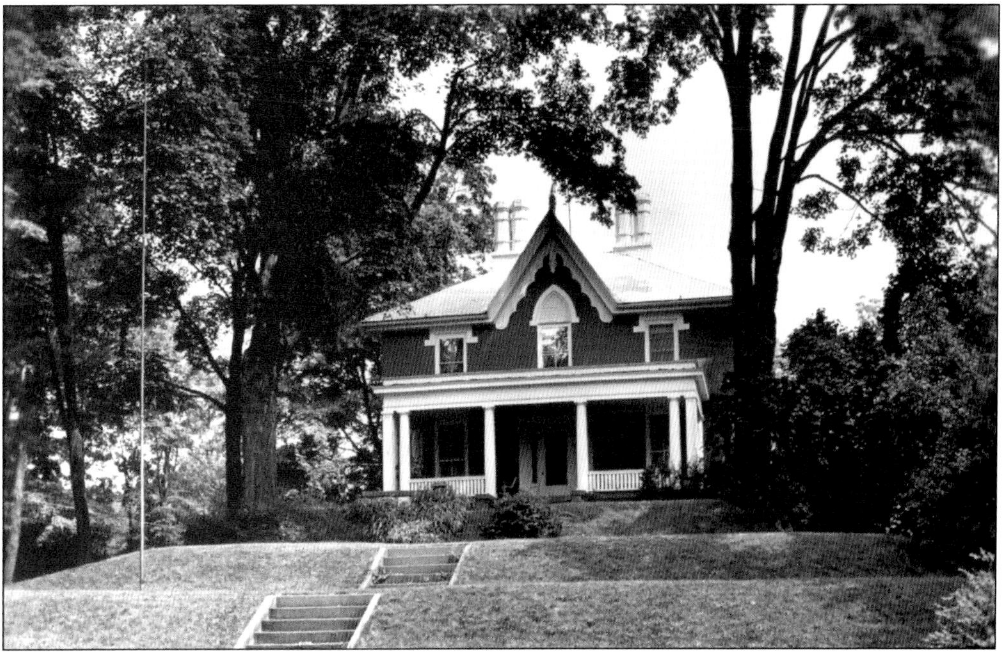

Hillside was built around 1843. During the early part of the 20th century, one of Michigan's most eminent women lived in this house. Maisey Miller was one of the first presidents of the Michigan League of Woman Voters. She entertained many famous national and state politicians in this home, and her Lilac Tea in May was definitely the must-have invitation, not only in Marshall but throughout the state.

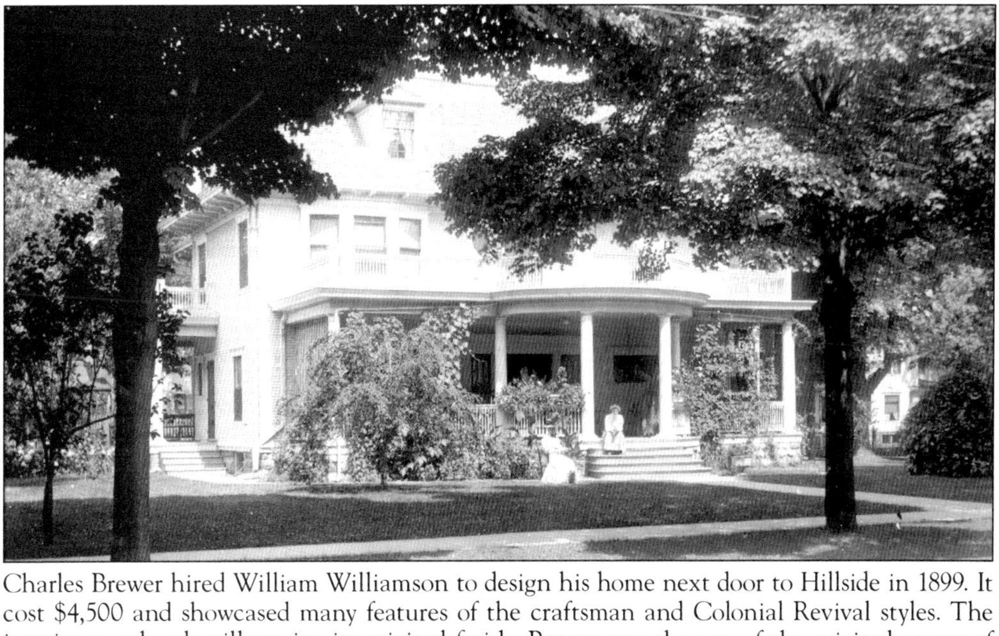

Charles Brewer hired William Williamson to design his home next door to Hillside in 1899. It cost $4,500 and showcased many features of the craftsman and Colonial Revival styles. The interior woodwork still retains its original finish. Brewer was the son of the original owner of Oakhill at the top of the hill behind the house. It is interesting to note that in this time, one of the current owners, Patricia Belew, is the daughter of Thomas Franke, the current owner of Oakhill.

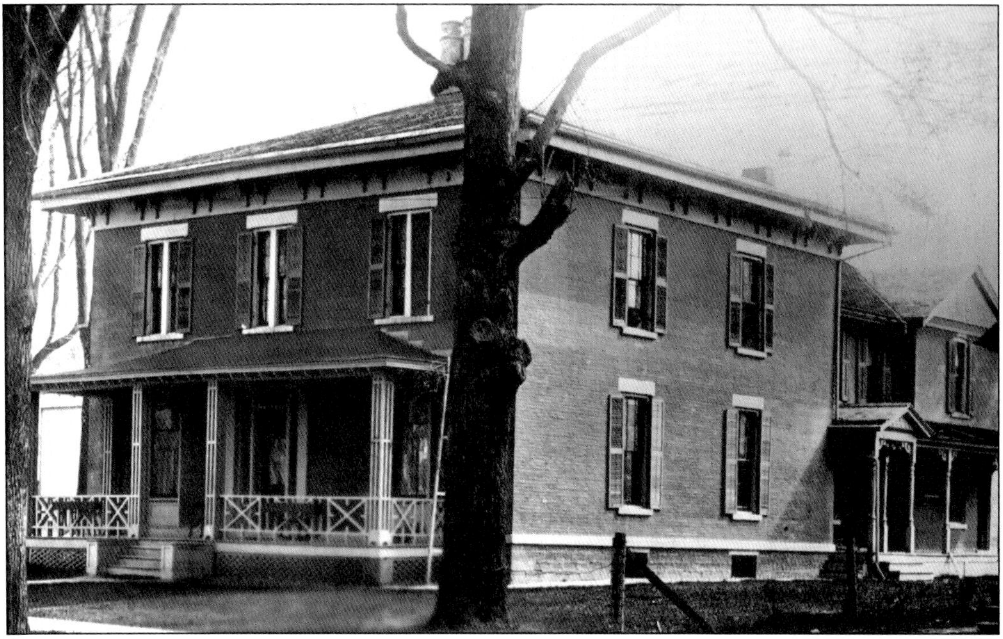

In 1850, Dr. John Montgomery and Mary (Schuyler) Montgomery built what was described in the *Ann Arbor Statesman* as a grand house east of Marshall. At 222 North Marshall Avenue, it is just two blocks north of Michigan Avenue. The new wing on the right in the photograph was added in 1889. The front porch was probably added at that time. It was removed in 1962. Dr. Montgomery was Marshall's second doctor and for sometime ran a chemist shop with his brother-in-law Dr. Henry L. Joy.

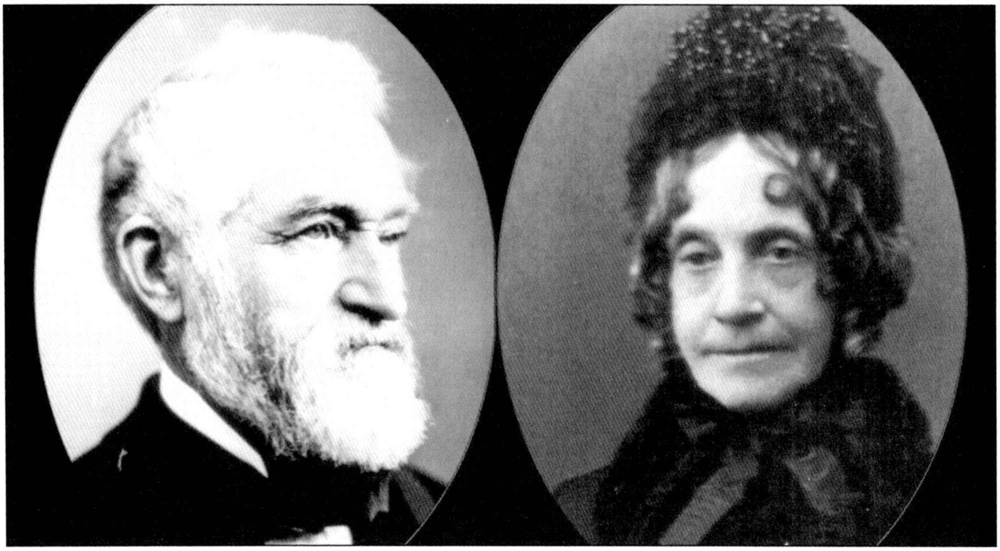

Mary Montgomery managed to get her entire family to follow her to Marshall and, like her, marry successful professional men. Her brother, Montgomery Schuyler, was the second rector at Trinity Episcopal Church. Dr. John Montgomery ran his medical practice from the north half of the first floor of his home. One of the founders of the Young Ladies Institute, Dr. Montgomery was also was the postmaster with a box in his desk. Serving as president of the school board and founding vestryman of Trinity occupied his other hours to keep him out of trouble.

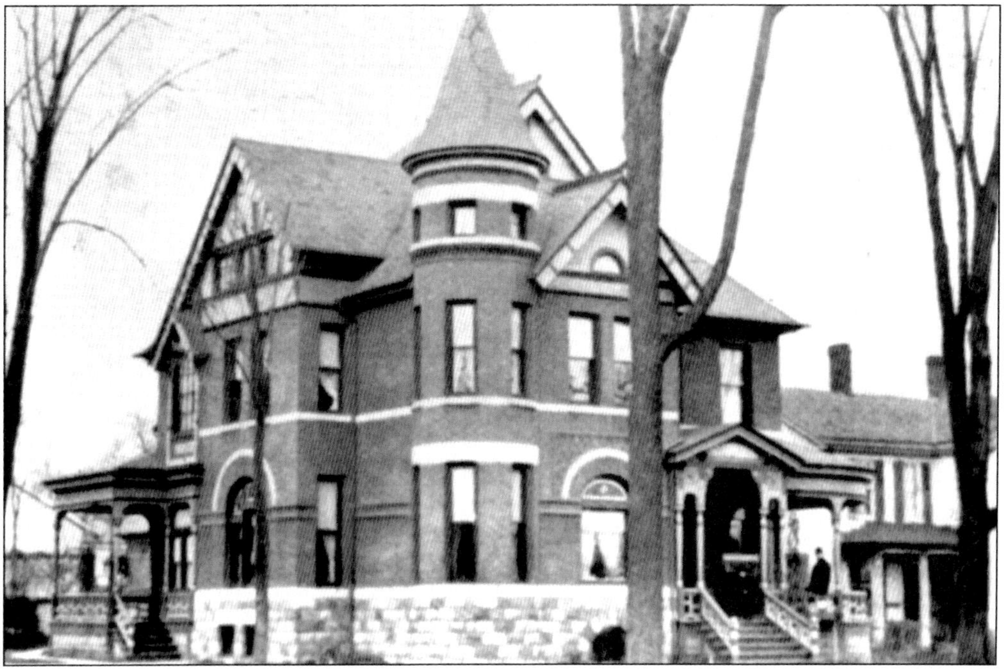

Clinton T. Cook hired the architectural firm Spier and Rohn of Detroit to design this home located at 401 East Mansion Street for his family in 1886, and the house was finished the next year. Every window, door, and fireplace features birds in the glass or tiles. The round-top windows have stained-glass panels, and the porches wrap around the house. Spier and Rohn is renowned for its railroad station designs. It designed at least five houses in Marshall, as well as the chapel at Oakridge Cemetery.

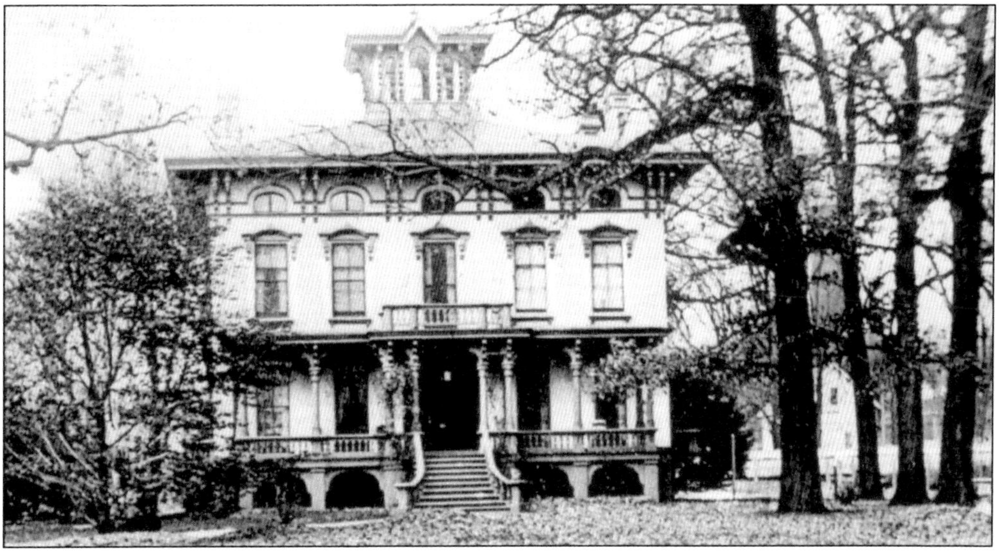

The Ketchum-Dibble mansion is how Marshall's famed Mansion Street earned its name. Town founder Sidney Ketchum built this, the second brick house in Marshall, in 1836. In the 1850s, it served as the residence for a ladies' finishing school. In 1861, Charles O. Dibble remodeled Ketchum's mansion into an Italian villa of the latest style, as it appears in this photograph. He then named the estate Oak Lawn. Oaklawn Hospital now occupies the site.

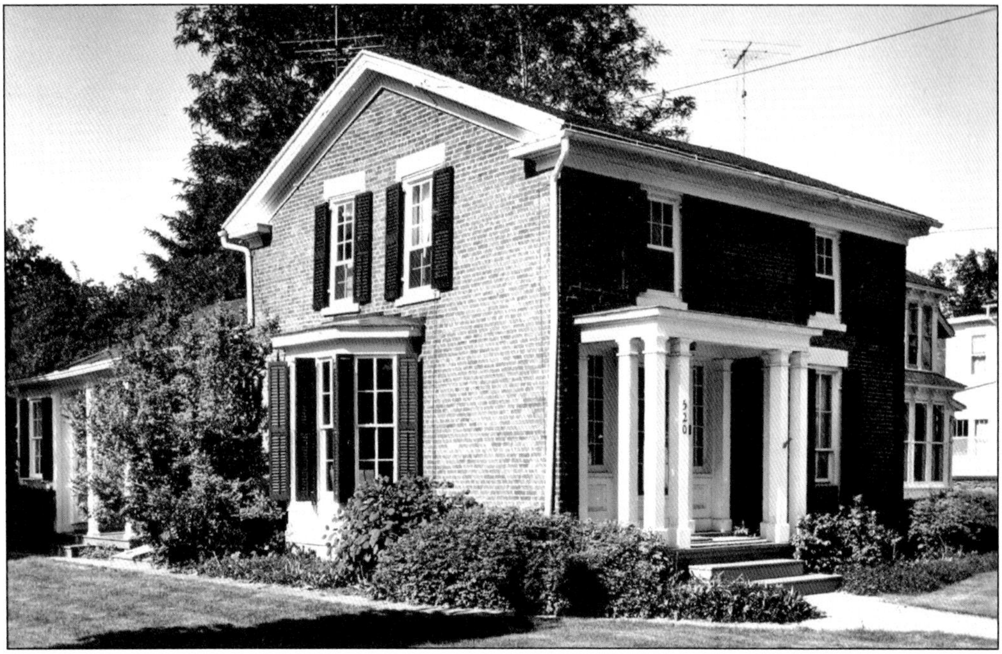

The Lord House at 520 West Michigan Avenue was built in 1838. It is now purported to be the oldest brick house still standing in the state. One of the many buildings that H. C. Brooks bought to preserve, it was sold by H. C. to his grandson Charles E. Brooks and his wife, Jan, in 1968. This house is typical of the Greek Revival style of the Midwest along with some early features of the Federal style so popular in the eastern United States.

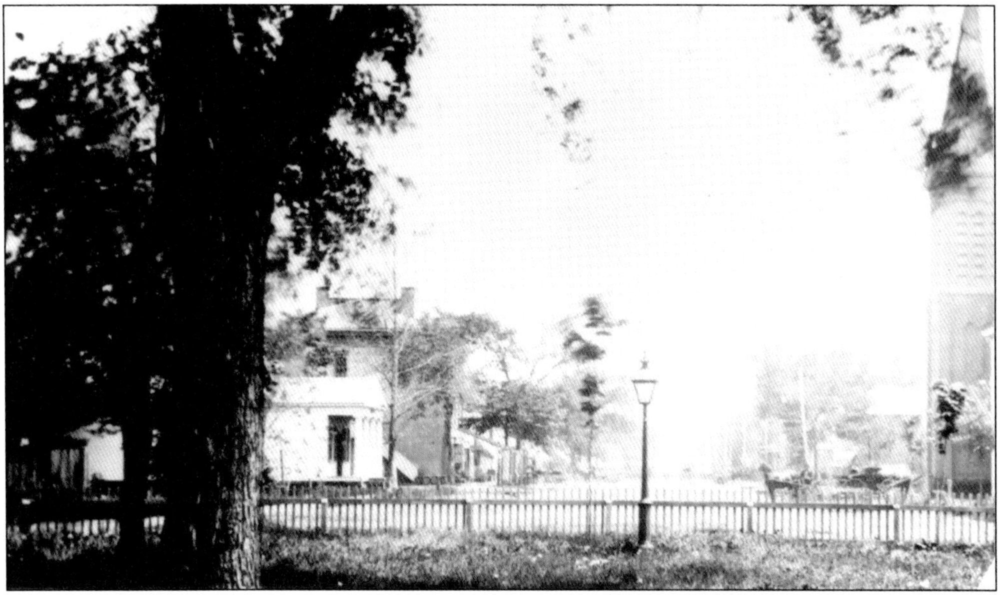

The small Greek Revival house on the left side of the street is Isaac Crary's law office. Crary was Michigan's territorial representative to the U.S. Congress and was also the first U.S. representative to Congress from Michigan. This small building stood next to his first Marshall home, hidden by the large tree to the left of the photograph. This office building still exists today as a small home on South Linden Street.

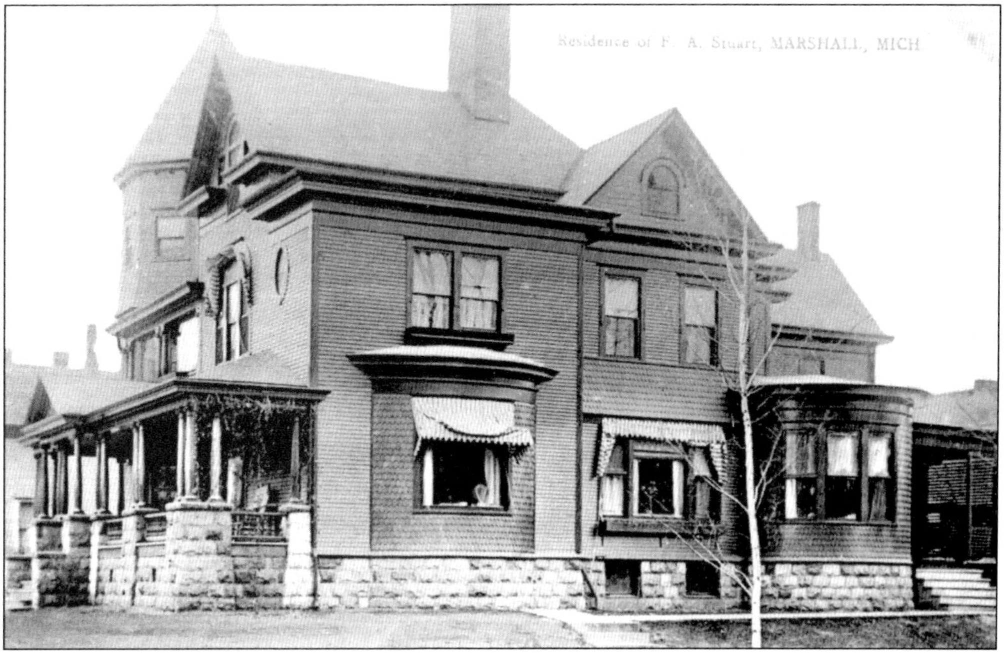

F. A. Stuart was the founder of one of the largest drug companies in the Midwest. His most famous product was Stuart's Dyspepsia Tablets. This concoction was the forerunner to TUMS antacid tablets. This grand brick house of his stood on Green Street in what is now the parking lot directly behind Schuler's Restaurant. The Stuart Block on Michigan Avenue still belongs to the Stuart family and has since it was built in 1852.

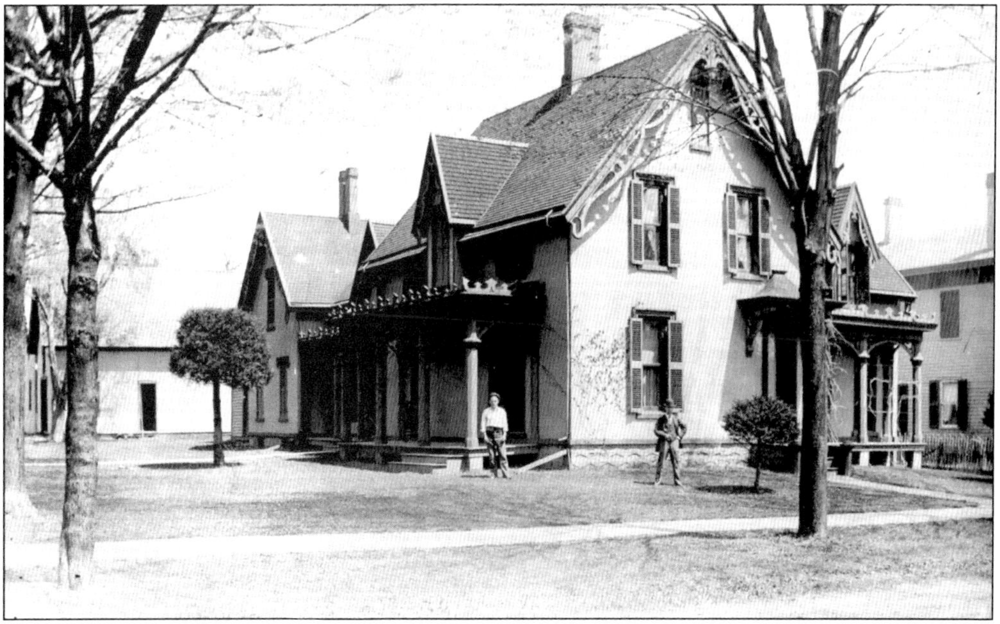

This brick house on the northeast corner of North Kalamazoo Avenue and Mansion Street is the only dwelling in Marshall to have two listings in the Historic American Building Survey. It has one for both the home and the carriage house behind it. It was built about 1853 and acquired by Abner Baker just two years later. Baker was a boot and shoe manufacturer.

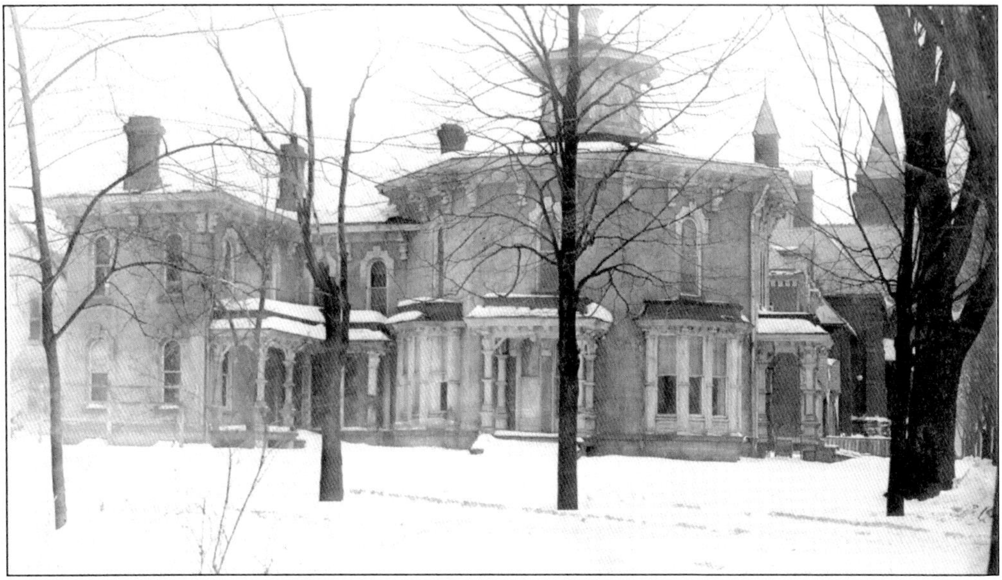

Orson Fowler came to Marshall for a week in April 1850 and lectured each evening at the Marshall House Hotel on either phrenology or sexology. He charged 12.5 pence per chair and spoke to a packed house every night. He is credited with the invention of the octagon form of architecture. Marshall resident Increase Pendleton thought Fowler had a good idea and built this quite substantial home at the corner of Eagle and Hanover Streets in 1856.

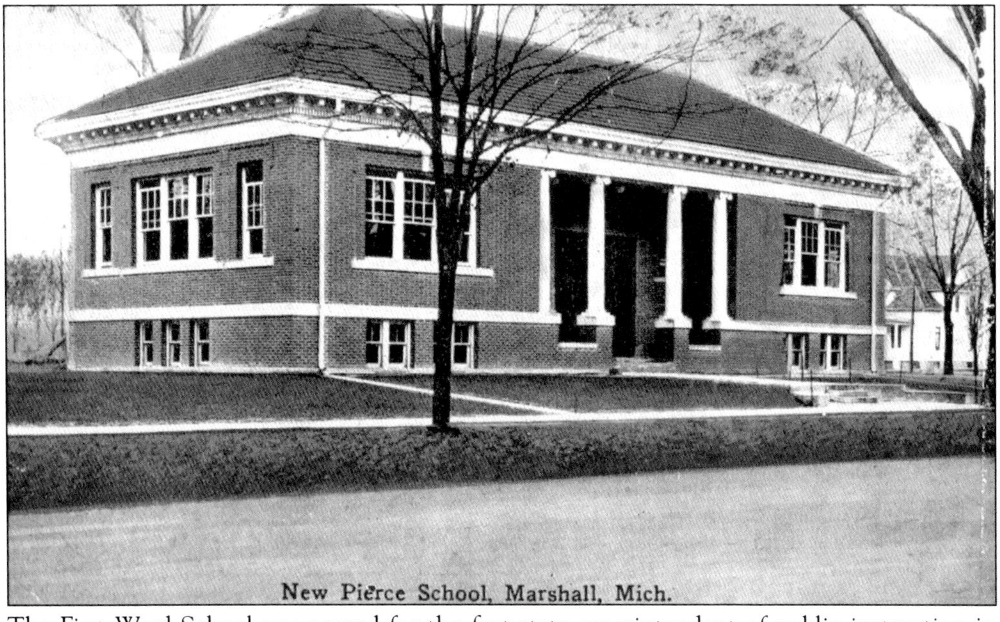

The First Ward School was named for the first state superintendent of public instruction in the United States, the Reverend John D. Pierce. The original 1860 school was torn down, and this replacement was built in 1911–1912. It was originally built for grades 1 through 3. It was purchased about 20 years ago and converted into a single-family dwelling. The new owners added a five-car garage that matches the school in scale and shape.

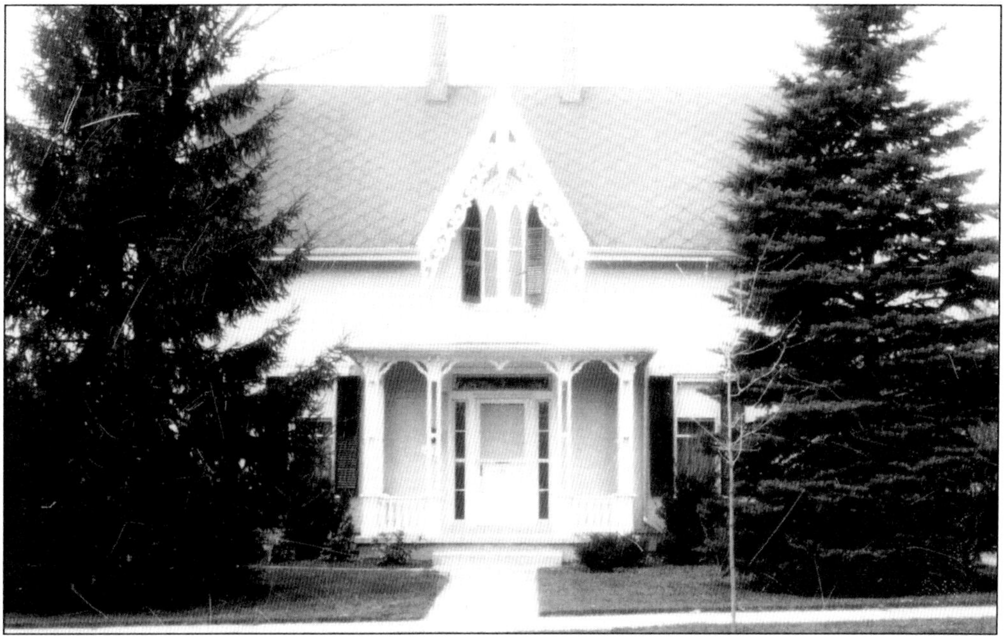

Chastain Mann was the editor of the local newspaper *Calhoun County Patriot and Democratic Expounder*. He built this wonderful example of a Gothic Revival house on the back of the Sidney Ketchum block in 1861. The interior floor plan is just as Mann recorded it in his diary while it was being built. The Foster family has owned the house since 1957. The large carriage house at the rear of the lot was added at a very early time.

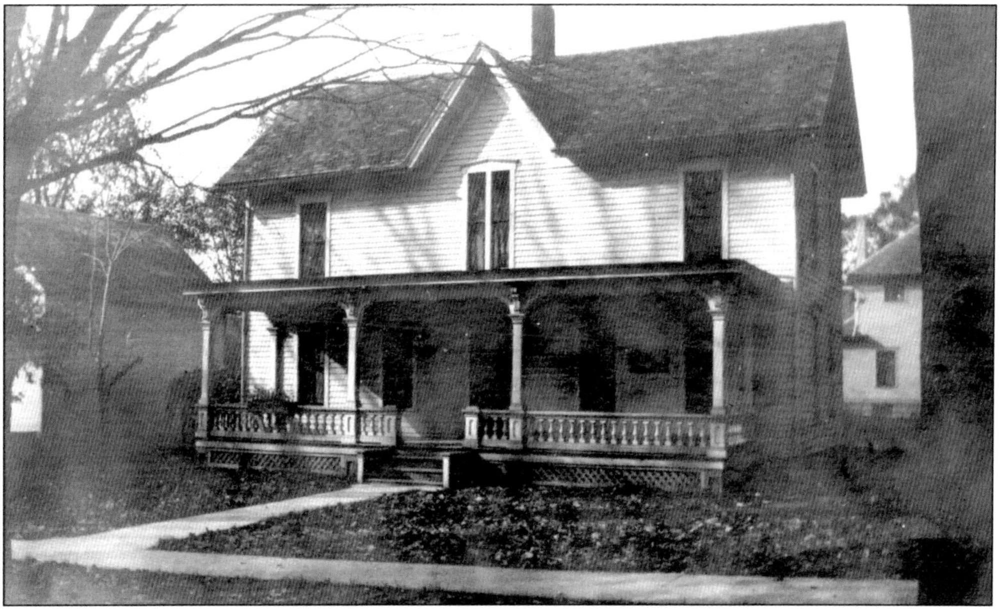

The Fletcher-Dickey house at 223 North Marshall Avenue is an excellent example of what a lot of tender loving care and a tasteful selection of colors can do for a lovely Gothic Revival–style house. From 1900 until the late 1970s, almost all of Marshall's houses were painted New England white with either black or dark green trim. This house is now a dark brick red with pale gold trim. It has made a dramatic difference.

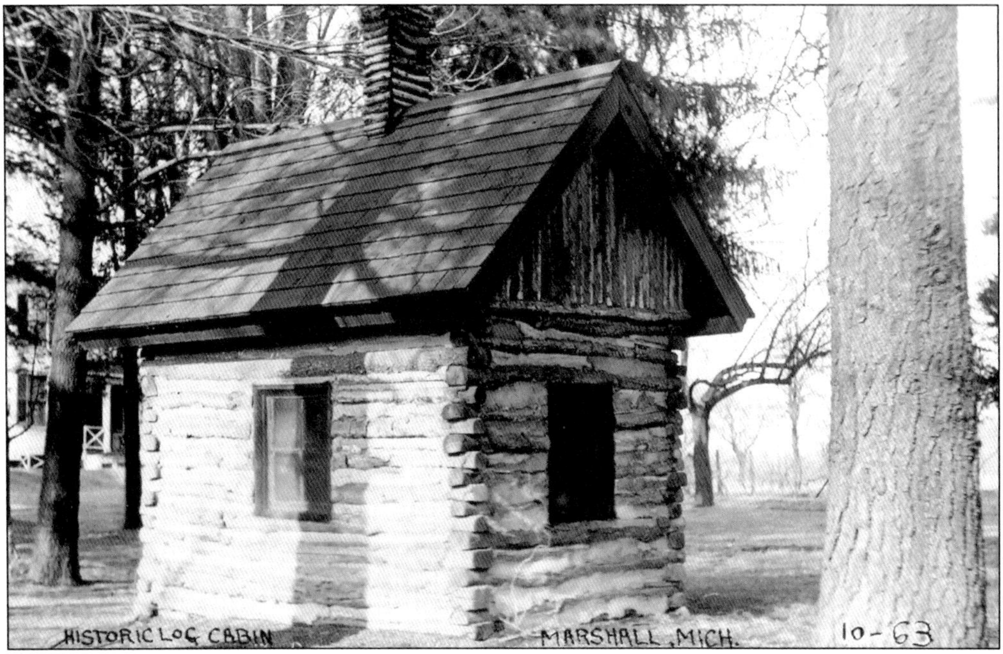

There were never very many log cabins in Marshall, so this early postcard has provided a good many laughs for the local residents. The first settlers of Marshall were wealthy politicians and business people. They built a sawmill during the summer they arrived and immediately began building frame houses in 1832.

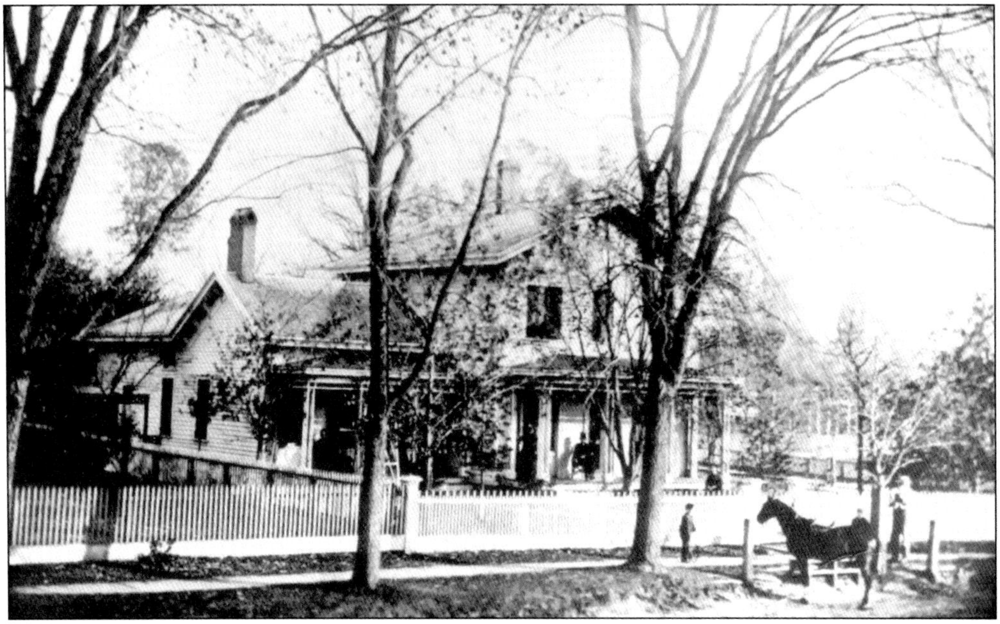

Lewis Wilmarth built this Greek Revival home on the northwest corner of Marshall Avenue and Mansion Street. It belonged to the Coleman family for about 85 years. Judge Creighton Coleman grew up in this house. Even though Judge Coleman went on to be a Michigan state senator, he is most famous for being the husband of the first female justice of the Michigan Supreme Court, Mary Coleman.

Three

FRIVOLITIES

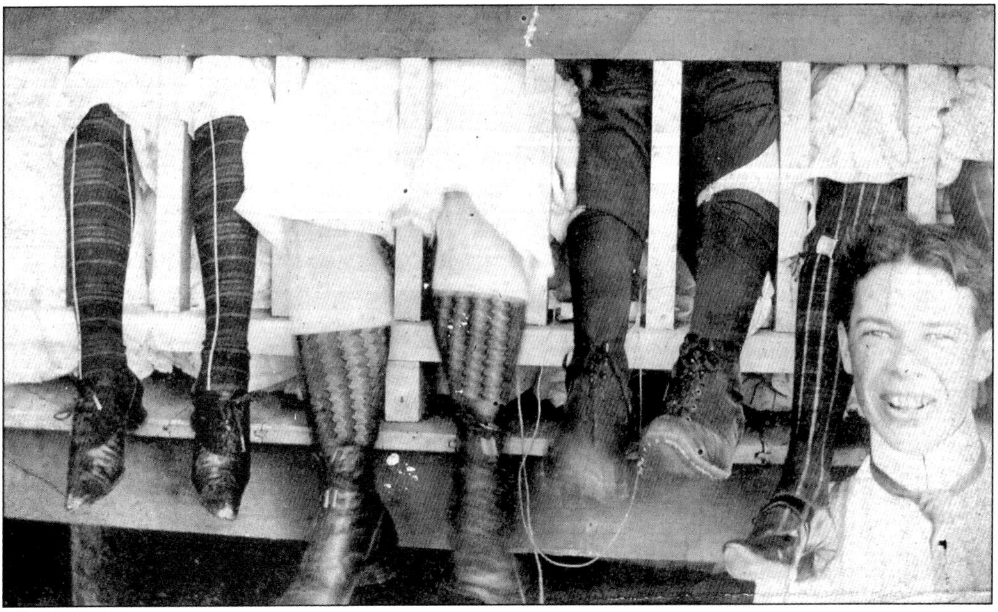

The look on this boy's face says that he is having fun, and in the days before television and electronic games, people gathered as a community to enjoy parades, the outdoors, picnics, church gatherings, and other get-togethers. This photograph, taken during the floral parade of 1904, is unique in that it gives an unusual view, showing not the faces but the shoes and socks of the viewers. Some of the feet featured in the photograph belong to Autumn Osborne, Gusta Casper, Wayne Casper, and Ethel Wright.

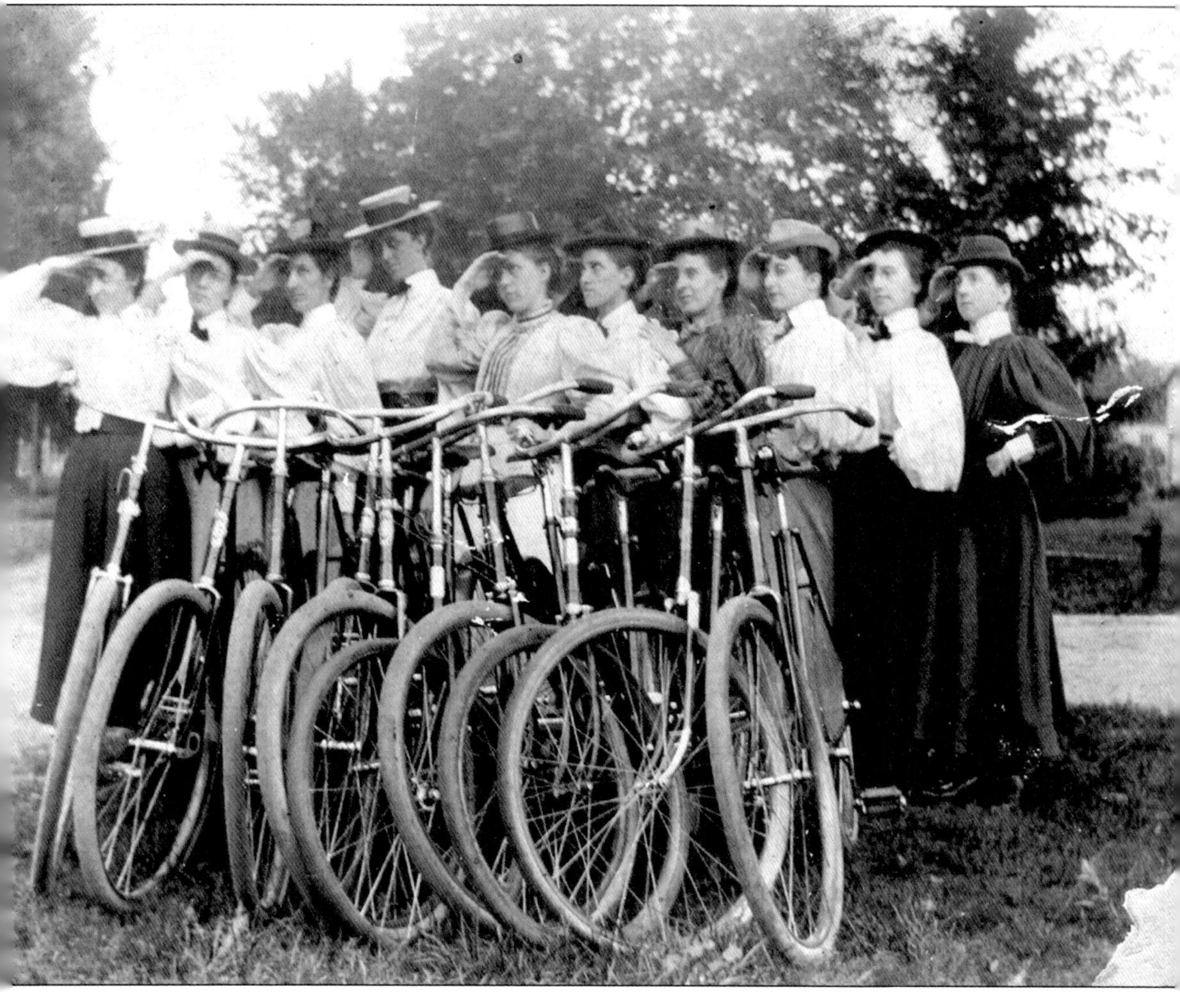

Bicycle clubs and bicycle riding were very popular in the late 1800s and early 1900s. These once-popular high-wheel bicycles, also known as penny-farthings, were dangerous and hard to maneuver and quickly lost favor to the new smaller, chain-driven models.

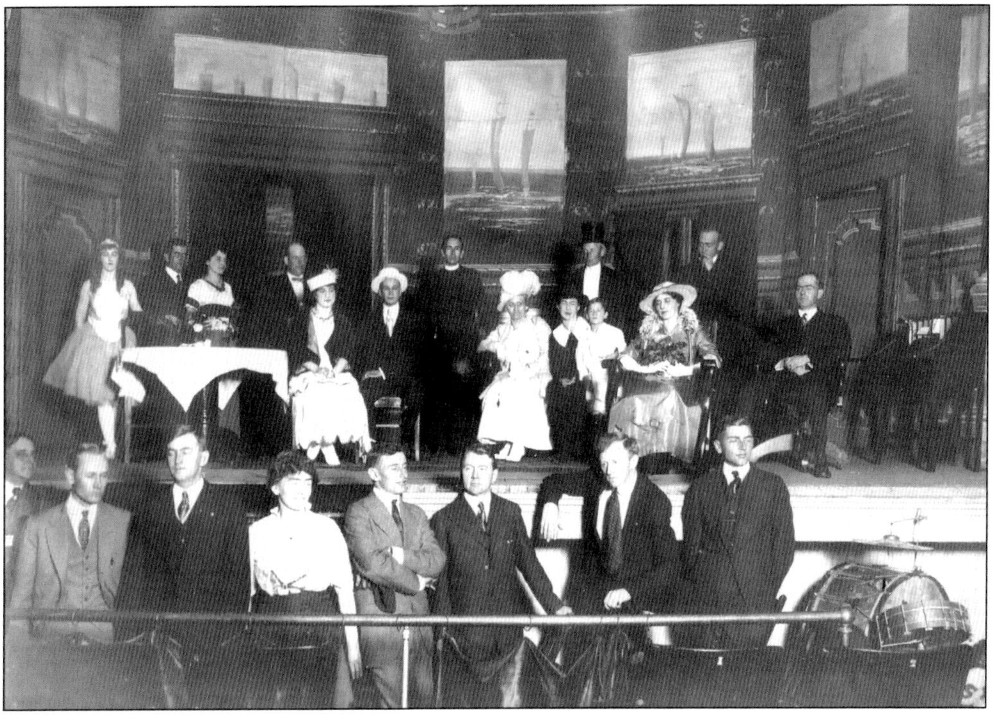

The cast and orchestra from a production of *Private Lives* take a bow after a performance at the Garden Theatre.

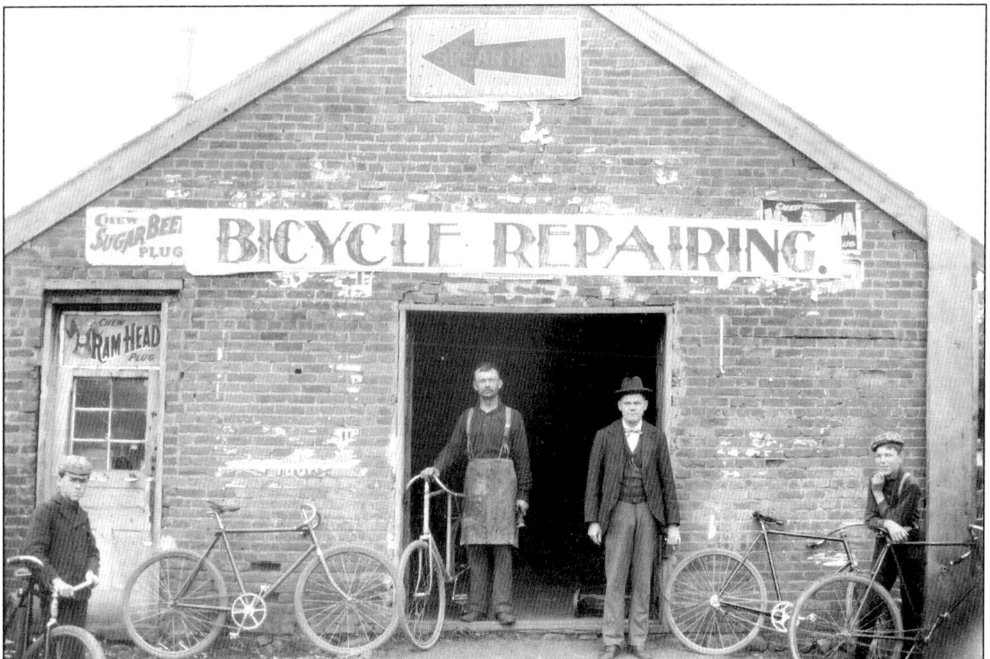

An old-time bicycle shop was one of many businesses in Marshall, which at one time had a windmill factory and an ice-cutting and storage business, as well as a buggy factory and several breweries.

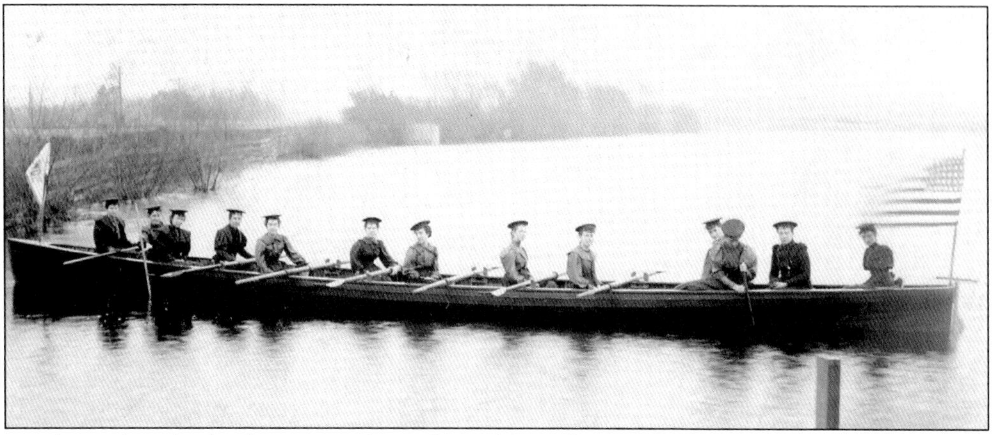

People tend to think of women as being less athletically active a century or so ago. But as this photograph of the Yawder Boat Club taken in the late 1890s shows, women liked to get out and do things. Note their jaunty caps. Listed on the back of the photograph are the following names: Annie Dennison, Ethel Wright, Charlie Phelps, Hattie Fletcher, Katherine Tremble, Bessie Fletcher, Mamie Spicer, Vic Monk, Nora Frick, Grace Hamilton, Hattie Woods, and Grace Geer.

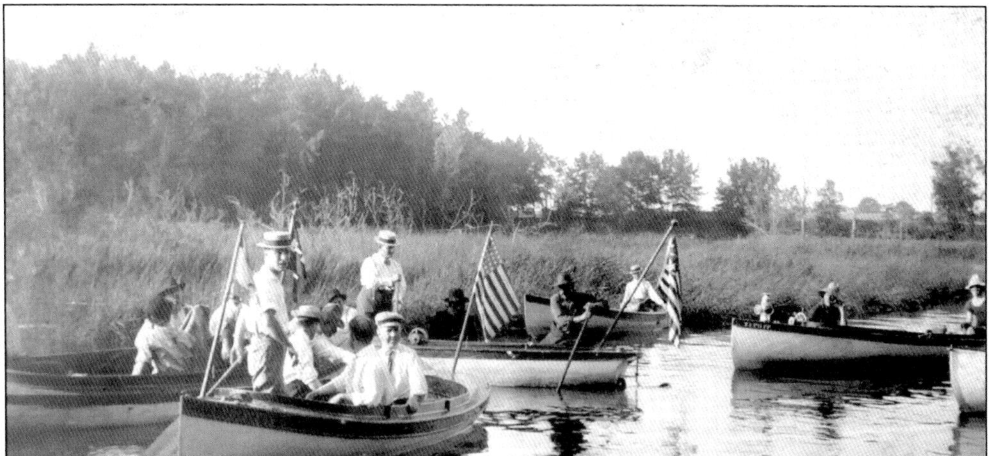

Inscribed on this photograph, dated 1910, are the words "Bad Bunch On the River." Water sports were popular in Marshall, which is on both the Kalamazoo River and Rice Creek. There were even steamboats, including the 75-passenger *S. J. Burpee*, that made their way along the Kalamazoo River.

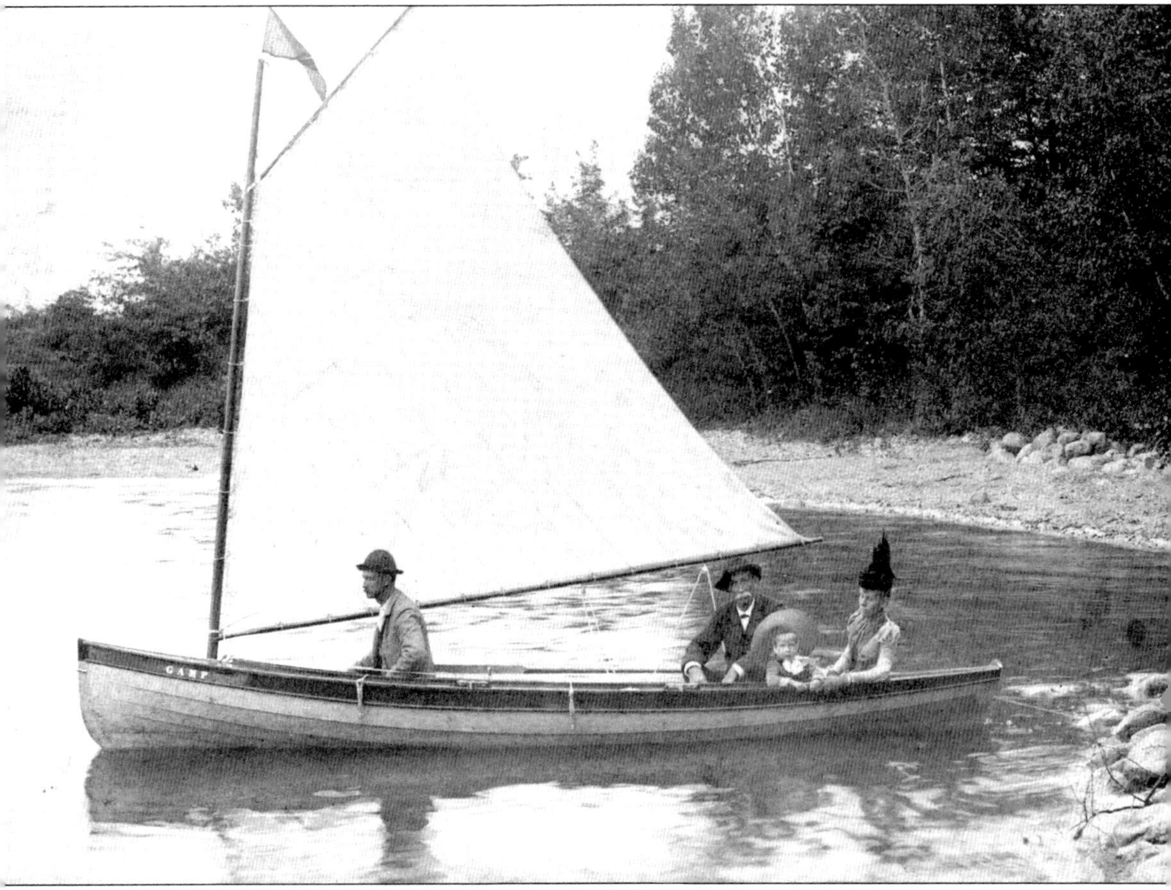

The well-known Gorham family, longtime Marshall residents, goes sailing. Note the woman's rather preposterous-looking hat.

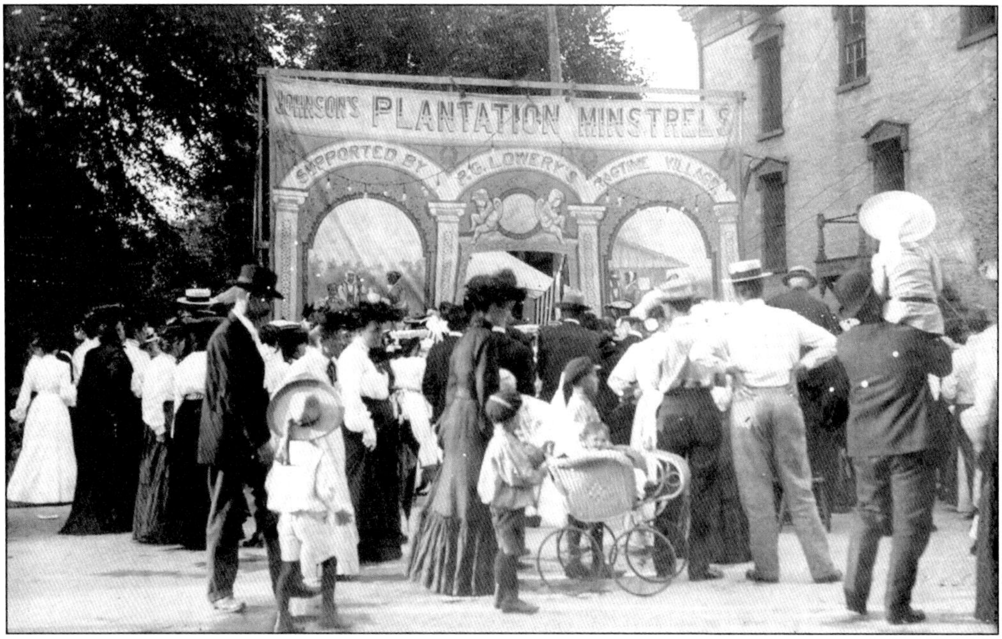

Crowds, including parents with babies in strollers, gather for some type of street fair in downtown Marshall. Circuses and other forms of entertainment traveled through the small towns and large cities, bringing entertainment.

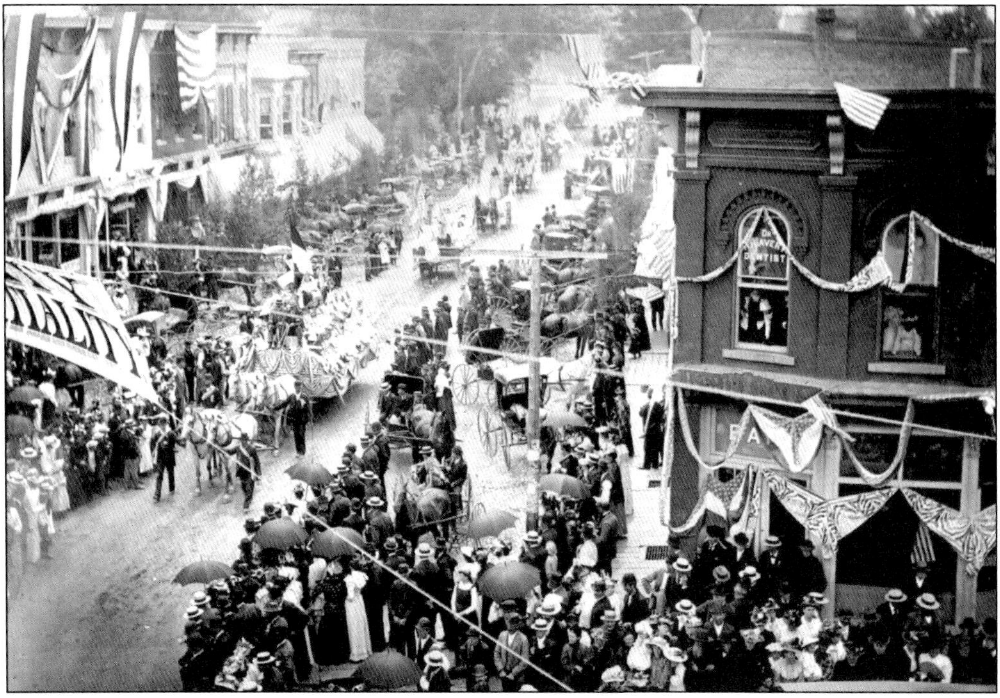

Downtown Marshall is shown at the late 1800s. Marshall was a switching center for the burgeoning Michigan Central Railroad, which kept it booming and growing during the Civil War era. Things slowed down in 1872 when the rail yards were moved to Jackson. Here it looks as if things are booming again.

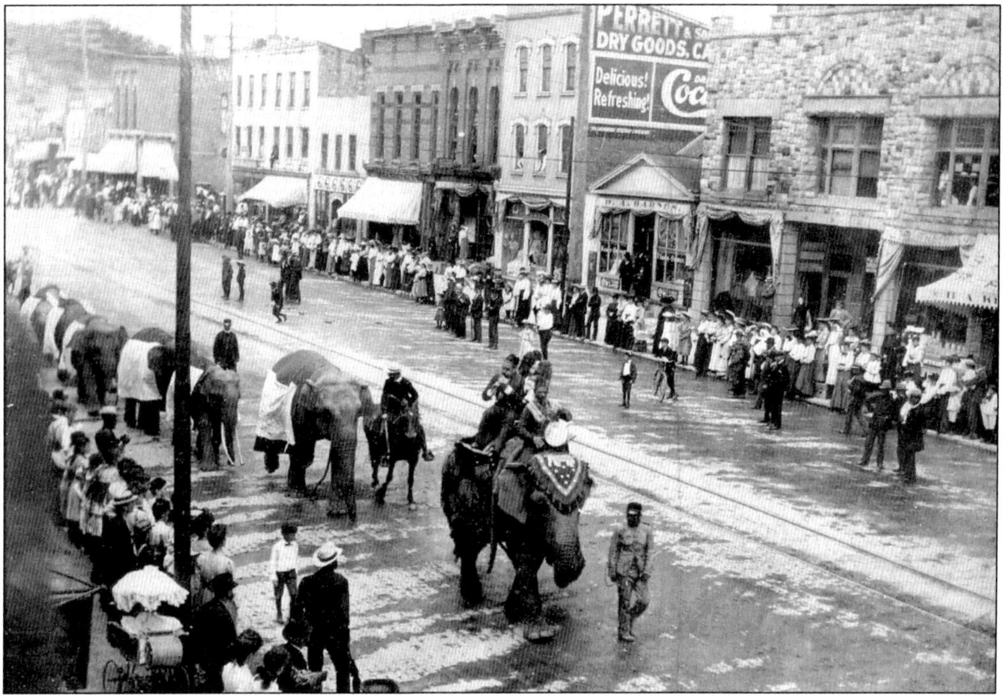

Circuses were a big part of city life, particularly in the summer when dozens of circuses, both big and small, made their way around the country. Here elephants march down Michigan Avenue, then called State Street. Note the sign for Perrett's Dry Goods in the background.

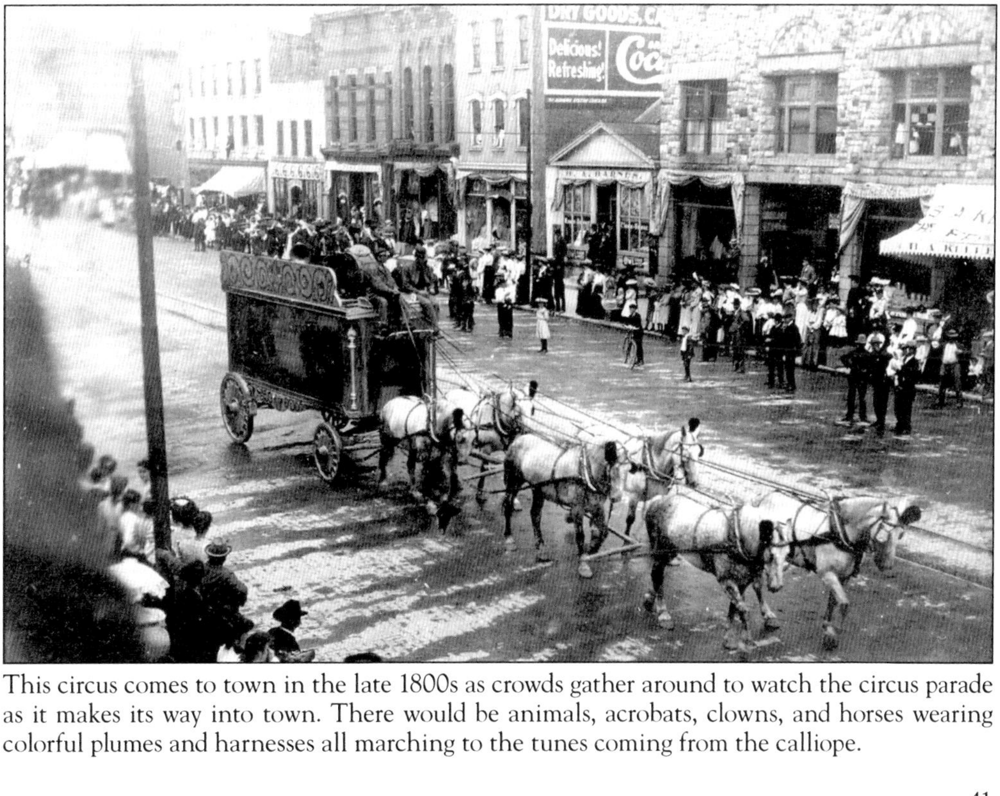

This circus comes to town in the late 1800s as crowds gather around to watch the circus parade as it makes its way into town. There would be animals, acrobats, clowns, and horses wearing colorful plumes and harnesses all marching to the tunes coming from the calliope.

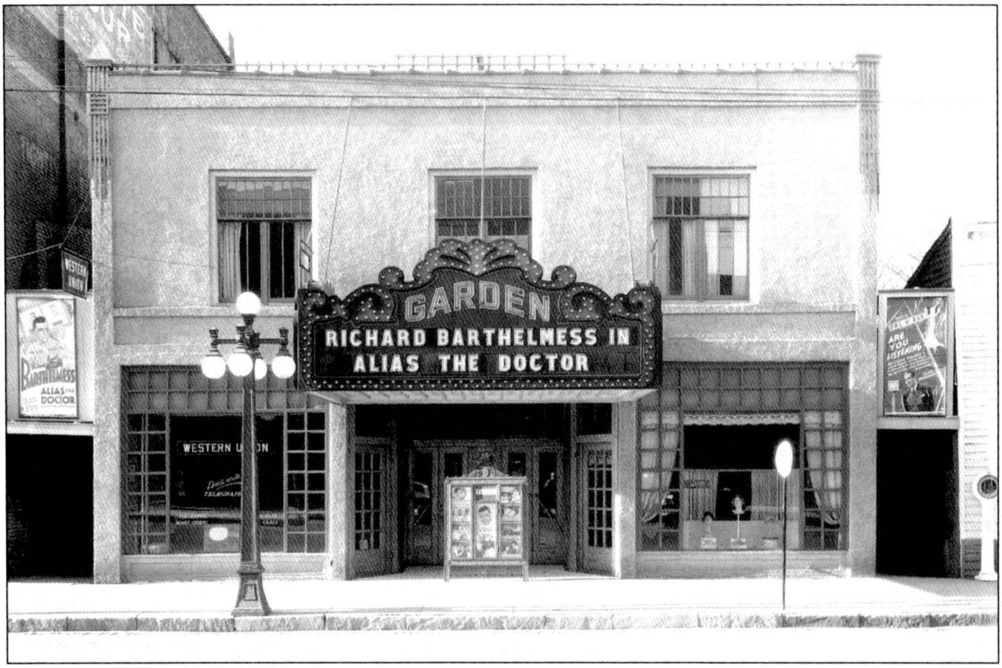

The Garden Theatre, located at 105 West Michigan Avenue and shown here in a 1940s photograph, was built in 1915. The organ from this theater is now across the street at the Mole Hole Gift Shop. It is now the site of five shops known as the Shops at the Garden Theatre.

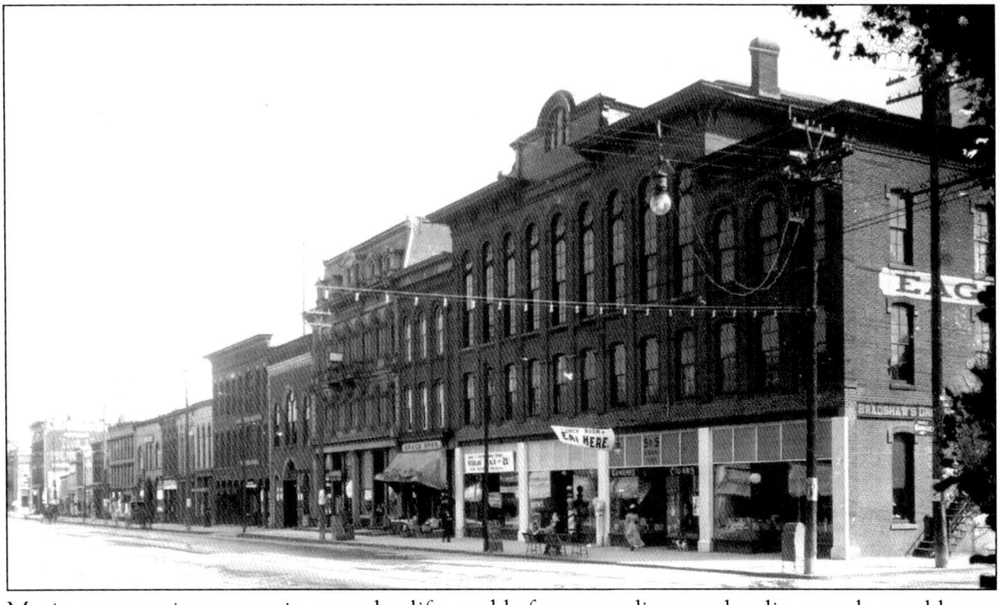

Music was very important in everyday life, and before recordings and radio, people would turn out for bands and orchestras. It was not uncommon for even small towns to have opera houses. Shown here is the Eagle Opera House, which is located at 151 West Michigan Avenue in downtown Marshall.

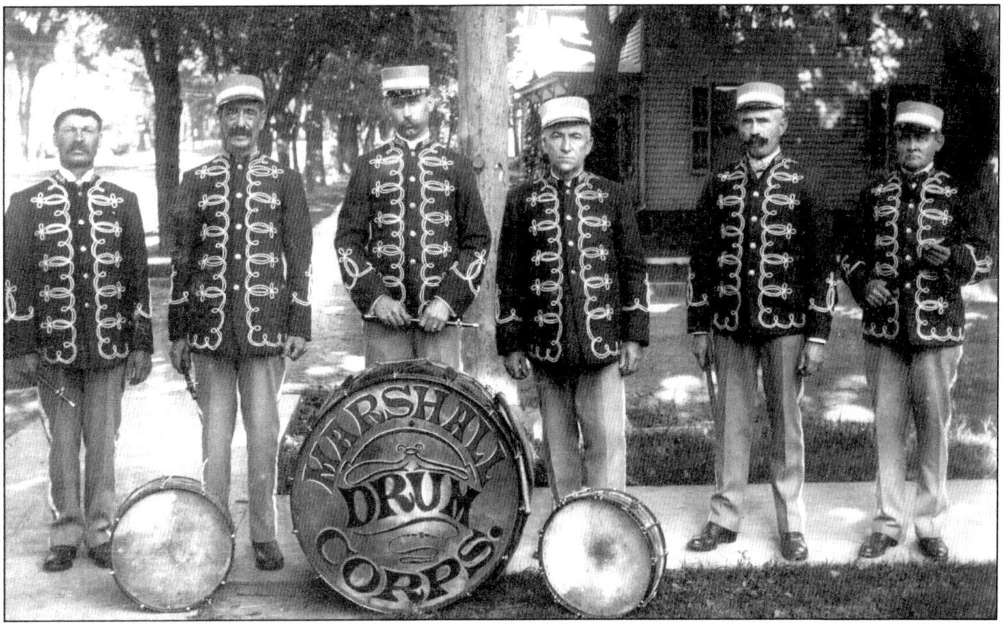

The Marshall Drum Corps was very popular not only in Marshall but throughout Calhoun County. The photograph was taken in the early 1900s. The drum in the photograph can be seen today in the GAR Museum in downtown Marshall. The museum, a repository of local history, is in the former Grand Army of the Republic Meeting Hall.

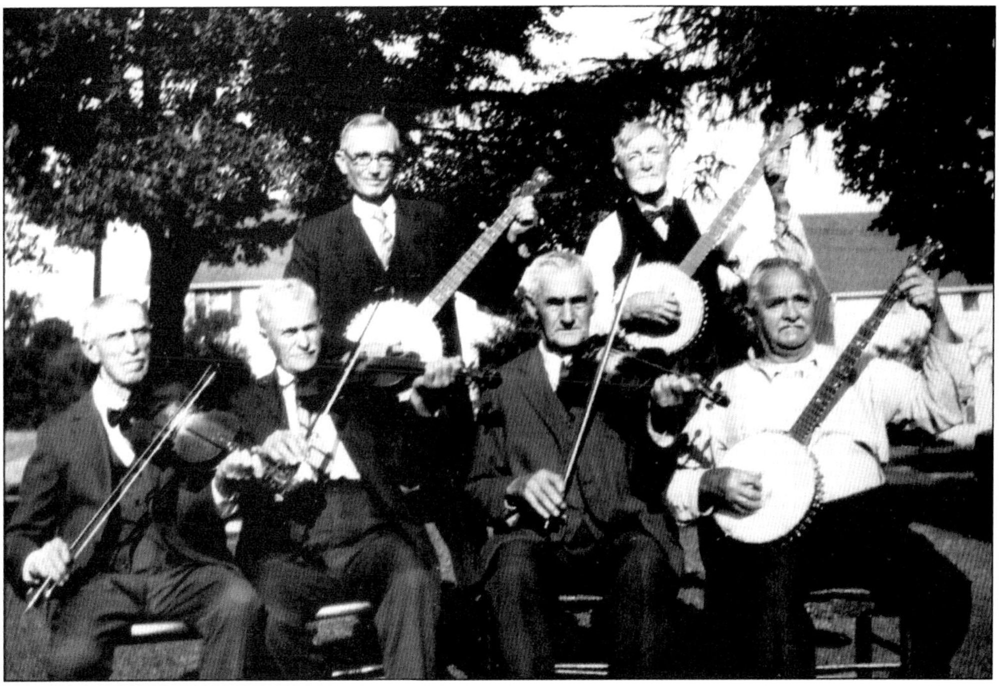

The Old Time Orchestra practices in Charles Grant's yard in this 1920s photograph. Shown here are Charles Grant (born 1840, died 1926), E. R. Priest (born 1846, died 1936), Apollo Lincoln (born 1853, died 1942), Edward Kipp (born 1853), Ralph Mann (born 1859, died 1932), and Charles Pierce (born 1869, died 1932).

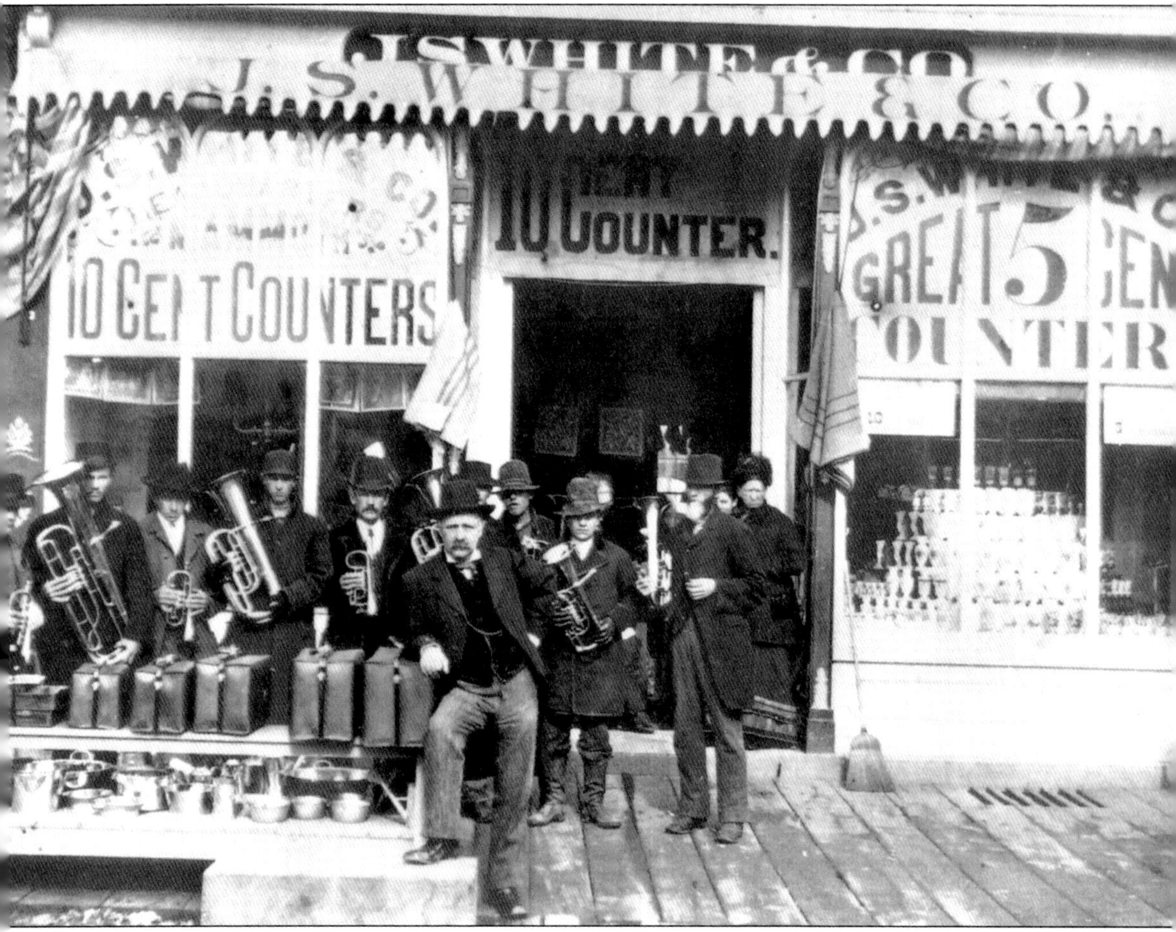

It appears they are having fun making music in this undated photograph that looks to be from the 1880s.

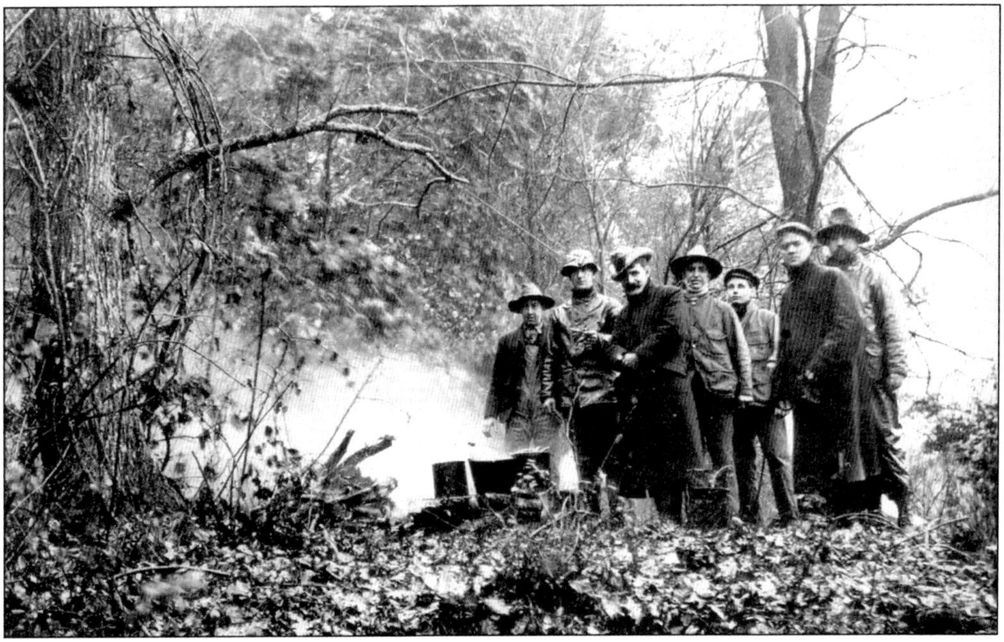

Although it was a stately city filled with marvelous buildings, rural activities were also a part of the social fabric of the community. In this undated photograph, from left to right, Sam Brewer, C. E. Gauss, L. Calkins, P. S. Joy, Rupert Bentley, D. Gorham, and C. W. Gasper watch as maple sap is boiled down into syrup.

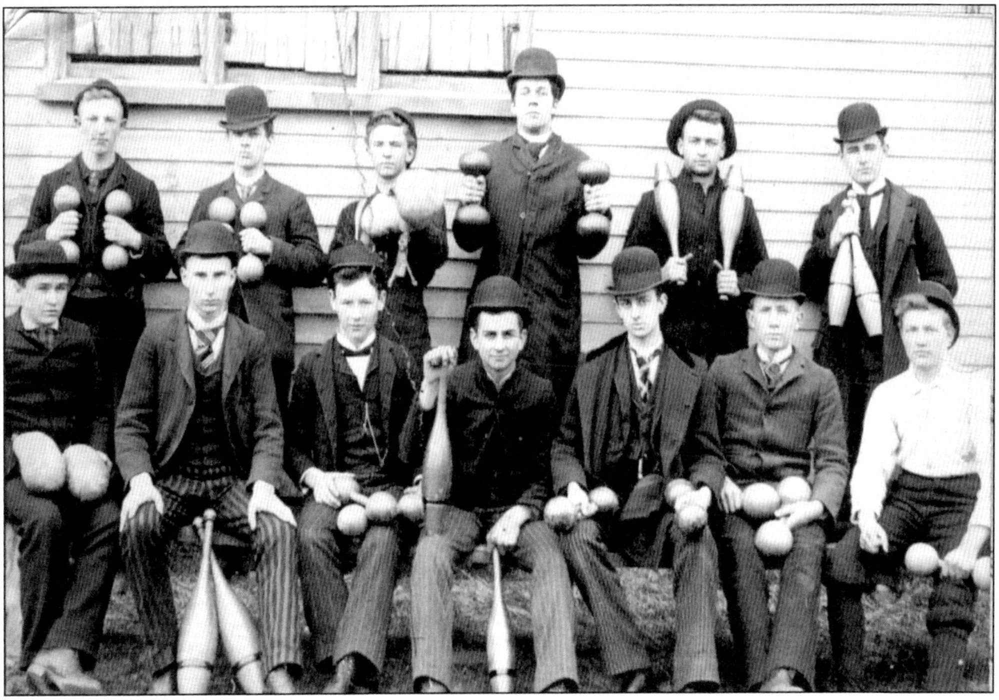

Here is a picture of the Marshall Bowling League. The following names are listed on the back: Henry Reed, Charles Day, Everett Evans, Lou Thompson, Frank Cathcart, L. B. Thompson, and Charles McPhearson.

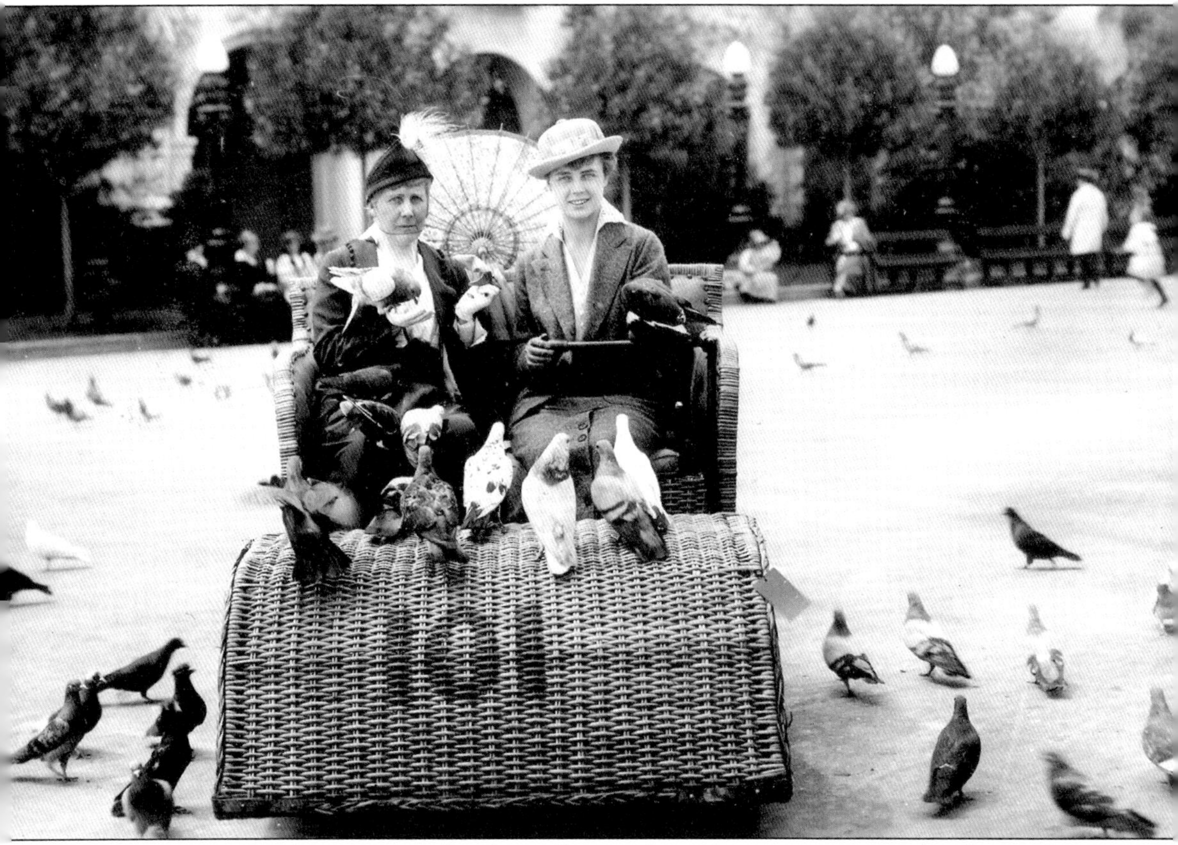

The Gorham family sure seemed to know how to have fun. Here are two family members traveling in style in a wicker carriage. Like the myriad of car models today, buggies came in different styles and sizes. This was probably taken while they were living in The Hague when Charles T. Gorham was the minister to the Dutch court.

Four

People

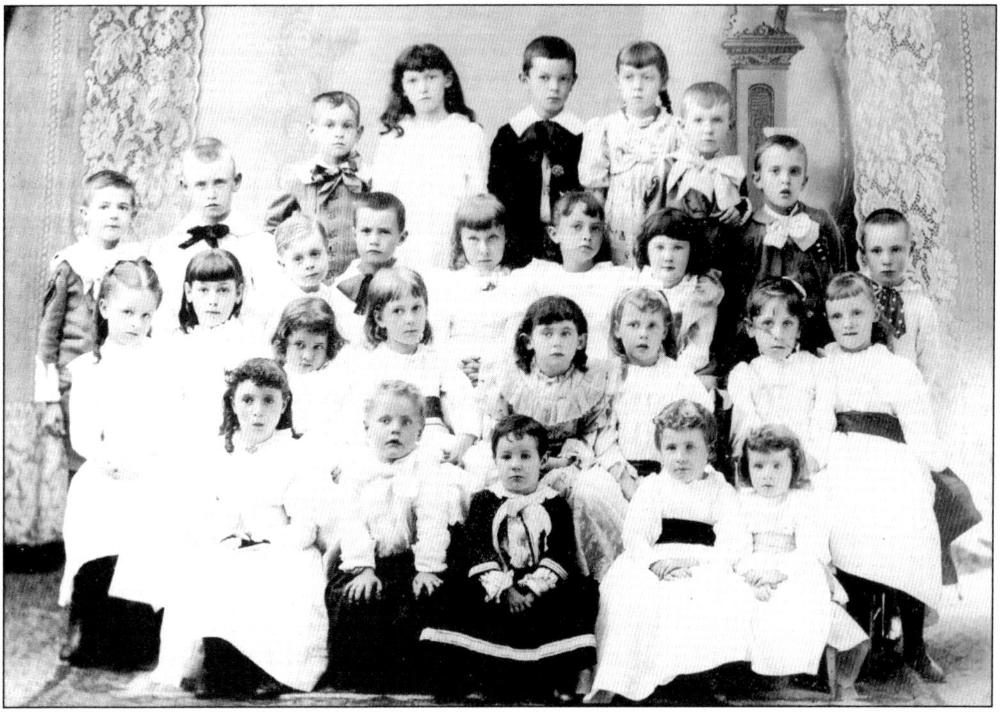

This photograph of J. Cunningham's Sunday school class was taken on Children's Day in 1893 at Trinity Episcopal Church. The children are, in no particular order, Dale Dobbins, Harold Dans, Glenn Freed, Jessie Stout, Jamie Cox, Ruth Brewer, Charlie Dobbins, Claude Merrill, Marie Winsor, Hewitt Coleman, Walter McKiver, Hazel Hoeltzel, Lilly McKiver, Helen Cook, Ray Cook, ? McKiver, Margery Dresser, George Eyre, Hester Cunningham, Flossie Prindle, Flossie Cunningham, Grace Brand, Leslie Cunningham, Hugh Cook, and ? Hinkle.

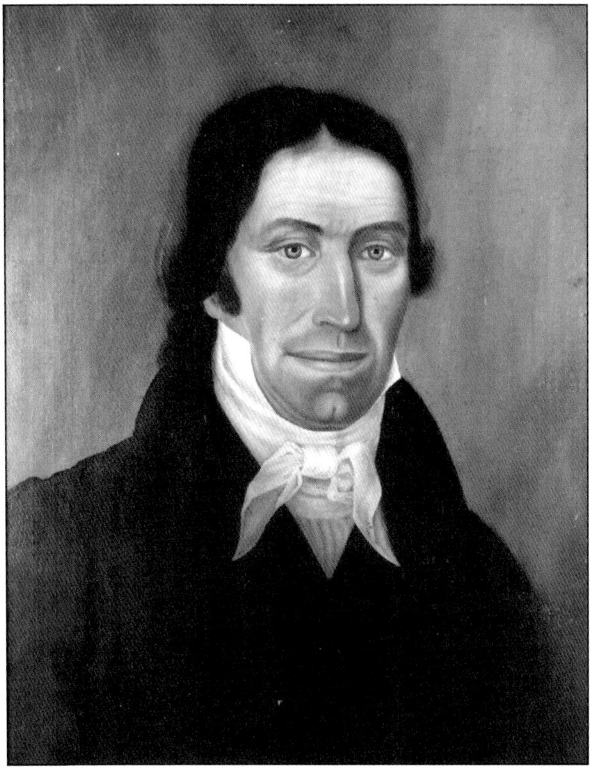

Seth Ketchum was the father of town founder Sidney Ketchum and Marshall's first settler, George Ketchum. He came with his sons to help settle the new business and political capital of the Michigan Territory. He is the only Revolutionary War veteran buried in Oakridge Cemetery.

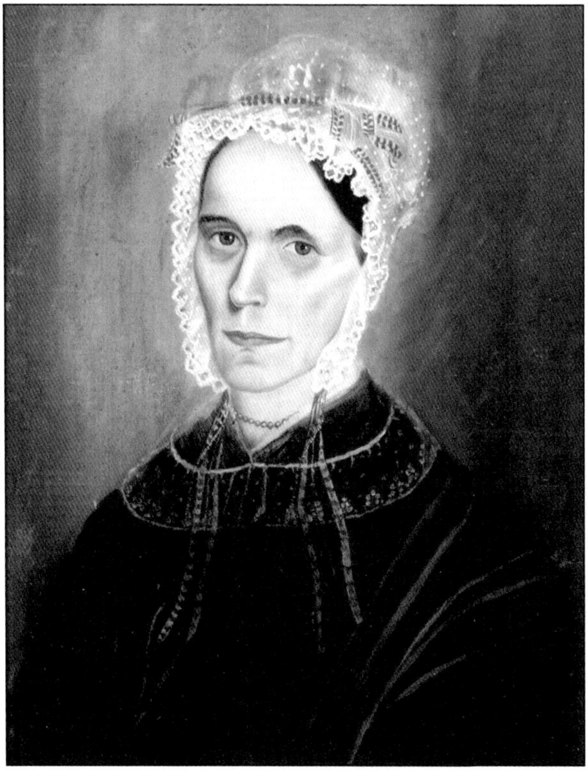

Lydia Ketchum was the matriarch of the Ketchum family. Her daughter, Eliza, was the teacher in Marshall's first schoolhouse in 1832. Both of the elder Ketchums are buried at Oakridge Cemetery in Marshall with their son Sidney. George went on to found Riverside, California, and is buried there.

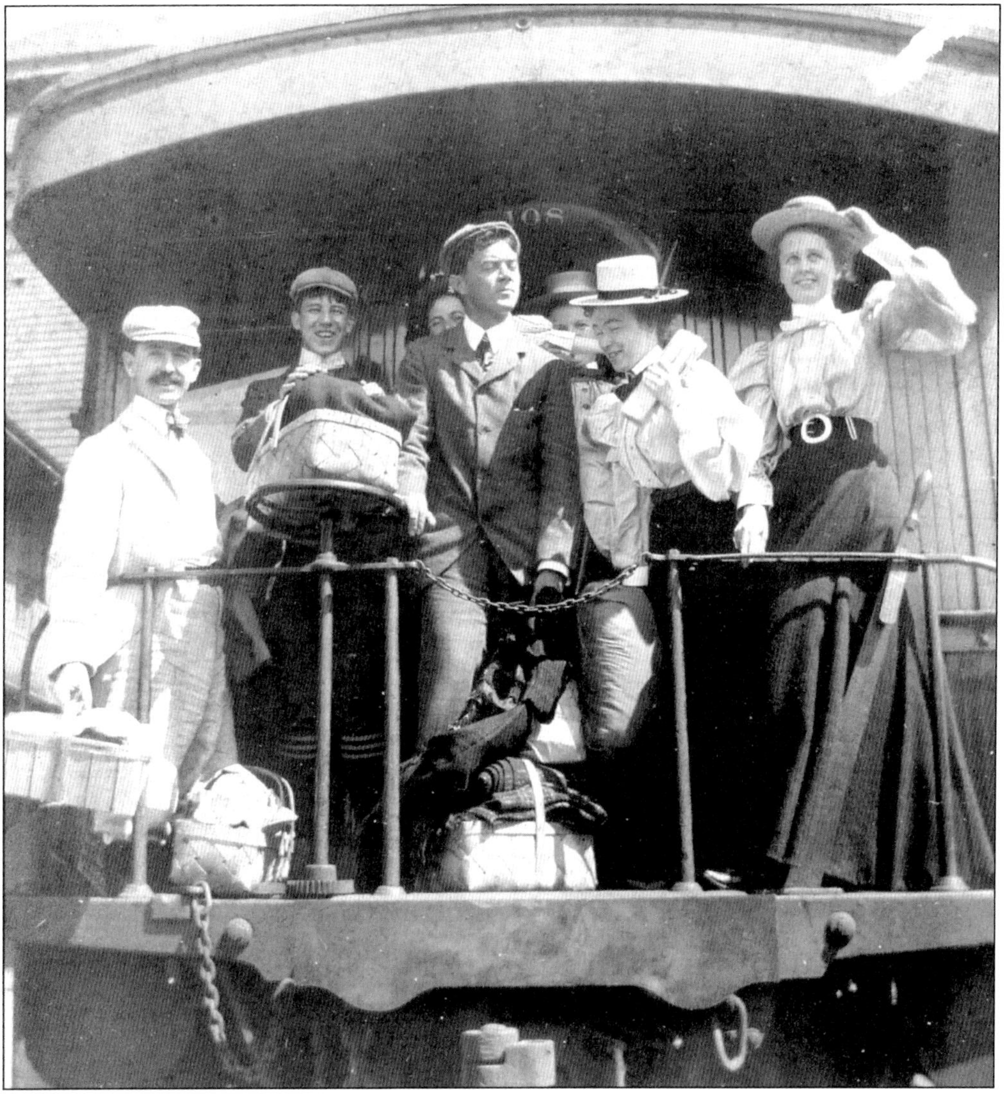

A picnic at Cold Springs Park between Marshall and Albion was a traditional hit with the young people of both communities around in the late 1800s and the early 1900s. A six-mile ride and back on the interurban to the park on the Kalamazoo River was a great day's outing.

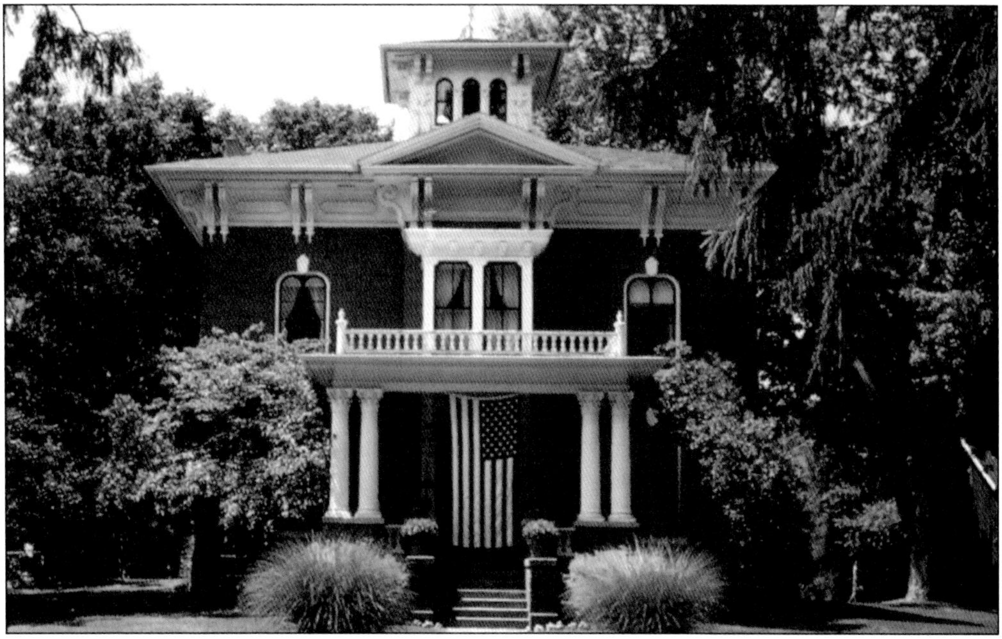

The Karstaedt-Cook house was built in 1869 at 603 North Kalamazoo Avenue. James Redefield was the architect for the Colonial Revival porch added in 1897. The most famous resident of this house was William Wallace Cook, who resided in the house from about 1900 to 1933. Cook was a novelist for Street and Smith in New York City. The exterior of this home has not changed much since the 1897 porch was added.

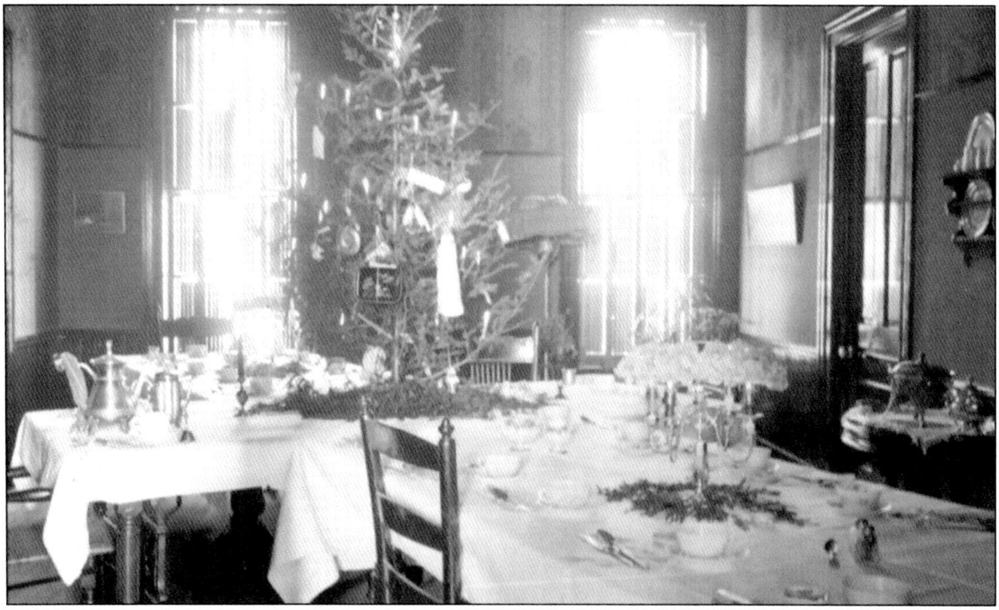

This interior of the dining room of the Karstaedt-Cook house shows it at Christmas in 1900. The interior of this room has been restored to the appearance in this photograph. However, the current owners do not have a tree with burning candles on the table for Christmas dinner. This is one of the few remaining interior photographs of the era. Notice the candelabra with shades in the middle of the table in the foreground.

William Wallace Cook was definitely Marshall's most famous author. Between 1900 and 1930, he wrote 60,000 words a week on what we would call a really old-fashioned upright typewriter. His genre was adventure stories of the Wild West. He wrote under a great number of pen names, such as Frank Merriwell.

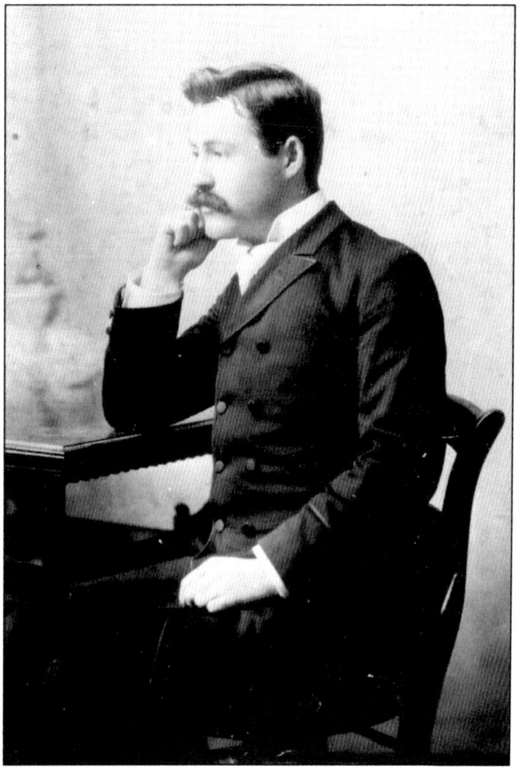

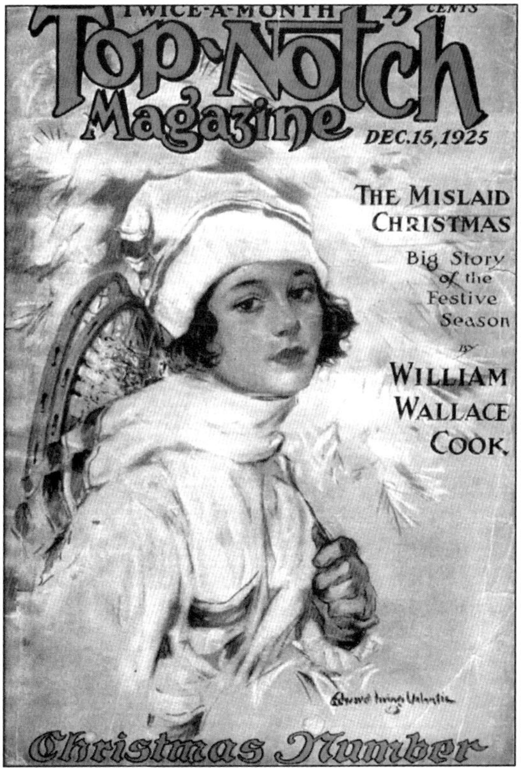

Many of Cook's stories appeared in Street and Smith's weekly magazines like this issue of *Top-Notch* from Christmas 1925. This is one of those rare occurrences where Street and Smith actually used Cook's own name. Even with his strenuous writing schedule, he still found time to be one of the charter members of the Marshall Rotary Club on February 29, 1924.

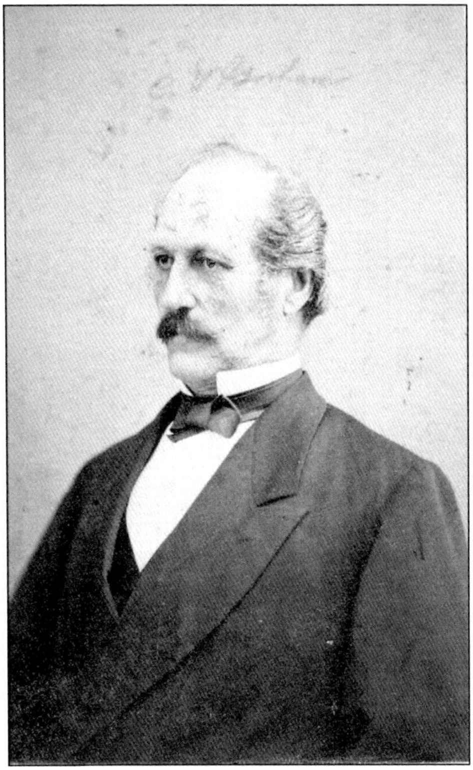

Charles T. Gorham made history all by himself. He was the first to step forward when it was asked who was responsible for shepherding escaped slaves and Marshall residents Adam Crosswhite and his family to Canada. He demanded that his name be put up in capital letters. What happened to the Crosswhite family caused Henry Clay, U.S. senator from Kentucky, to push the Fugitive Slave Act through the U.S. Congress, an act that caused the Civil War. Gorham began his life in Marshall as a dry goods merchant in partnership with Chauncey Brewer. When he sold his half of the business, he formed the First National Bank of Marshall. That bank went through many manifestations before it merged in the mid-20th century with seven other banks to become once again the Michigan National Bank.

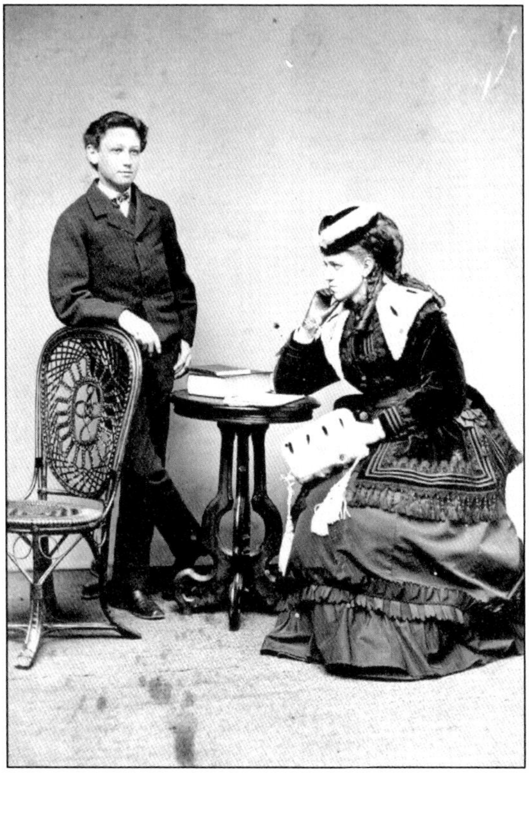

Belle Gorham, shown here with her son Charles E., was also active in the community. She was the secretary of the Marshall Ladies Library Association that raised $15,000 to build the library at the corner of Mansion and Madison Streets. She enjoyed her time in The Hague while her husband was the U.S. minister to the Netherlands. When they returned to Marshall in 1851, they settled into the grand five-columned home at 300 North Kalamazoo Avenue, currently referred to as the Brooks House.

Thomas J. O'Brien was born in Jackson but grew up in Marshall. He went on to study law at the University of Michigan and came home to practice. He became counsel for the Grand Rapids and Indiana Railroad. He ended up in the U.S. Diplomatic Corps and married the daughter of the ambassador from the United Kingdom. He served as ambassador to Italy, Japan, and Denmark. During his tour in Denmark, he successfully negotiated the purchase of the U.S. Virgin Islands in 1917 for $25 million.

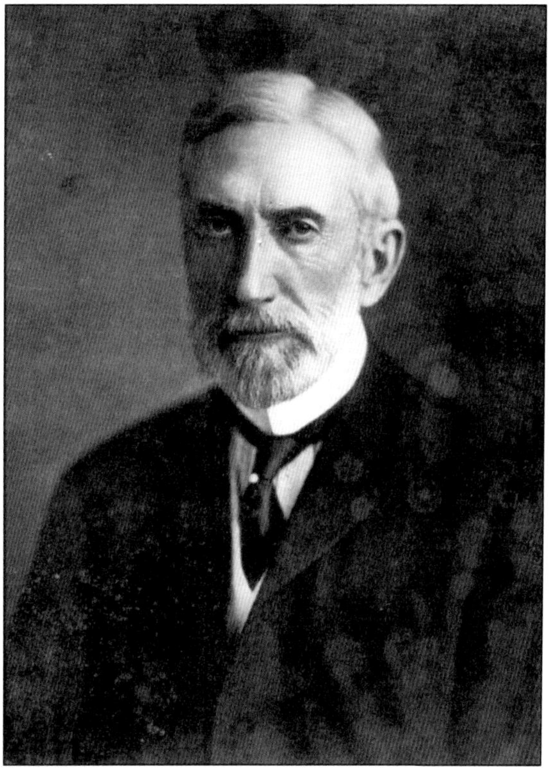

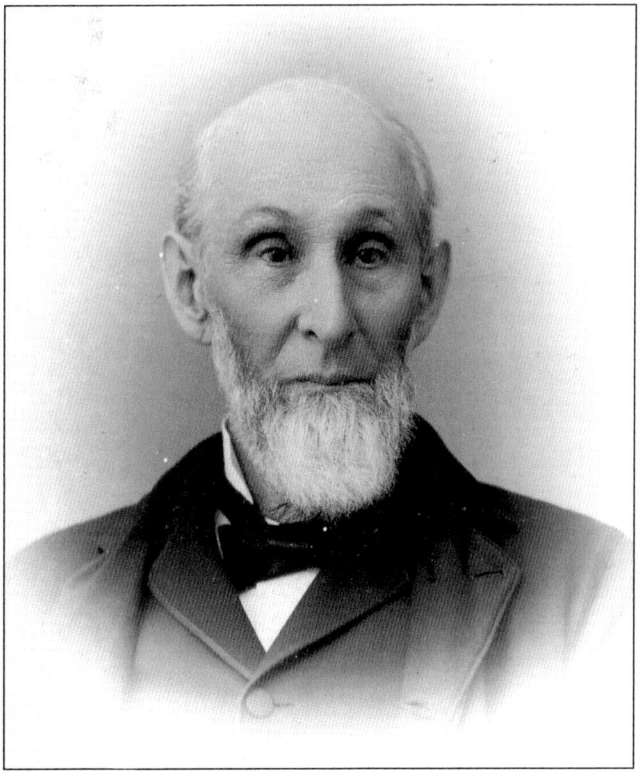

The people in Marshall were avid abolitionists, and Judge George T. Ingersoll led the Crosswhite family to Ketchums Mill on the Kalamazoo River in the southeast portion of Marshall when the family's owner tried to reclaim all of them. Ingersoll was also one of the original owners of the Young Ladies Institute housed in the old Ketchum mansion. The Ingersoll house still stands at the northwest corner of Grand and Mansion Streets. He lived there from 1850 until he died in 1902.

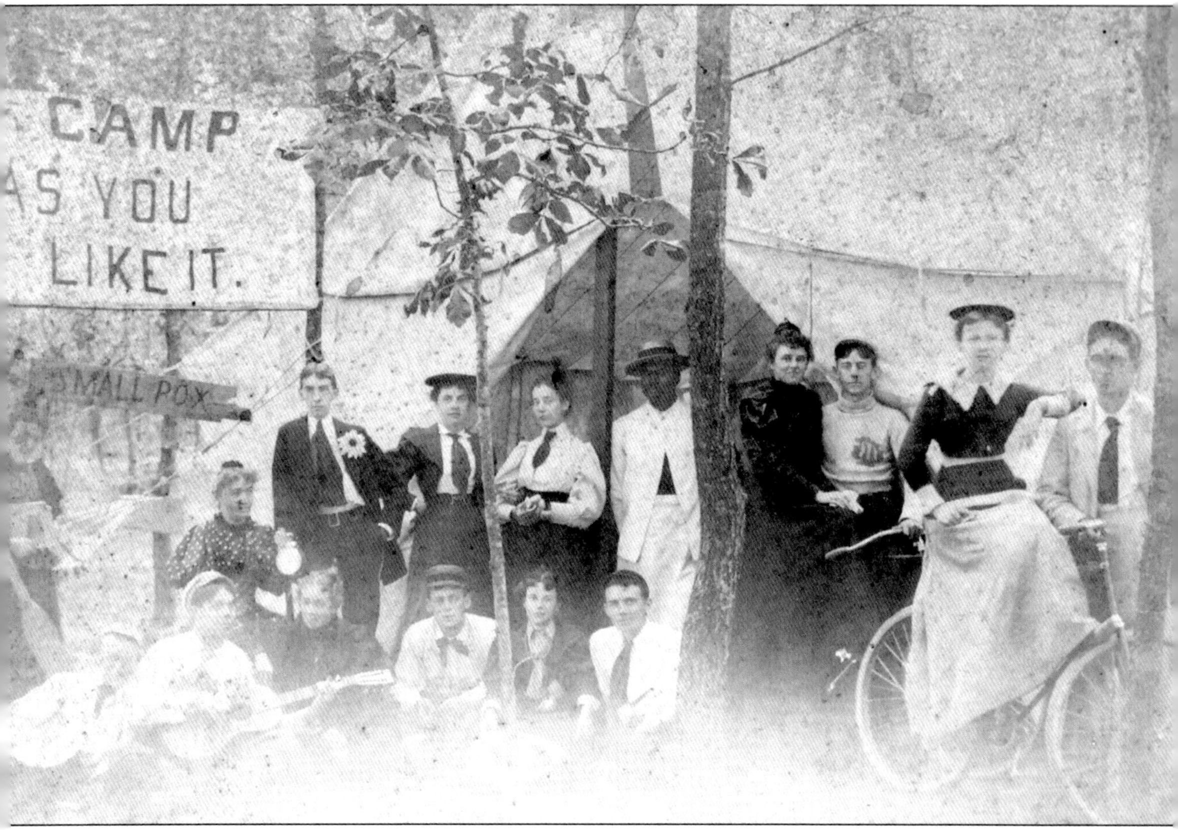

Camping at Lyon Lake south of town seems to be a big pastime in the late 1800s and early 1900s. "Camp as You Like It" and "Smallpox" are questionable signs for the era's ethics. Six miles on one of those bicycles really took a lot of energy, especially while trying to avoid catching one's skirt in the bicycle chain.

"Two Contented Johns" is the title on the picture to the right. John Harther (left) and John Fischer are the two contented gentlemen. One might refer to them as Mutt and Jeff. Below are John Gottlob (left) and John David. Gottlob was a shoemaker by trade. David was a farmer. Judging by the appearance of Gottlob's shoes, one has to wonder about the difference in cleanliness standards between then and now. All four of these citizens are listed as pioneers of Marshall. Harold C. Brooks included both of these photographs in his 1930s history of Marshall. The photograph to the right was one of the 15 photographs included in the series of postcards he created for Marshall's centennial celebration. The collection was created to promote the history of Marshall he was working on at that time. He never finished it before he died in the early 1980s.

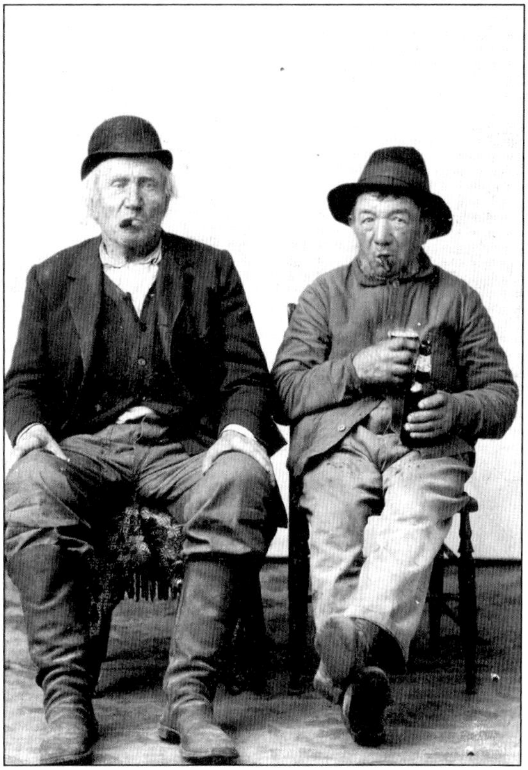

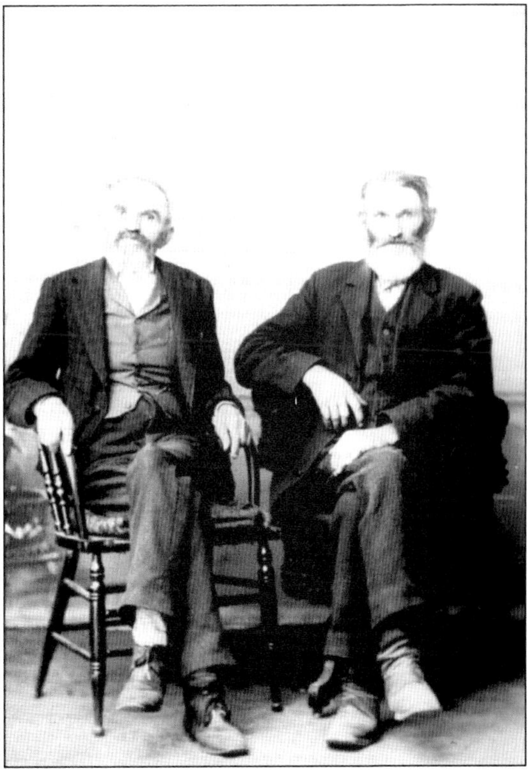

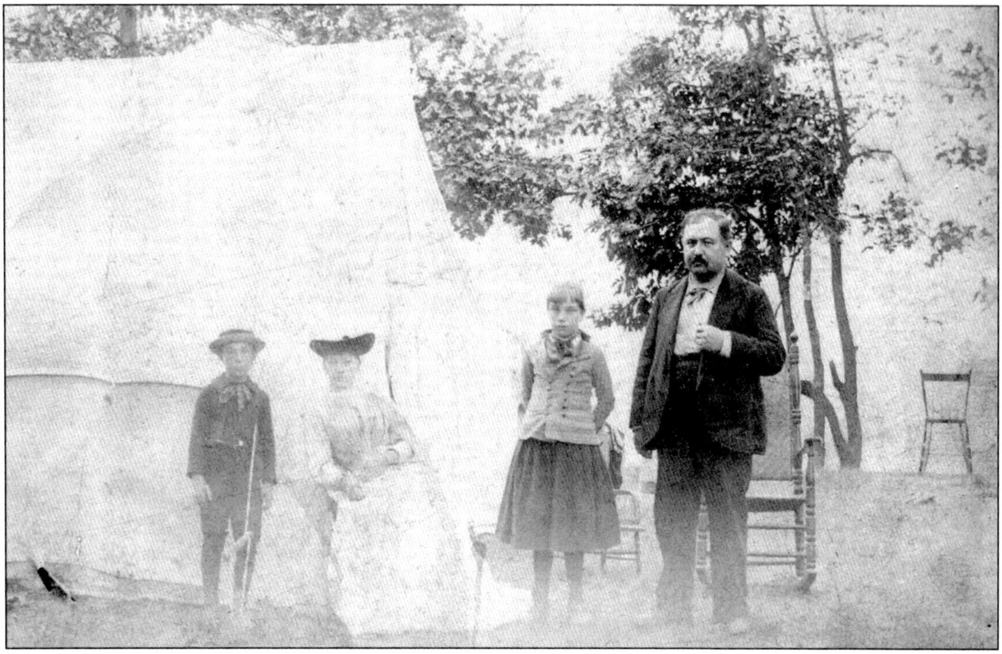

The Martin "Cap" Wagner family enjoys a little camping at Lyon Lake several miles south of Marshall. The Wagners are the ones who hired the famous muralist F. A. Grace from Quincy, Illinois, to paint the frescos in their already opulent home, the Honolulu House, between 1885 and 1888. Seeing them beside a tent at the lake seems a little out of place for a family so accustomed to a life of ease. Notice they did not forget to bring the rocking chairs to use at the lake.

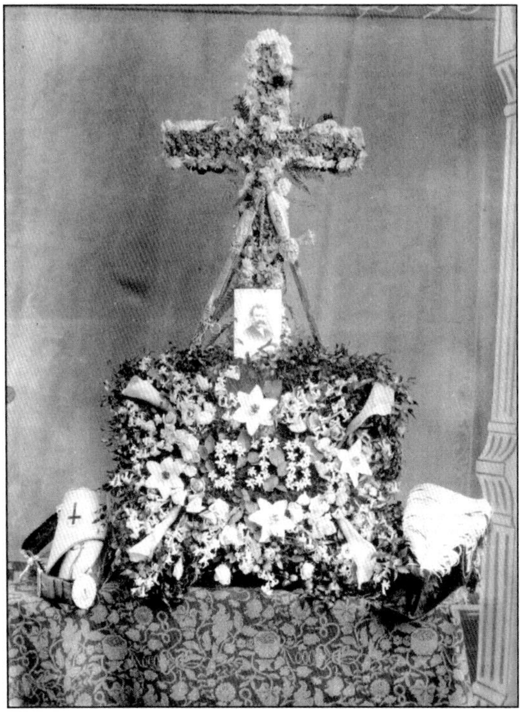

This elaborate floral display was presented at Cap Wagner's funeral by his fraternal organization. When one thinks of the lack of refrigeration available around 1900, it is amazing that something like this could be made and kept until the funeral.

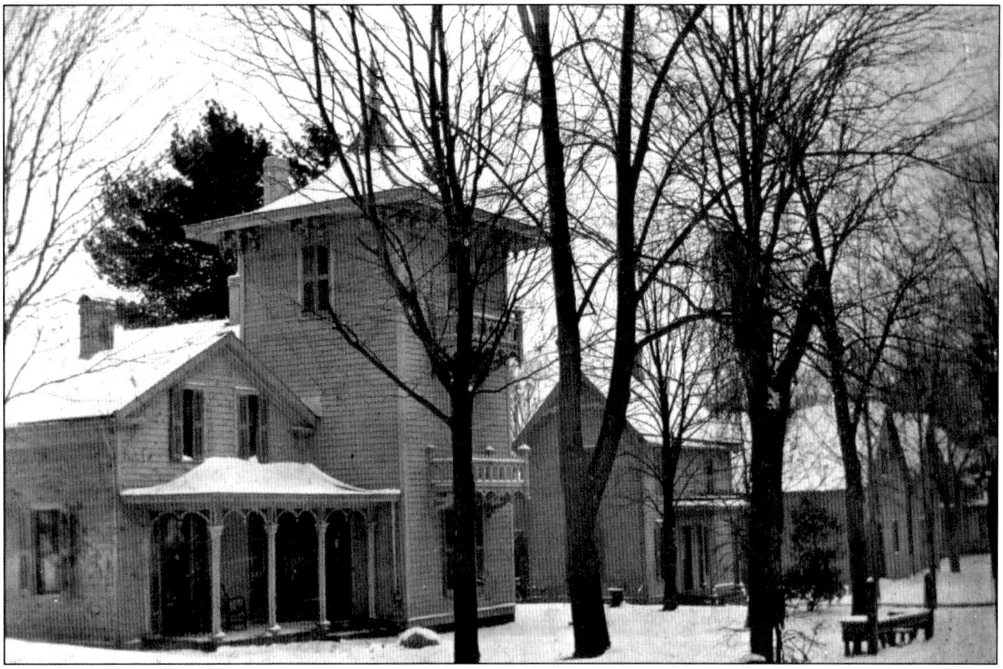

Dr. Henry L. Joy built this house on the corner of Kalamazoo Avenue and Prospect Street in 1844. Joy was married to Carolyn Schuyler. They expanded the house and added the tower in 1857. The only room in the tower is on the third floor. The rest is just a circular stair leading to that room. The house is so distinctive that it was featured on the cover of Mabel Cooper Skjelver's *Nineteenth Century Homes of Marshall, Michigan*.

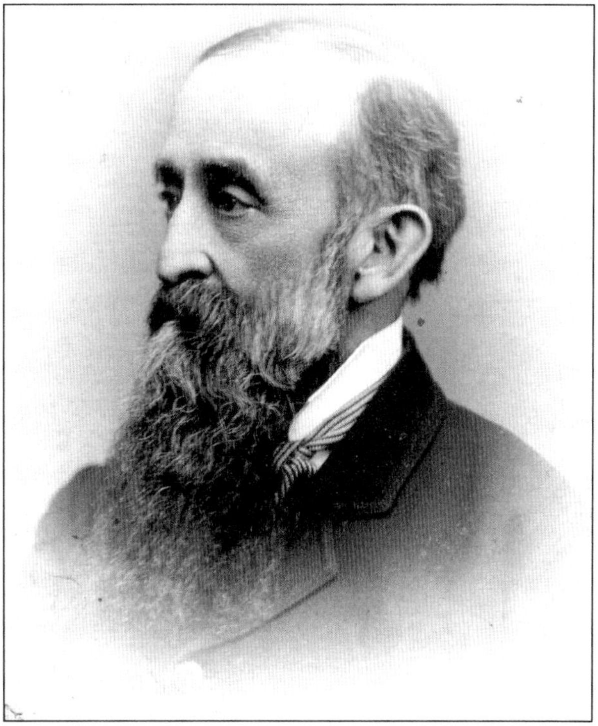

Dr. Joy was quite active in many facets of the community. He jointly owned a drugstore with his brother-in-law, Dr. John Montgomery. He was on the vestry of Trinity Episcopal Church and later on the school board. He was also one of the founders of the Young Ladies Institute.

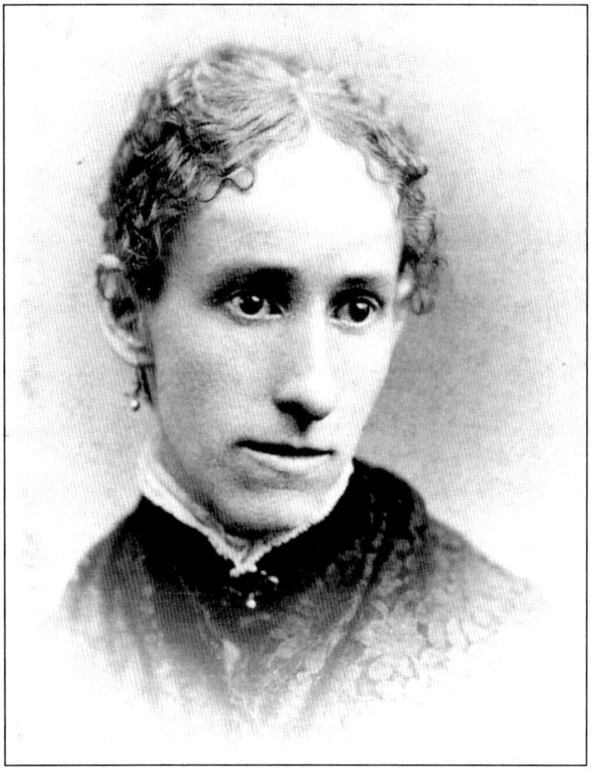

Gertrude Smith was one of several female professional photographers. This self-portrait is not exactly flattering, but she was brave to break the gender gap and pursue a career. The most famous lady photographers in Marshall were Wright and MacKay, who took several of the photographs in this book along with two or three by Smith.

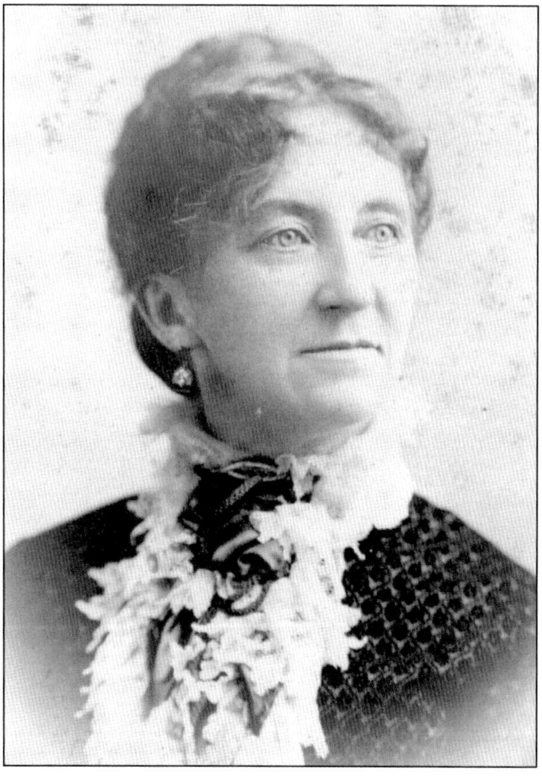

Susan Jones pursued a more traditional female occupation and served as an executive secretary. Her claim to fame is the truly unusual burial plot she designed for her family. She never married, but she created a plot outlined by concrete logs. There is a 10-foot-tall tree stump in the center of the site with the family name. There are log chairs also made from concrete. Every grave in the plot is marked by a small horizontal log inscribed for each family member.

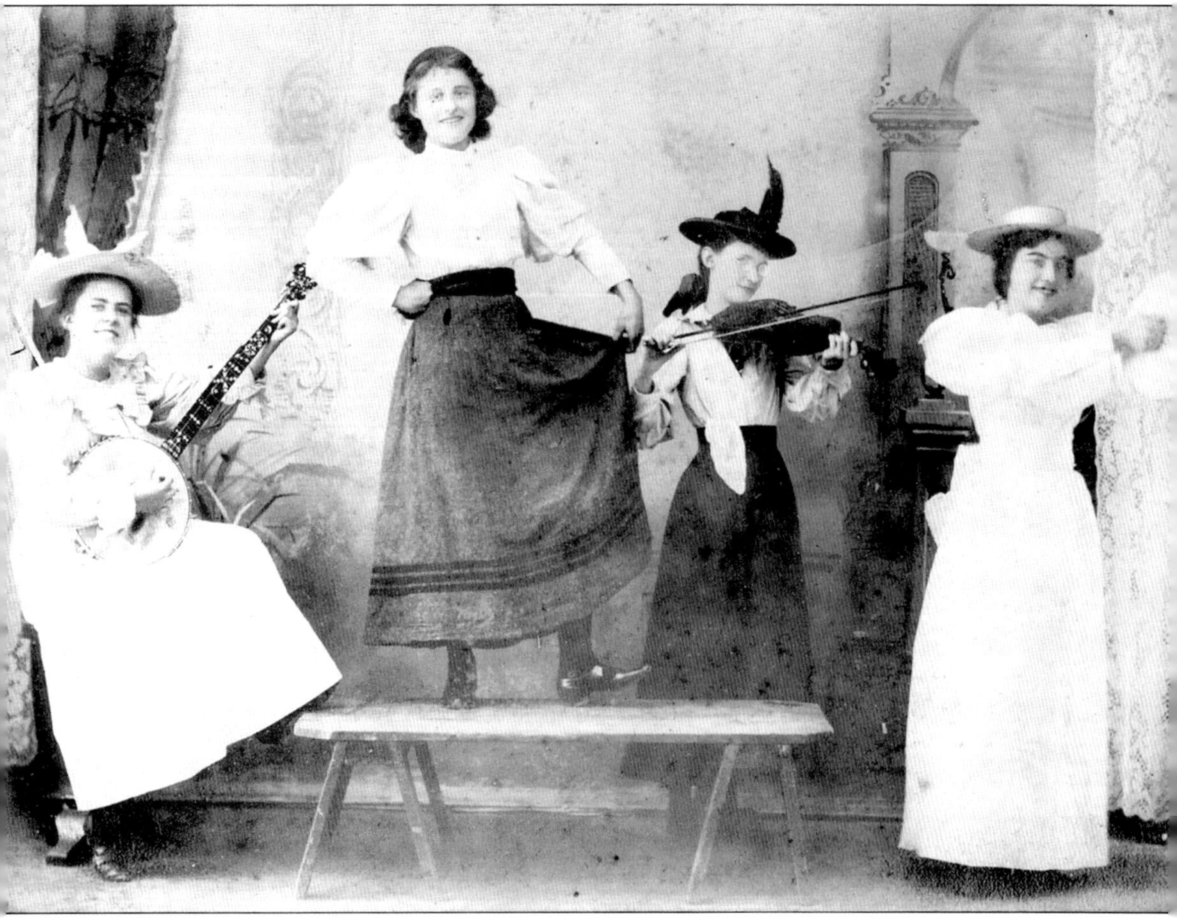

These young ladies must be very talented to perform at the Eagle Opera House. The same backdrop appears in many old photographs taken at the opera house.

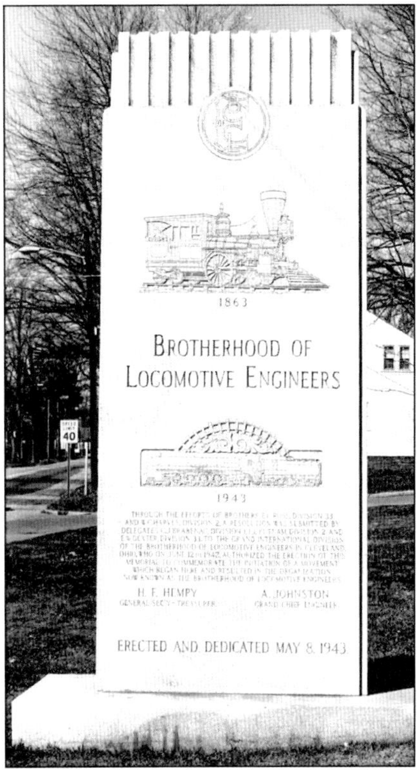

Marshall seems to have markers everywhere. It is not a new phenomenon, as shown by this 1943 marker dedicated to the Brotherhood of Locomotive Engineers. The organization was founded in 1863 as the Brotherhood of the Footboard. This was one of the first unions in the world and was founded by the workers in the roundhouse and railroad yards at the end of South Linden Street.

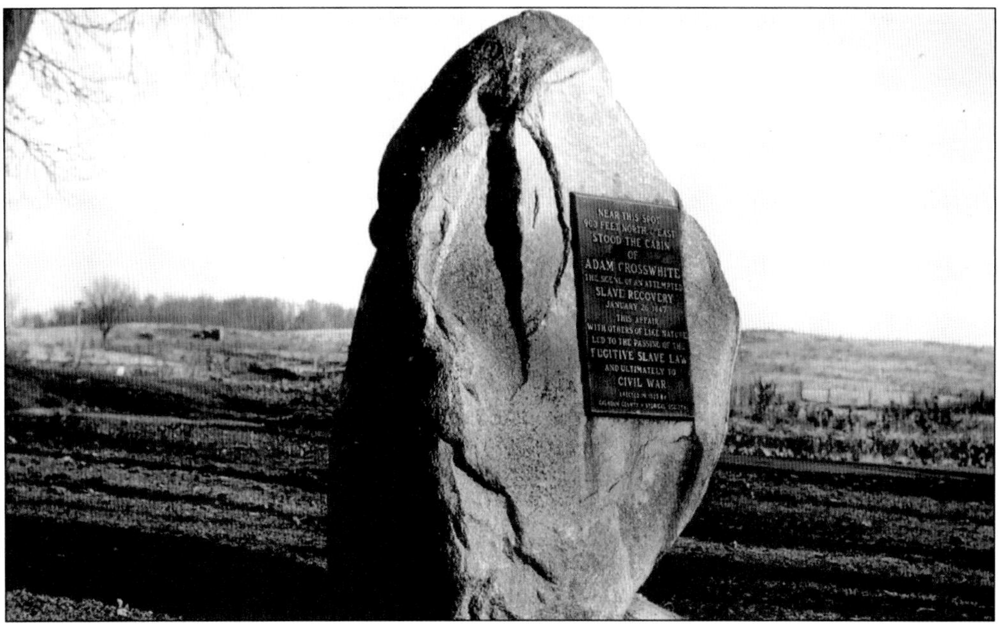

Adam Crosswhite was an escaped slave living in Marshall with his wife and family when a representative for his former owner came looking for him. He and several other former slaves had a system worked out with the leading citizens of Marshall to send up an alarm when someone showed up to reclaim "former property." Crosswhite sent the alarm, and Charles T. Gorham, Isaac Hurd, and Oliver C. Comstock Jr. were among those that came to his immediate rescue.

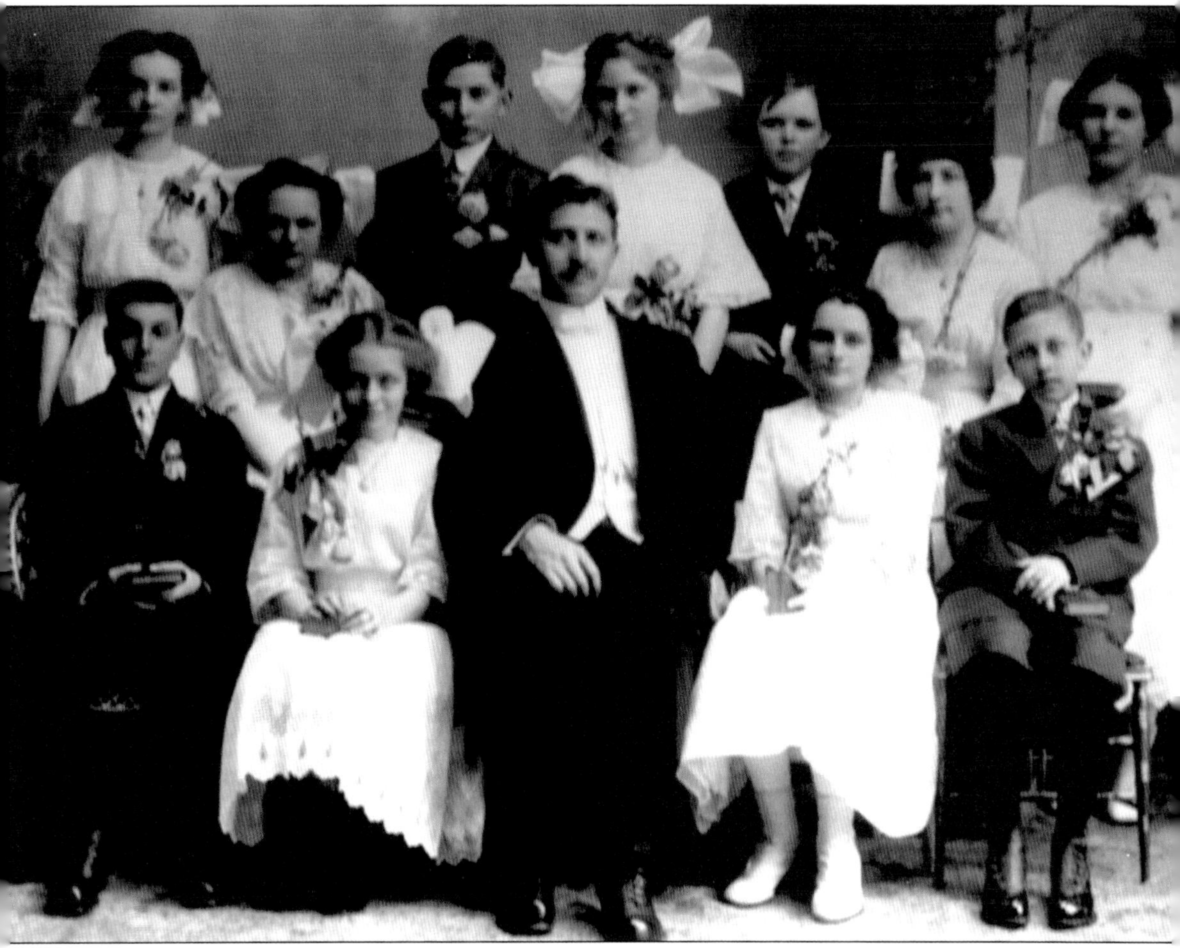

Confirmation class at Zion Lutheran Church is shown about 1927–1932. Dr. Christopher Heidenreich was the minister at Zion from 1896 to 1946. From left to right, the members of the class are (first row) Erwin Noneman, Pearl Luscher, Dr. Heidenreich, Bessie Voght, and Theophile Heidenreich; (second row) Neva Eipper, Margaret Rentschler, Rudy D. Vogelreuter, Nellie Zanger, Harold Noneman, a Schutz girl, and Betty Reyer. Many of these young people still have descendents living in Marshall today. This photograph was taken by Young and MacKay.

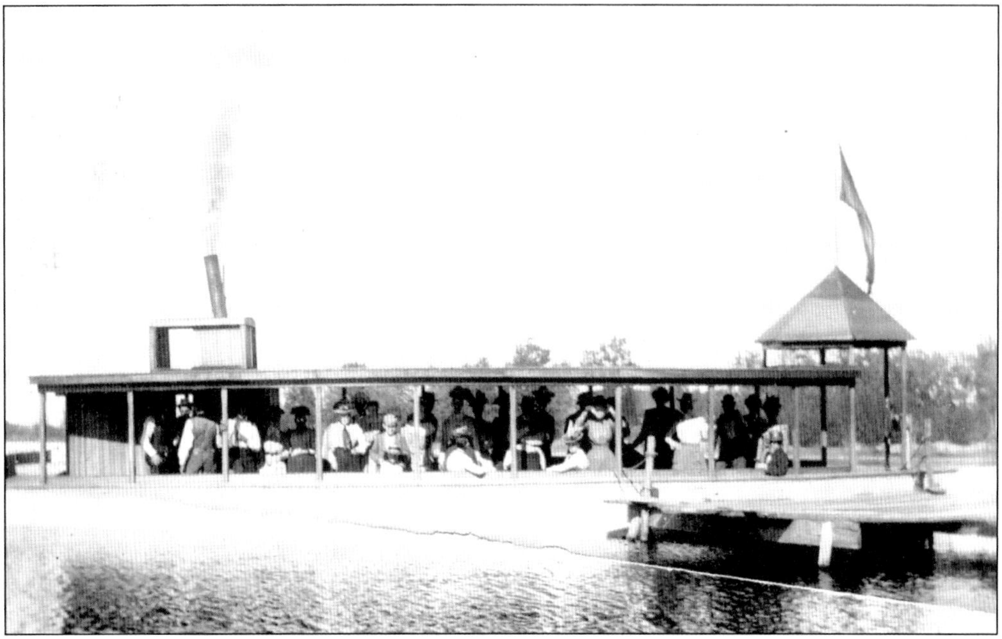

The *S. J. Burpee* plied the waters of the Kalamazoo River between Marshall and Cold Springs Park. It was advertised as being a full-size side-paddle steamship. It did provide a great deal of entertainment in the days before video games.

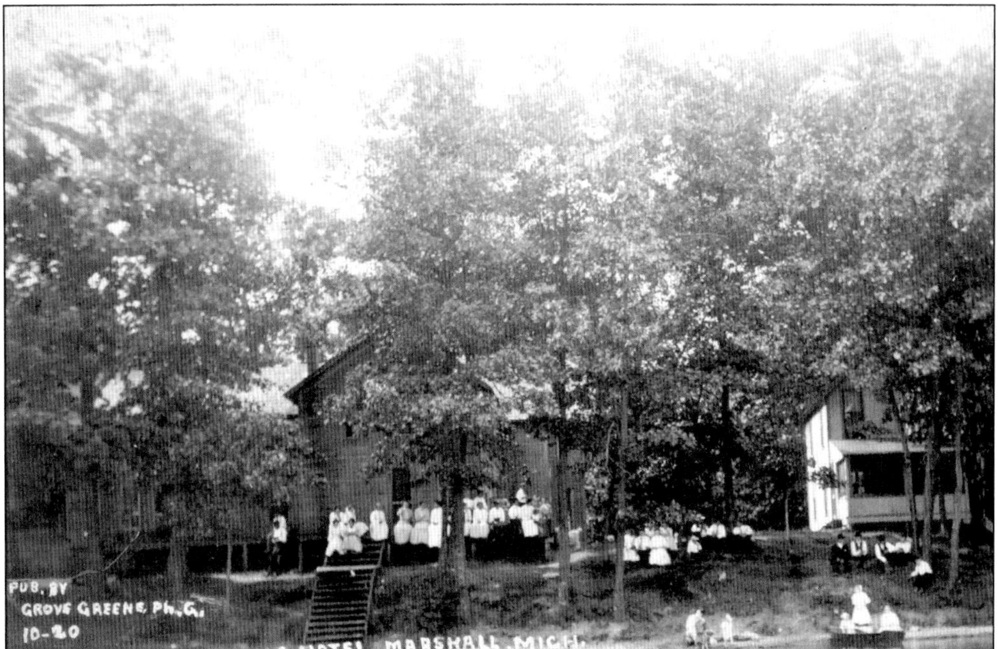

Lyon Lake was definitely the "in" place to be in the summer. It is hard to imagine staying cool with all that material in the white dresses worn by these ladies. The hotel is now a single-family home. The postcard was produced by Grove Greene Pharmacy, which is now Hemmingsen's Rexall in downtown Marshall.

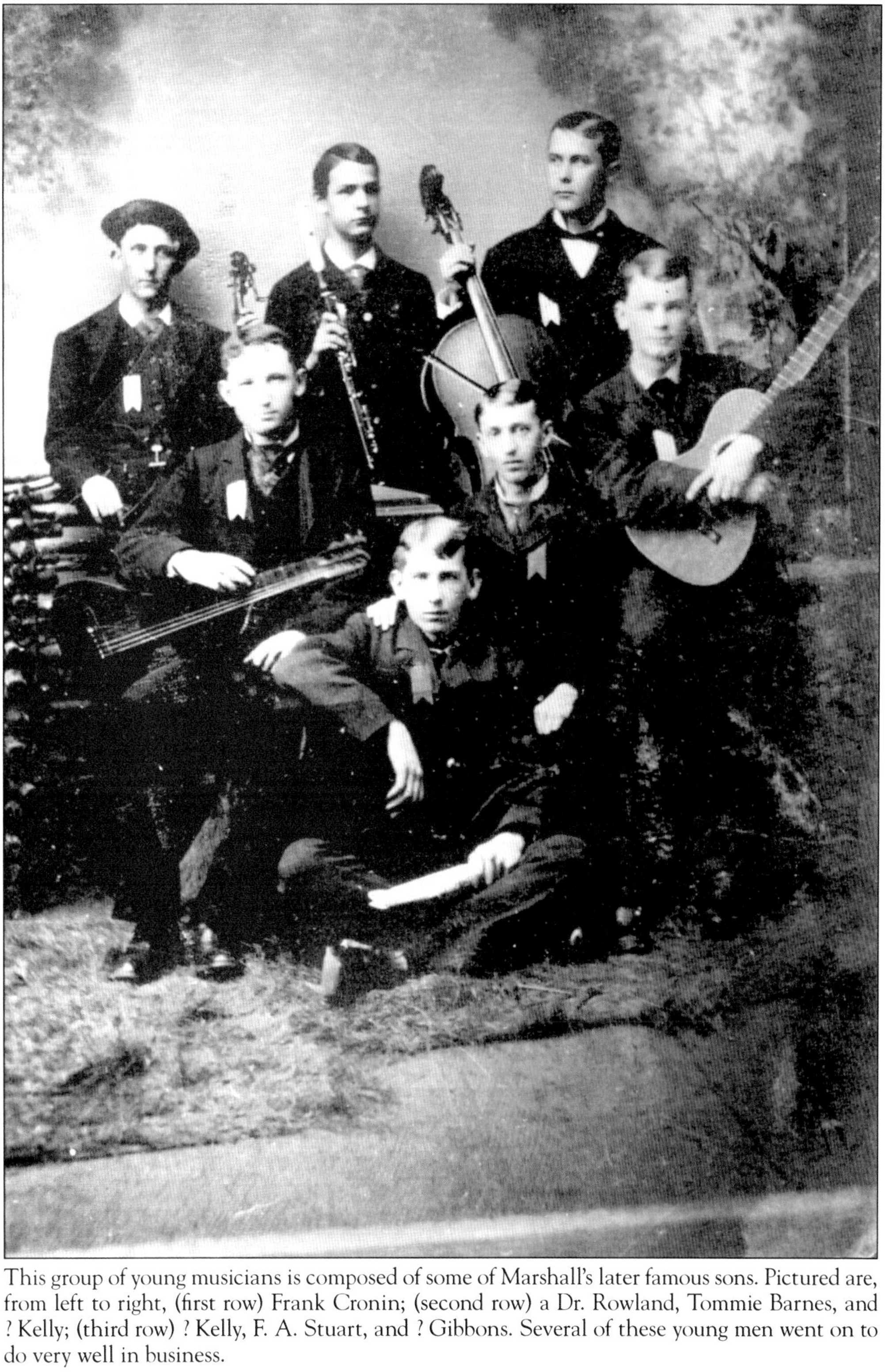

This group of young musicians is composed of some of Marshall's later famous sons. Pictured are, from left to right, (first row) Frank Cronin; (second row) a Dr. Rowland, Tommie Barnes, and ? Kelly; (third row) ? Kelly, F. A. Stuart, and ? Gibbons. Several of these young men went on to do very well in business.

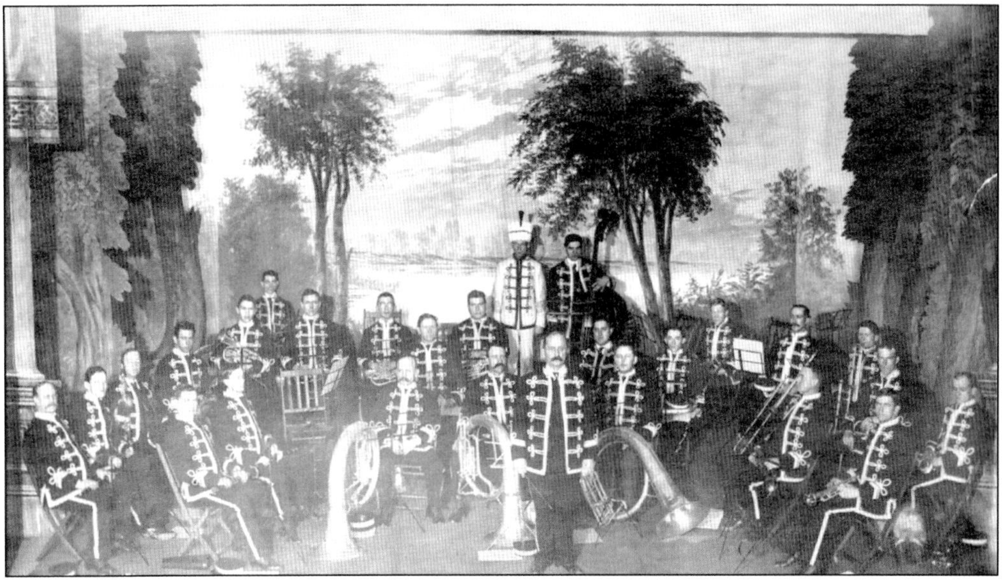

The Marshall Cornet Band was very popular. It had its own backdrop at the Eagle Opera House, as shown here. Obviously it allowed some tubas to join its ranks.

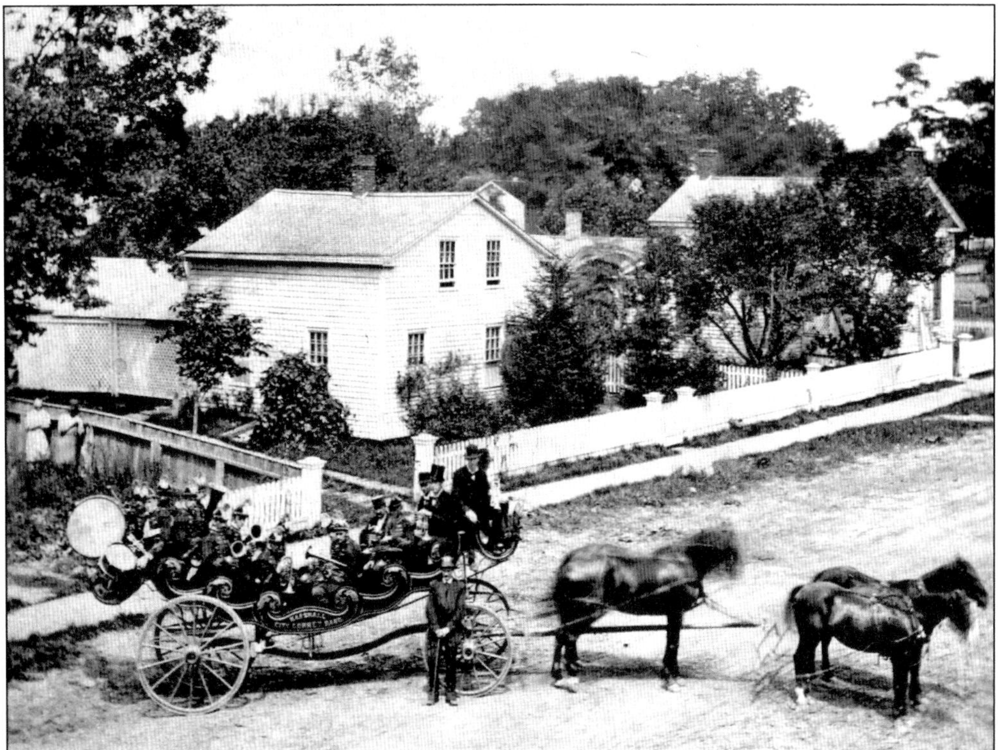

The Marshall Cornet Band also had its very own bandwagon used in parades all over the area. It was well renowned throughout southern Michigan. The drummers had the best seats, playing while hanging their drums off the back of the wagon. This picture was taken on Mansion Street before it was paved.

Five

Churches and Schools

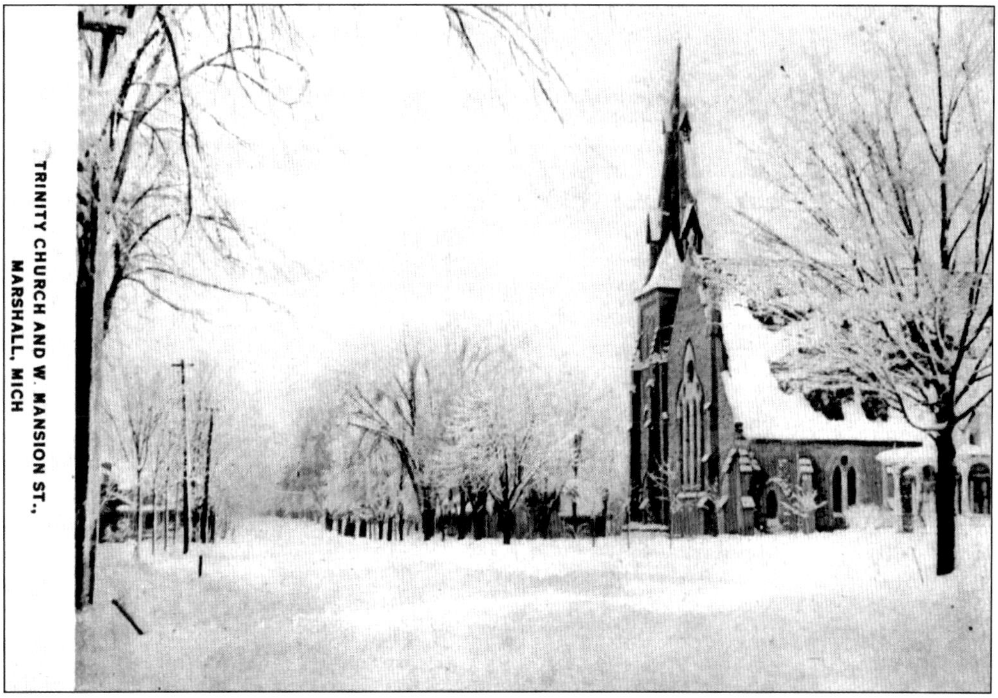

Founded in 1836, Trinity Episcopal Church is one of the oldest congregations in Marshall. The original church was located on the southeast corner of Hamilton and Green Streets. That site was sold to the Lutherans so that this building could be erected on Mansion Street in 1860–1863 at a cost of $8,000. Montgomery Schuyler was the second rector of Trinity.

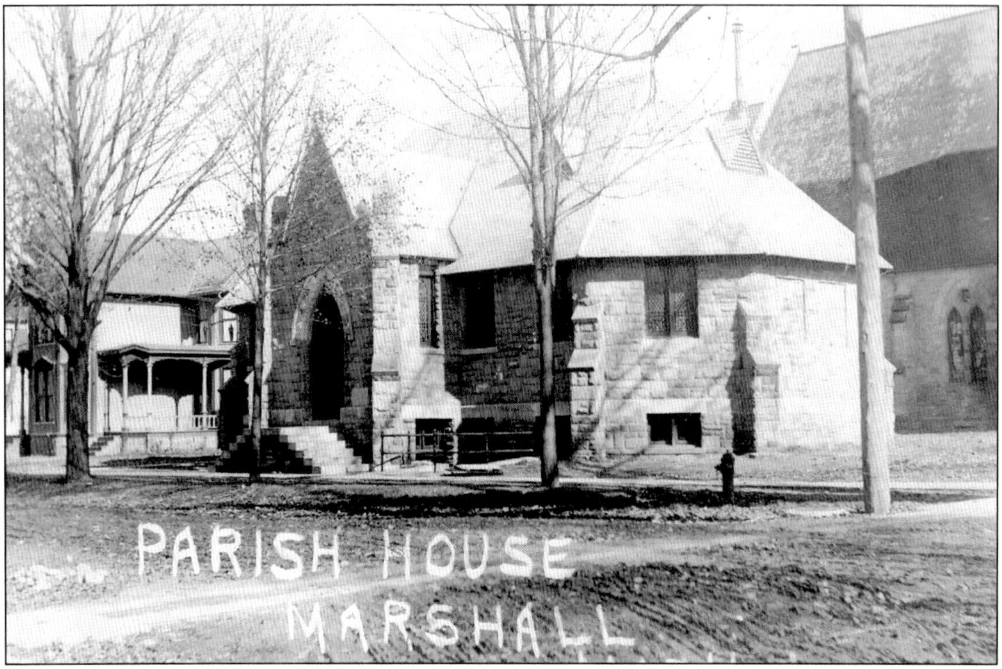

The parish hall and chapel for Trinity Episcopal Church was constructed in 1905. An oft-told story goes that the project was put out for bid and several contractors bid on it. One man's bid was considerably less than the others, and he was awarded the job. After it was completed, one parishioner asked him how his bid could be so much lower than all the others, and his reply was, "Forgot the roof!"

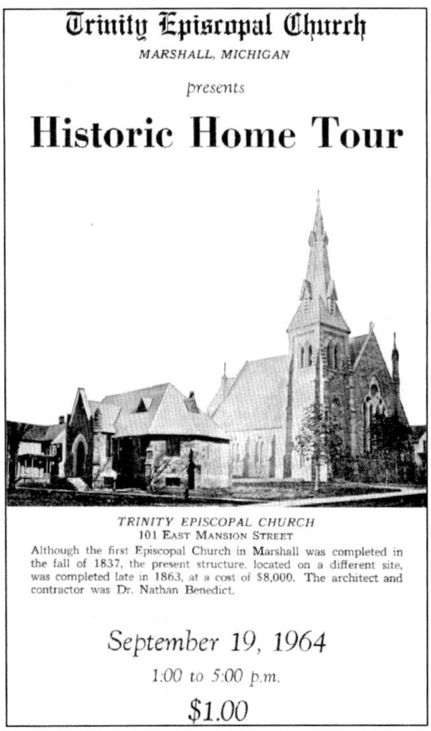

Trinity Episcopal Church

MARSHALL, MICHIGAN

presents

Historic Home Tour

TRINITY EPISCOPAL CHURCH

101 EAST MANSION STREET

Although the first Episcopal Church in Marshall was completed in the fall of 1837, the present structure, located on a different site, was completed late in 1863, at a cost of $8,000. The architect and contractor was Dr. Nathan Benedict.

September 19, 1964

1:00 to 5:00 p.m.

$1.00

This festival is a significant part of life in Marshall. The first home tour in the Midwest began right here in Marshall as a fund-raiser for Trinity Episcopal Church. The event began as a kitchen tour after World War II. It was expanded to include the rest of the house in 1964. It grew rapidly and was turned over to the Marshall Historical Society to run as a community-wide event in 1967.

The First Presbyterian Church moved to this building in 1873. The congregation still exists at that location but is no longer associated with the Church of Scotland. The first pastor, the Reverend John P. Cleveland, was an uncle of Pres. Grover Cleveland. In 1903, a huge windstorm came through and knocked over the steeple and several of the smaller spires.

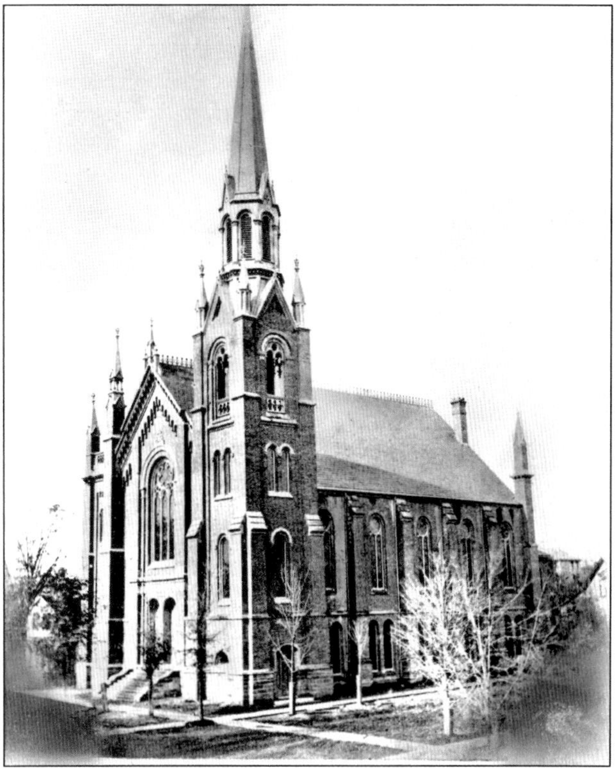

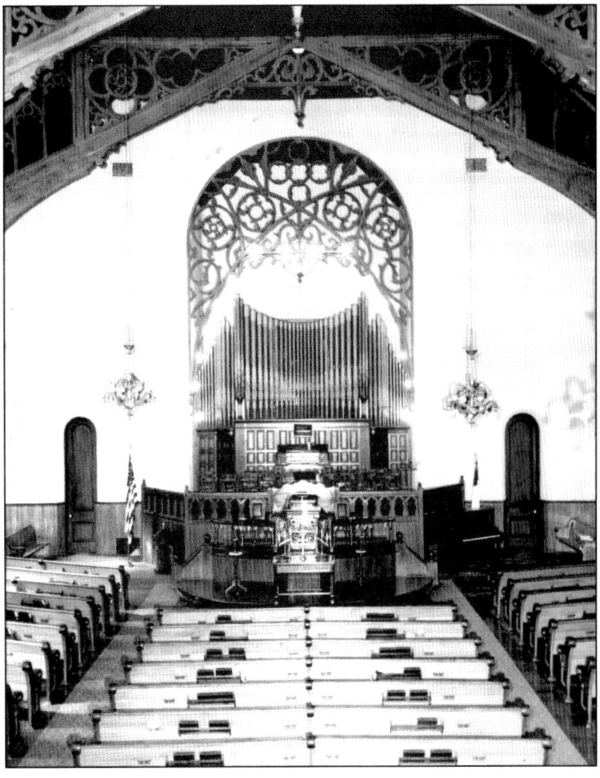

The chancel was glorious after the second remodeling. The wonderful overhead arches were added at that time. The huge fretwork over the altar has since been removed, and the Gorham Brass Pulpit has been moved to the rear of the sanctuary.

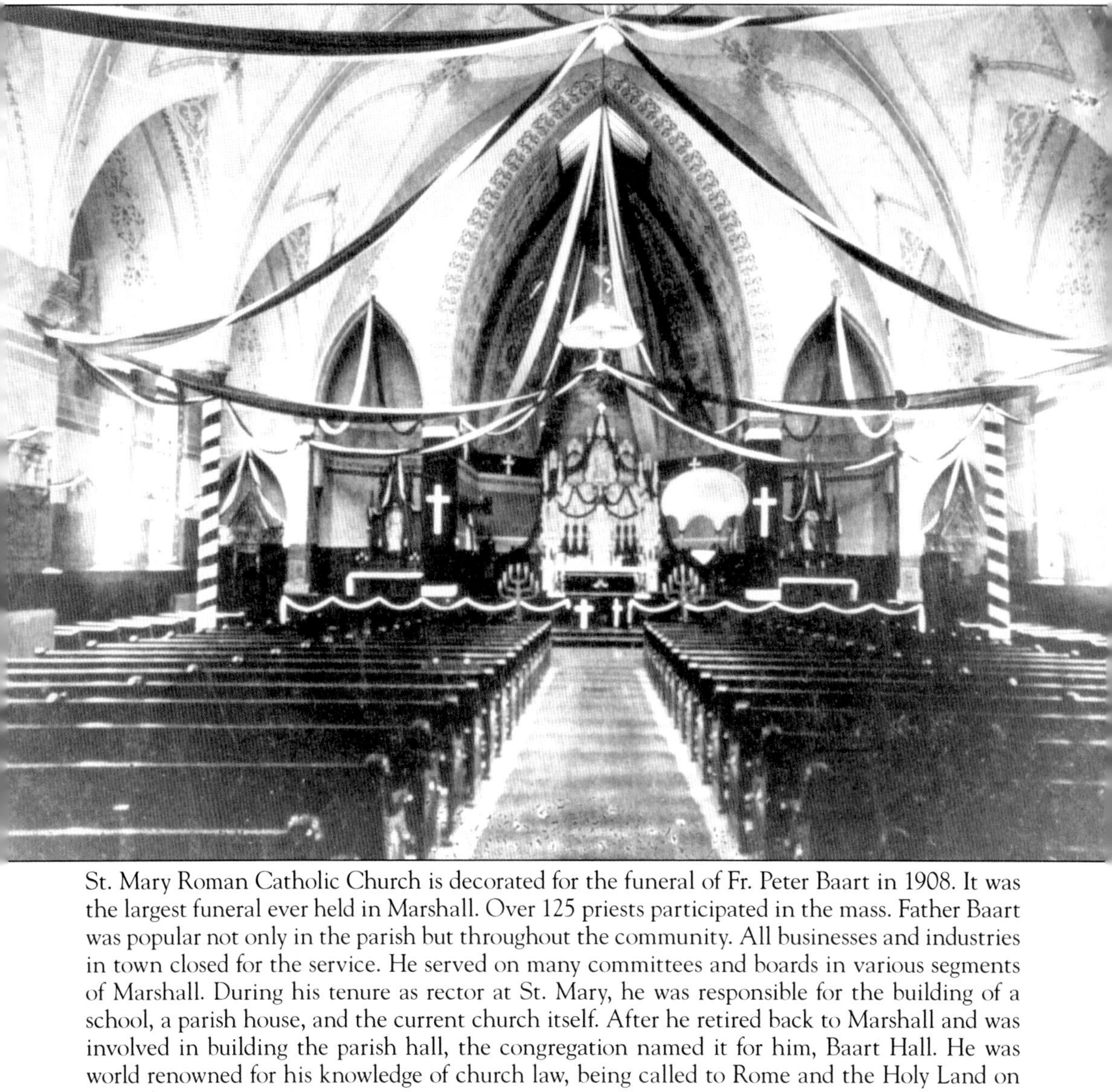

St. Mary Roman Catholic Church is decorated for the funeral of Fr. Peter Baart in 1908. It was the largest funeral ever held in Marshall. Over 125 priests participated in the mass. Father Baart was popular not only in the parish but throughout the community. All businesses and industries in town closed for the service. He served on many committees and boards in various segments of Marshall. During his tenure as rector at St. Mary, he was responsible for the building of a school, a parish house, and the current church itself. After he retired back to Marshall and was involved in building the parish hall, the congregation named it for him, Baart Hall. He was world renowned for his knowledge of church law, being called to Rome and the Holy Land on more than one occasion.

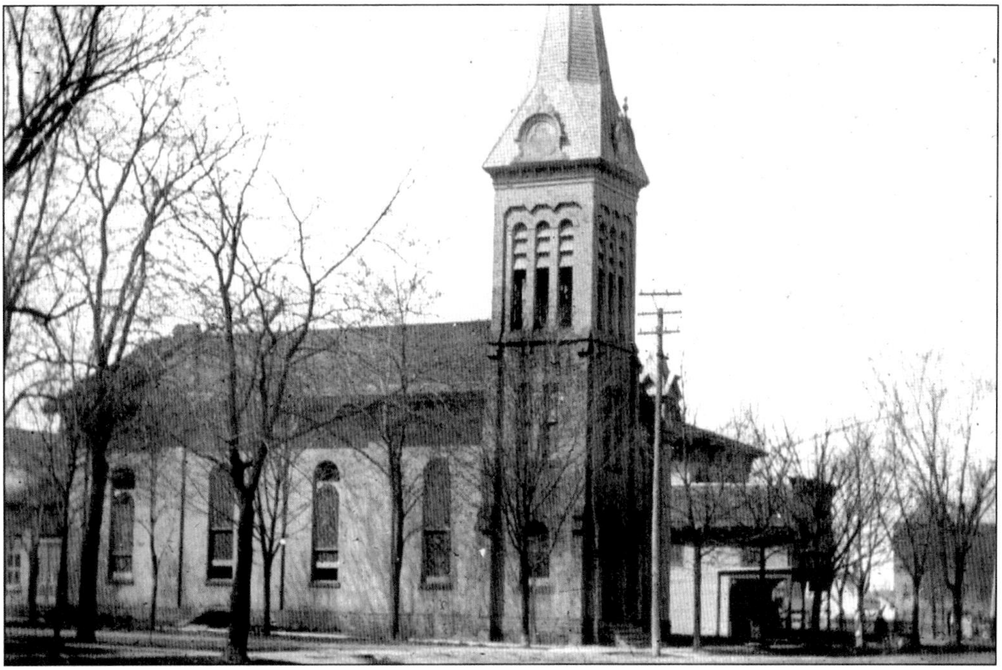

Founded in 1840, the Baptists moved to this corner just off Fountain Circle in 1852. That makes it the congregation that has been meeting in the same location for the longest time in Marshall's history. The 1915 steeple was recently re-created by Jeff Gardner and his roofing company while the community gathered to watch. It was quite a sight to see the new steeple lifted up by a crane. It was a long cry from the original construction technique!

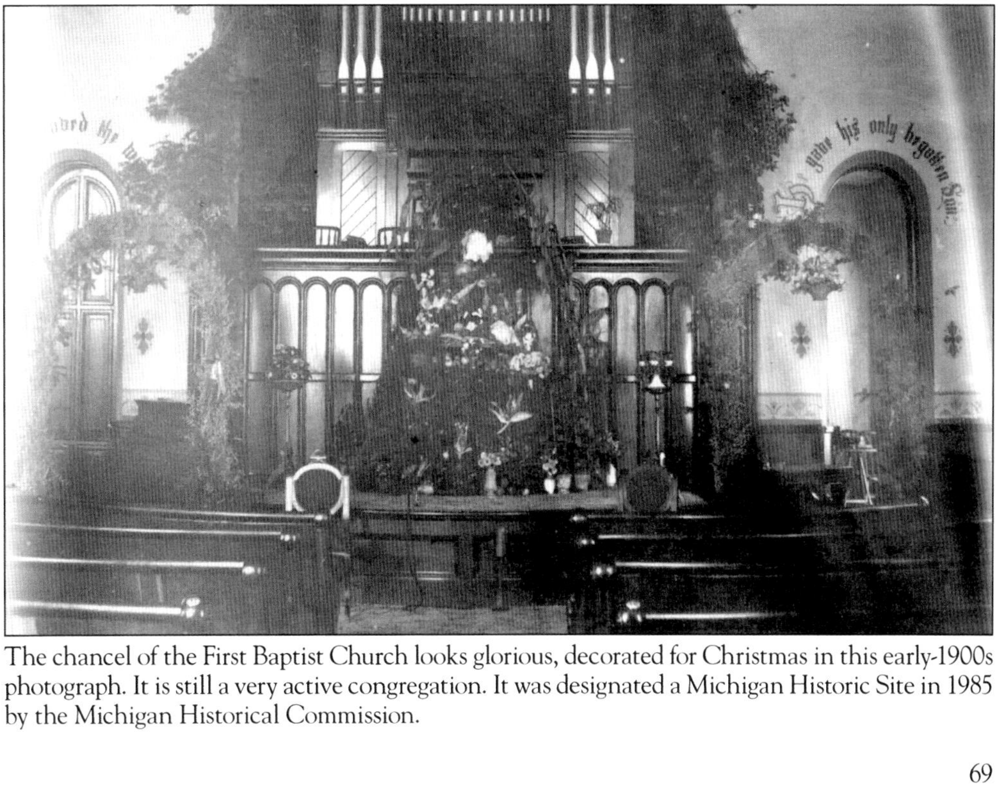

The chancel of the First Baptist Church looks glorious, decorated for Christmas in this early-1900s photograph. It is still a very active congregation. It was designated a Michigan Historic Site in 1985 by the Michigan Historical Commission.

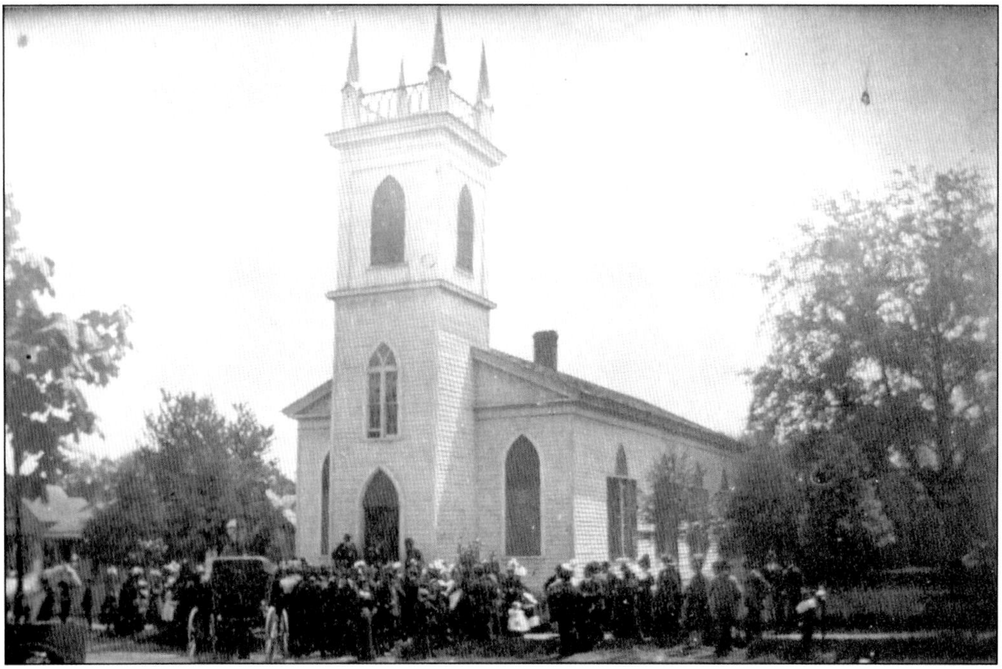

This great little Gothic Revival frame church was built by the congregation of Trinity Episcopal Church in 1837 at the southeast corner of Eagle and Green Streets. Just 20 years later, Trinity sold the property to Zion Lutheran for the sum of $2,000. The Lutherans later demolished the building to erect the current large brick Gothic Revival building that still stands in 2007.

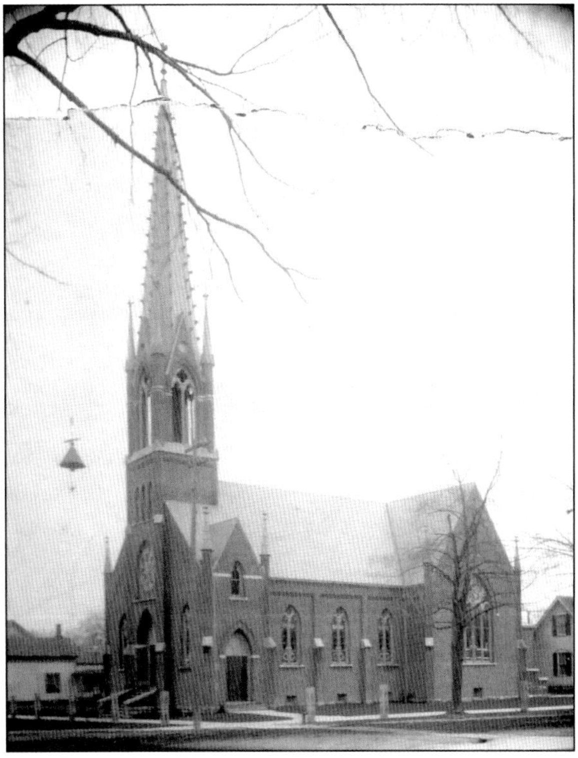

The year 1848 was when Zion Lutheran Church met with a circuit preacher from Ann Arbor who came to Marshall every six weeks. Much to the delight of the local families, the services were conducted in German. The current building, which cost $10,000, was completed in December 1901. By then there was a congregation of about 500 people. The church joined the Missouri Synod in 1935.

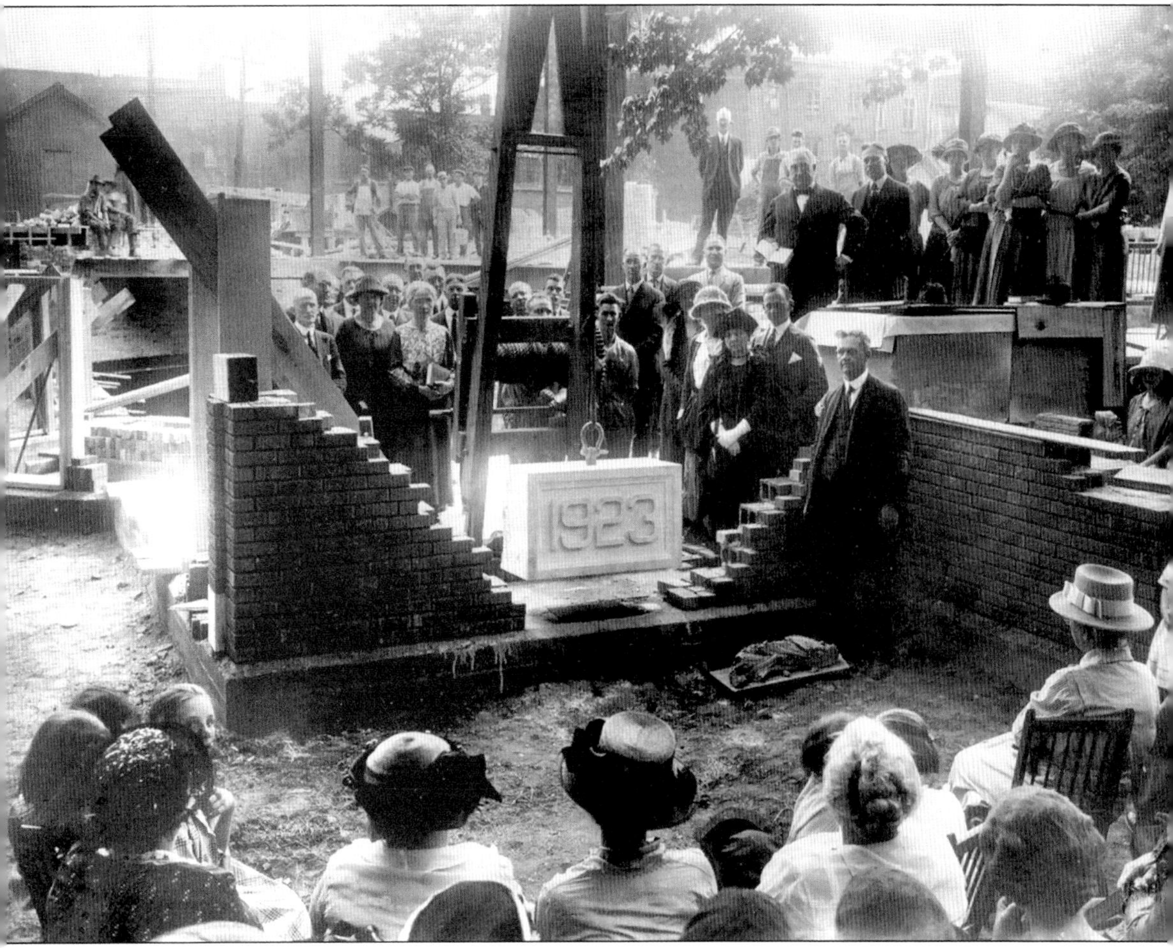

This image shows the First Methodist Church laying the cornerstone for another new church in 1923. It was named the Brooks Memorial Methodist Episcopal Church in memory of Charles Esseltyn Brooks. The building served the needs of the congregation for over 40 years before it built again north of town. In 1969, the Marshall Civic Trust was formed to raise money to buy the structure for the Civic Players. The trust eventually gave the building to the city. In 2001, the newly formed Marshall Civic Center Trust negotiated with the city to sell it to the trust rather than have it torn down for more parking. It is now the Joyce and Lucy Franke Center for the Arts. The center attracts all sorts of top performers from around the world.

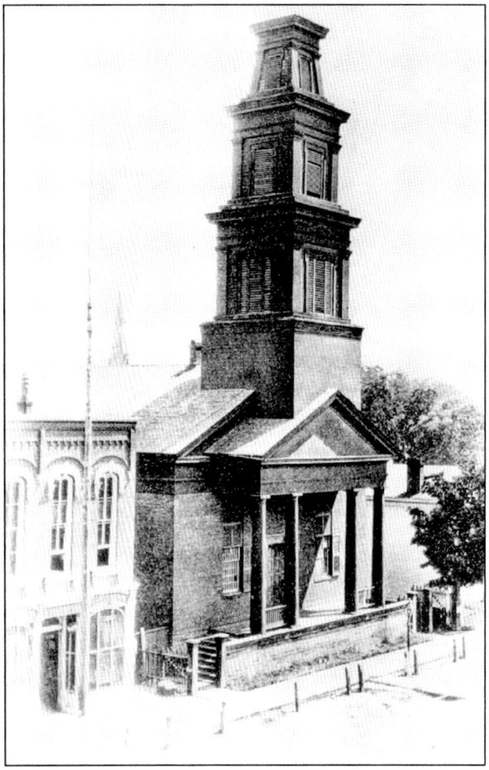

The Presbyterian church was originally downtown right in the middle of what is now known as "the big block." It was roughly where Hemmingsen's Rexall is now and was definitely the centerpiece of the block. During the construction, one of the walls collapsed, killing the contractor. That was a fairly common occurrence in those days, but because it was a church, the story still lives on.

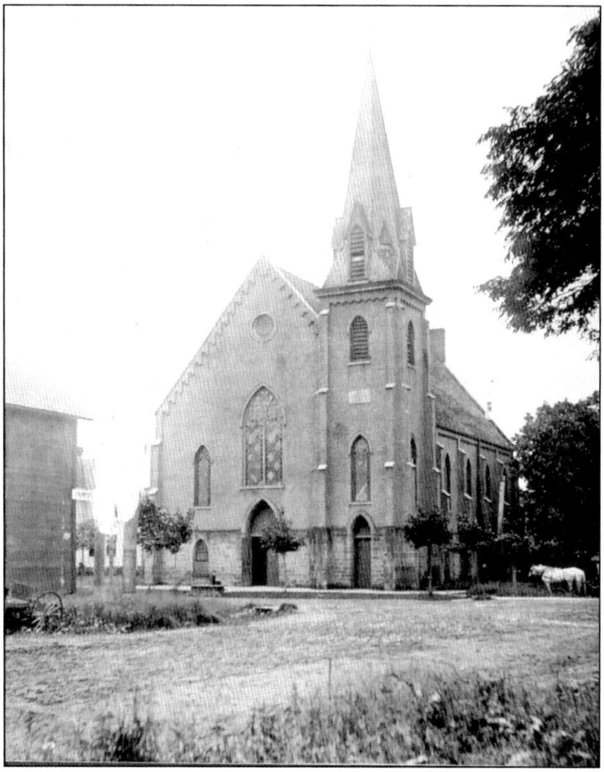

The Methodists seemed to move more than any other congregation. This is the first large church they built at the southeast corner of Green and Hamilton Streets. They worshipped here from 1871 to 1924. From here they went to what is now the Franke Center for the Arts.

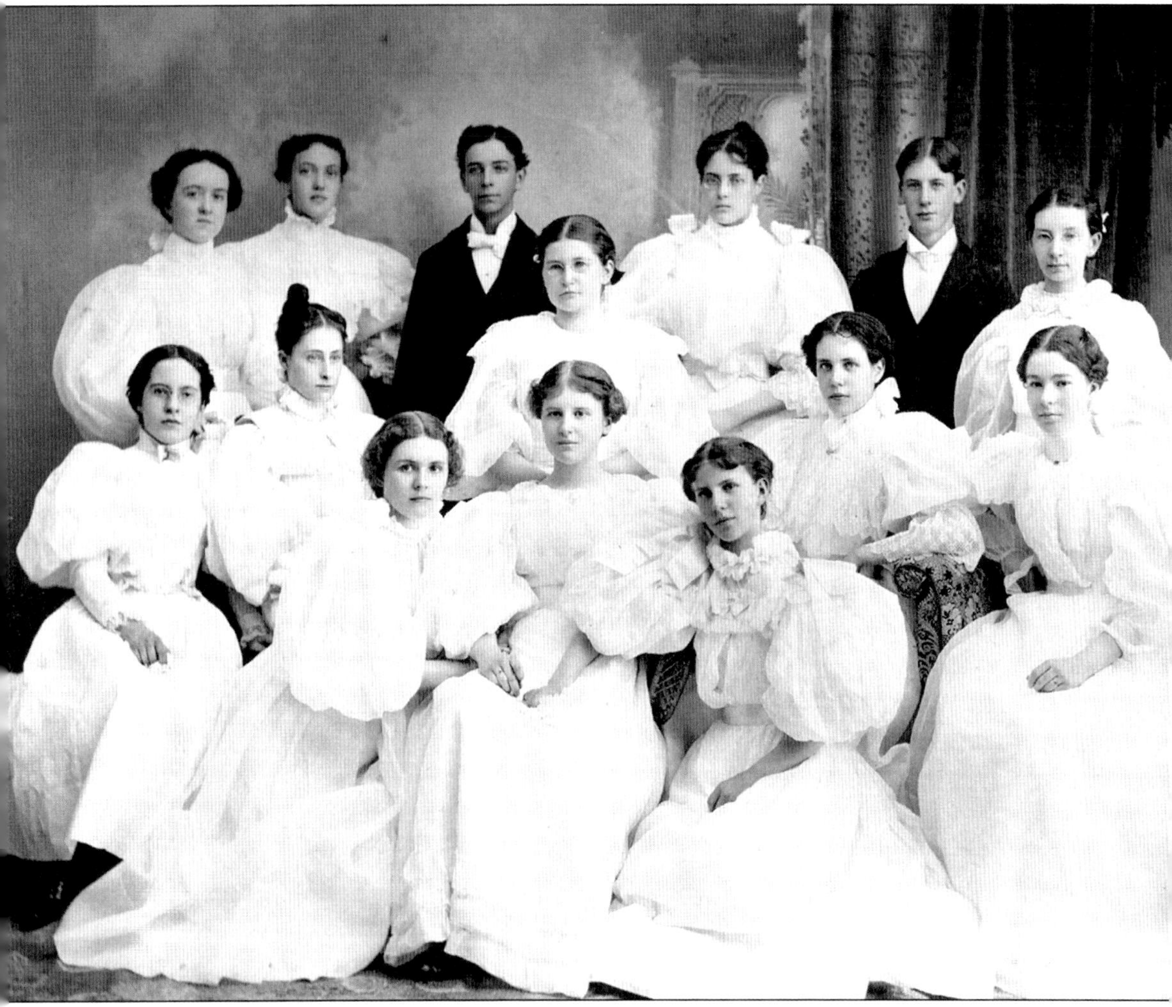

This photograph of the class of 1897 shows, from left to right, (first row) Thera Cox, Mabel Davis, and Bertha Crossman; (second row) Nellie Tilton, Sadie Blanchard, Ada Hirth, Lilly Wells, and Della Mumaw; (third row) Vera Lockwood, May Chister, George Chapin, Mary Wells, Ernest Vernor, and Agnes Rossa.

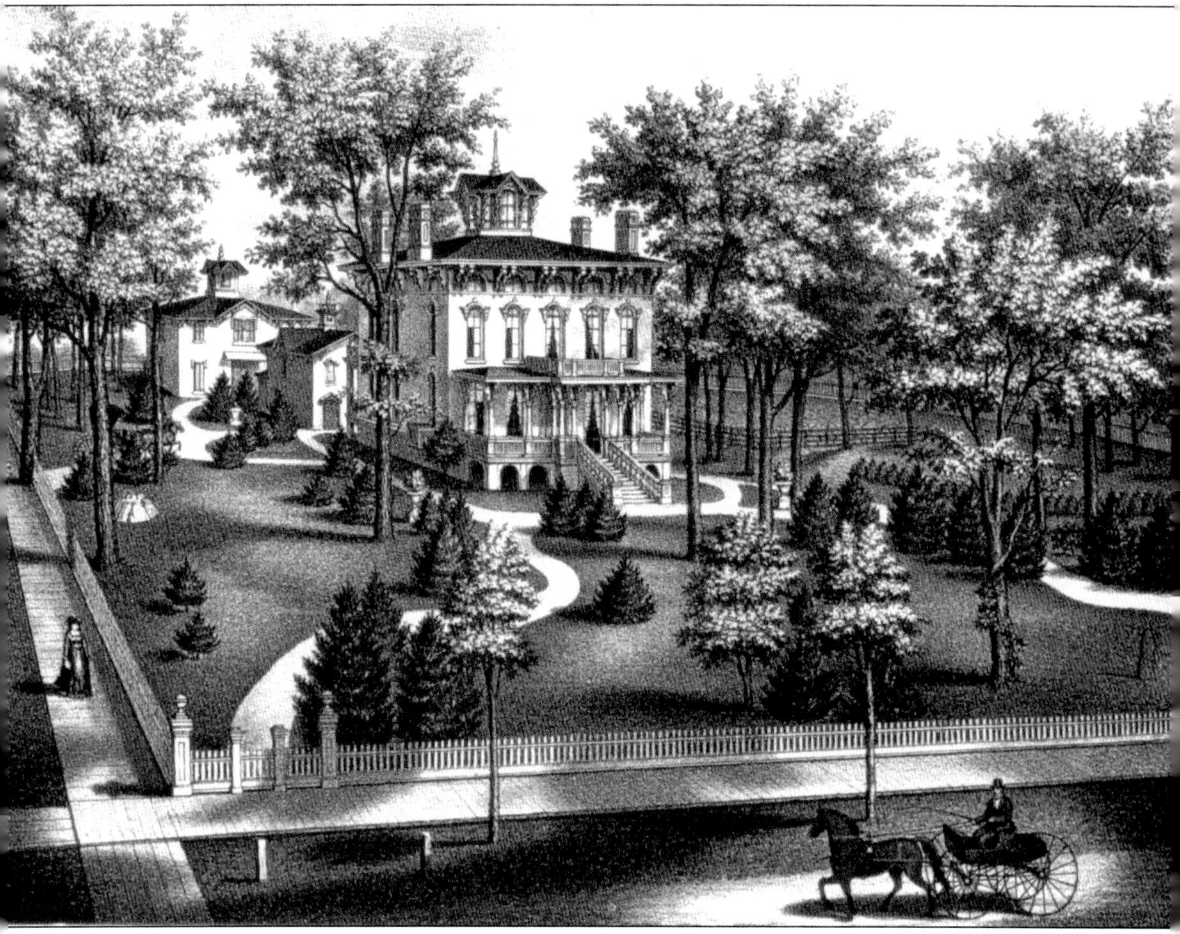

In 1855, a group of local citizens purchased the Sidney Ketchum mansion to open the Young Ladies Institute. It was the largest boarding school Marshall ever had. The girls attending the finishing school were housed a block away in the old Marshall House Hotel. Later the Dibble family bought the school and enlarged and embellished it to make it appear as it does in this illustration.

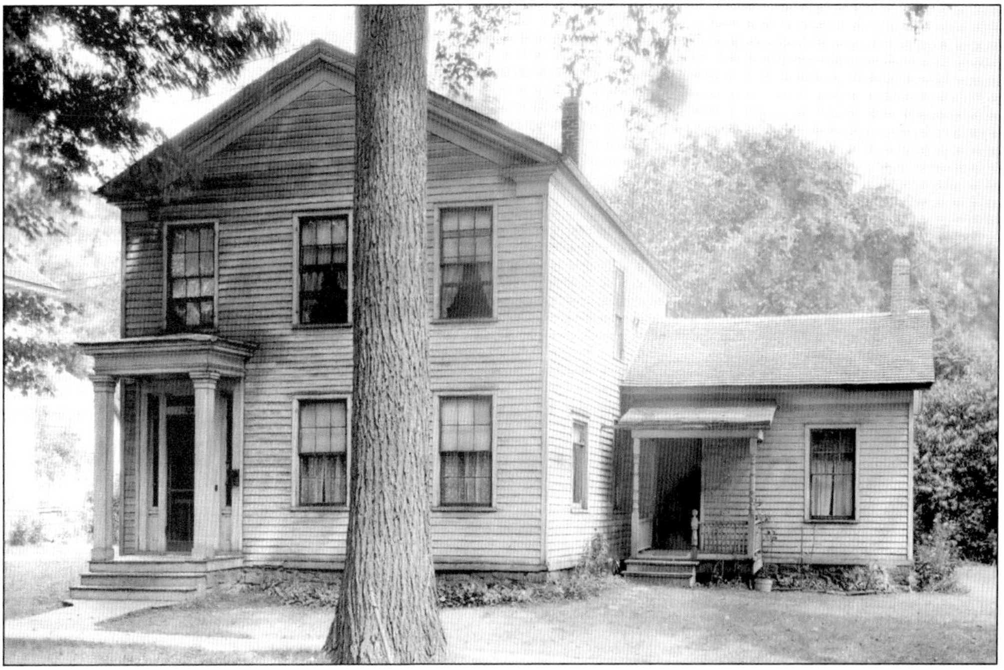

The Marshall Academy was erected to house a boys' preparatory school. It was considered a great school and drew young men from all over. It later served as the Presbyterian manse.

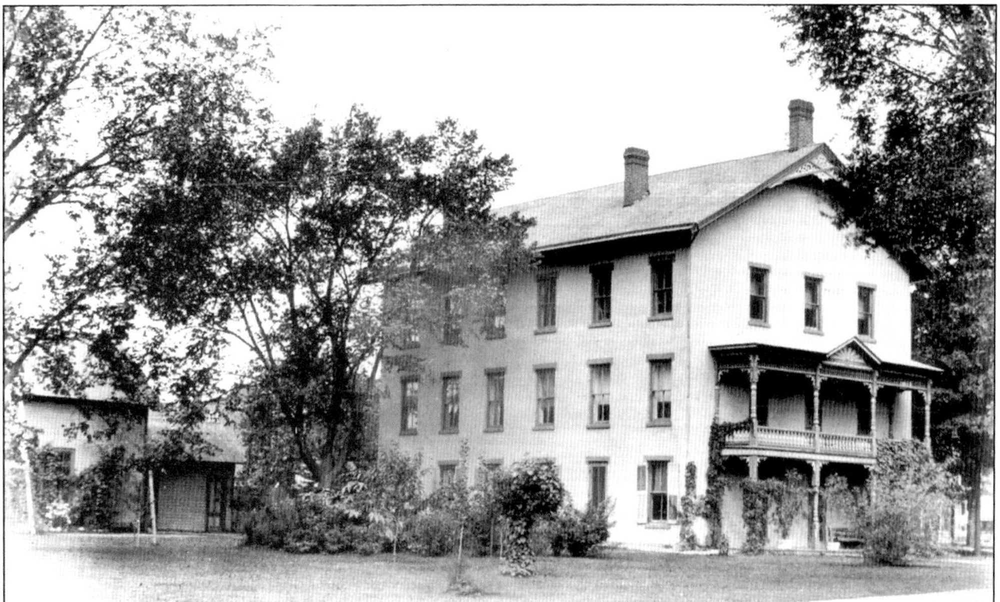

The Marshall House Hotel on the east end of town was once the largest hotel between Detroit and Chicago. After a devastating fire destroyed 60 percent of the building, this portion is what remained. It was converted to a school and dormitory for the young ladies attending the Perrin Collegiate Institute founded by industrialist Horace J. Perrin. Later it housed the young ladies attending the Young Ladies Institute, the finishing school a block away in the old Ketchum mansion.

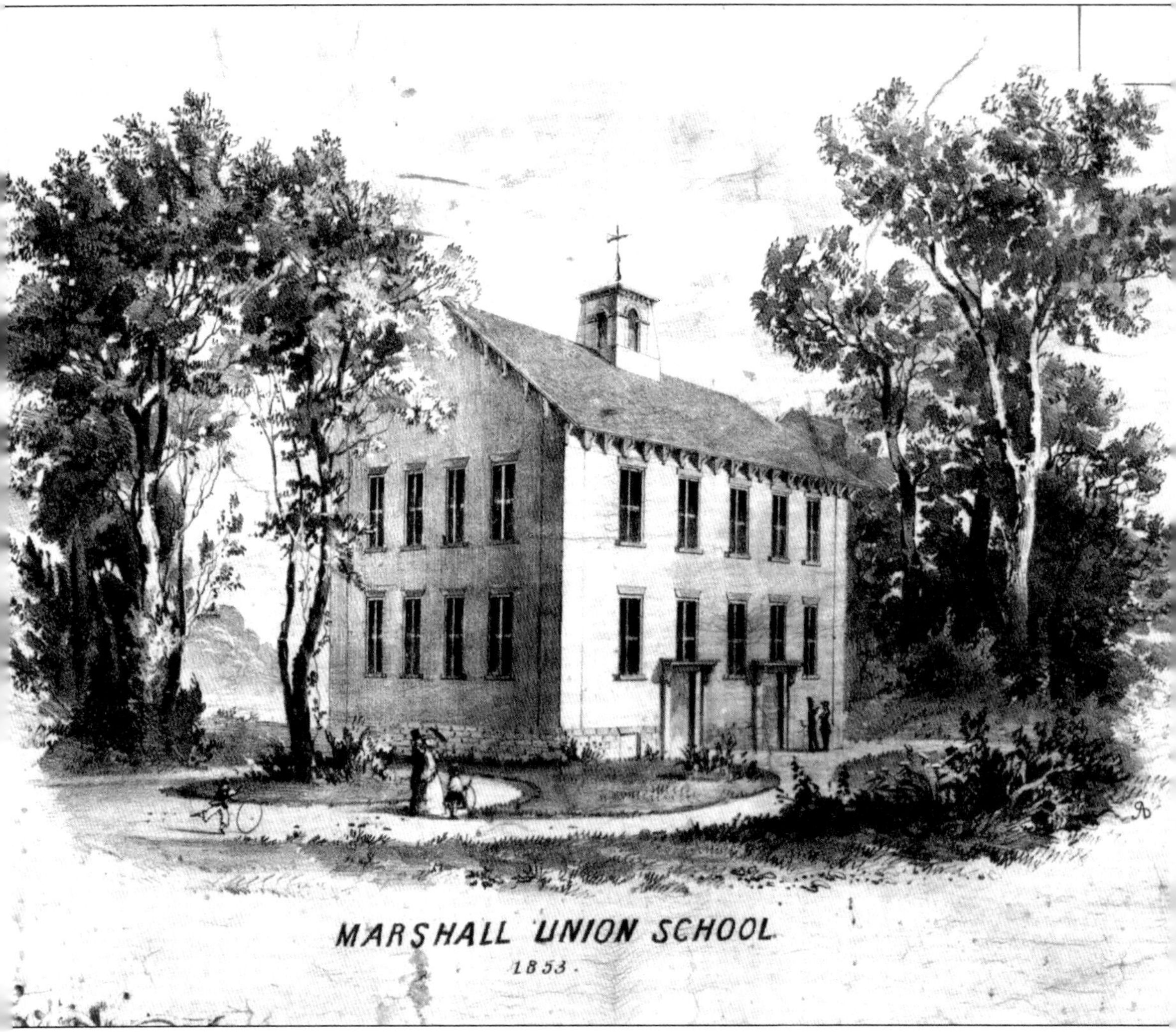

Because Marshall was settled by educated people, schooling has always been important to the citizens of Marshall. In 1851, this school was built to educate all age levels of children from both the upper and lower villages of Marshall. Because it was uniting children from both villages, it was given the name Union School and was placed in the middle of the community on the courthouse square. At one time, there were 33 students in the high school alone.

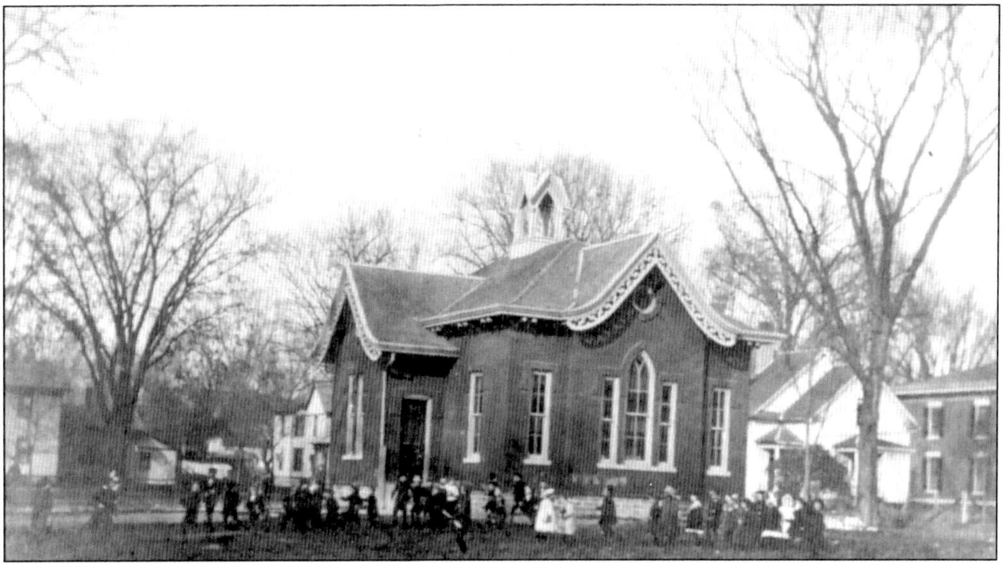

The year 1860 was a very big year for building in Marshall. The community built three small two-room schoolhouses for a grand total of $8,000. The one pictured above is the East Ward School, which later became Pierce School. The other two were Capitol Hill and Crary. The architect was Sheldon Smith. Smith's son went on to found the firm Smith, Hinchman and Gryls of Detroit, which is still one of the largest architectural firms in Michigan.

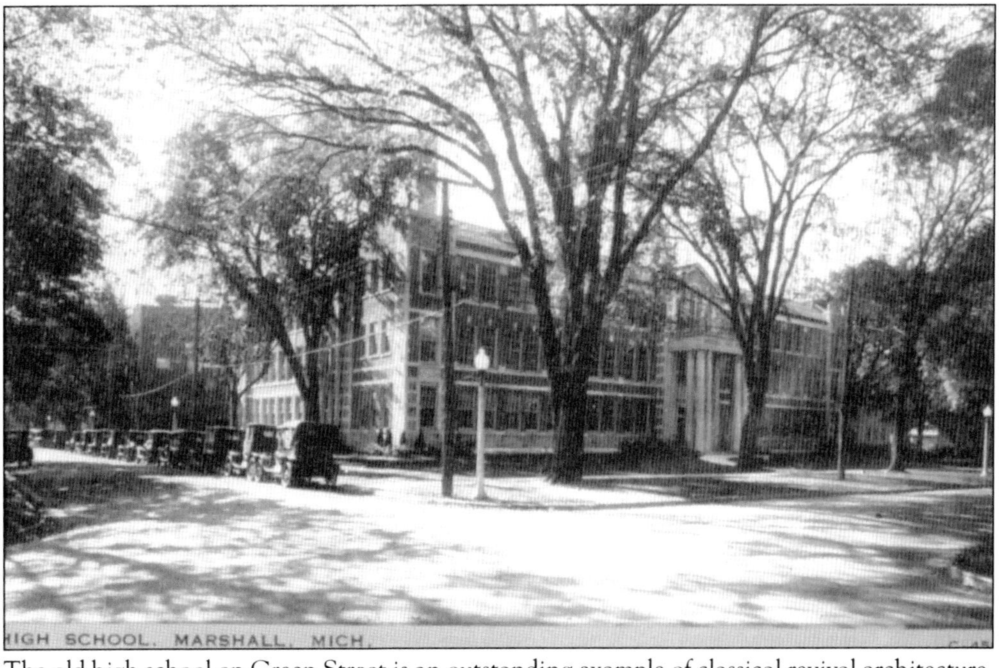

The old high school on Green Street is an outstanding example of classical revival architecture. It was the third high school and is now the administration building and part of the middle school. It was built in 1929 and cost $268,000. That is quite a difference from $8,000 for three buildings in 1860.

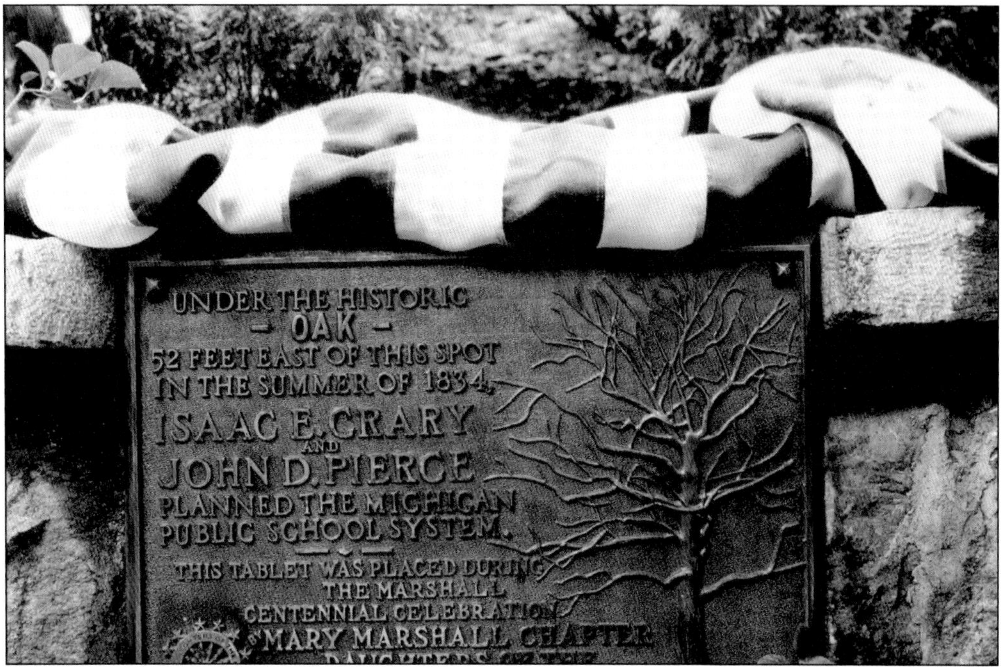

In 1930, in celebration of Marshall's centennial, the Mary Marshall chapter of the DAR commissioned several bronze markers around the community. This one was mounted in the wall at the foot of the steps leading up to the Gorham-Brooks house. It commemorates the Education Oak standing at the top of the stairs.

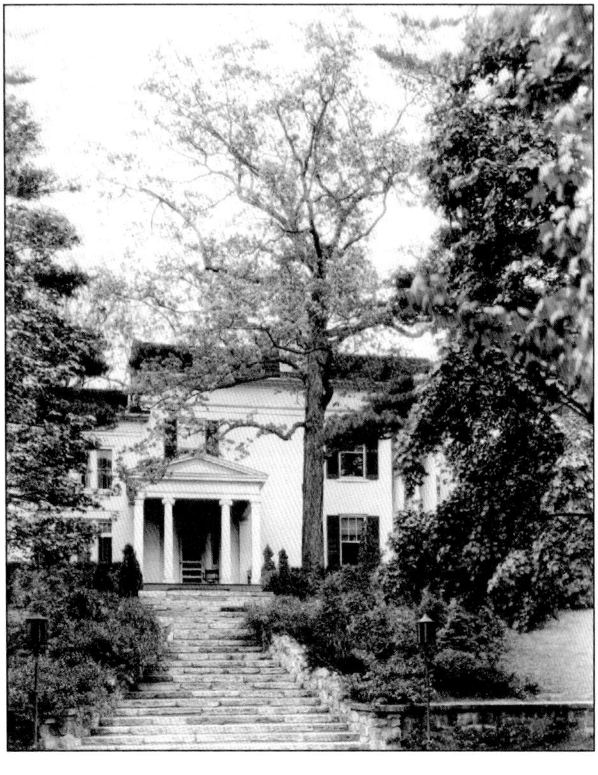

The Education Oak can be seen to the right of the porch at the top of the stairs leading to the front door of H. C. Brooks's home on North Kalamazoo Avenue. It was under this tree that Michigan's first representative to Congress, Isaac Crary, and the Reverend John D. Pierce sat in 1837 while they designed the school system for the state of Michigan. The Reverend Pierce went on to become the first state superintendent of public instruction in the country.

Six

BY ROAD AND RAIL

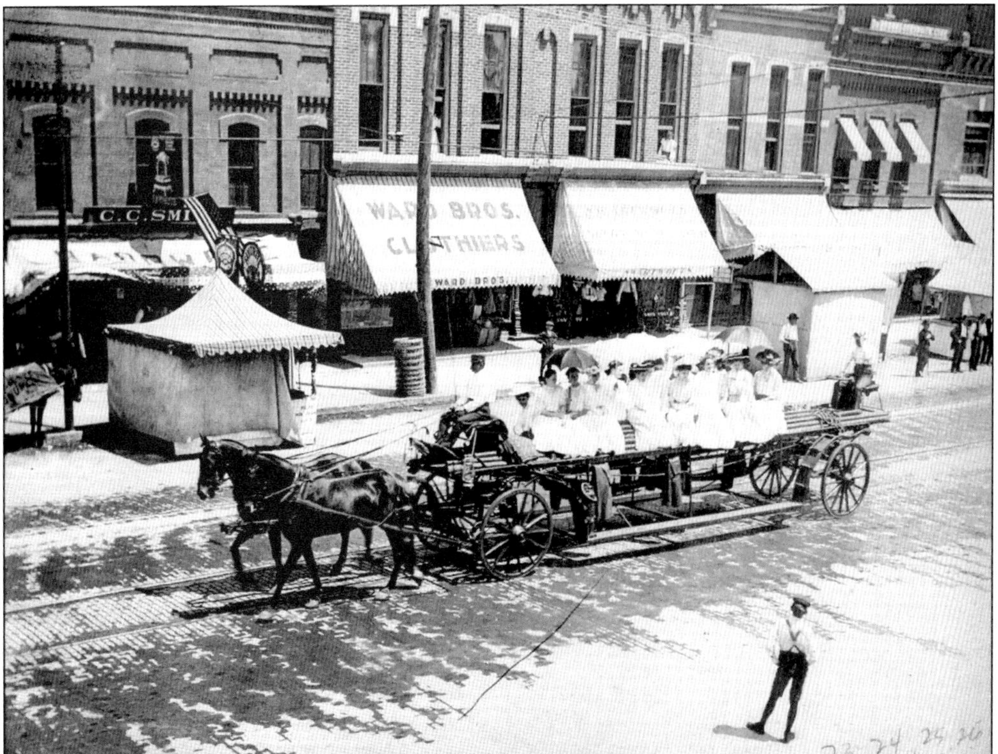

In a photograph labeled "Hook and Ladder," women in frilly white dresses with matching parasols parade down Michigan Avenue.

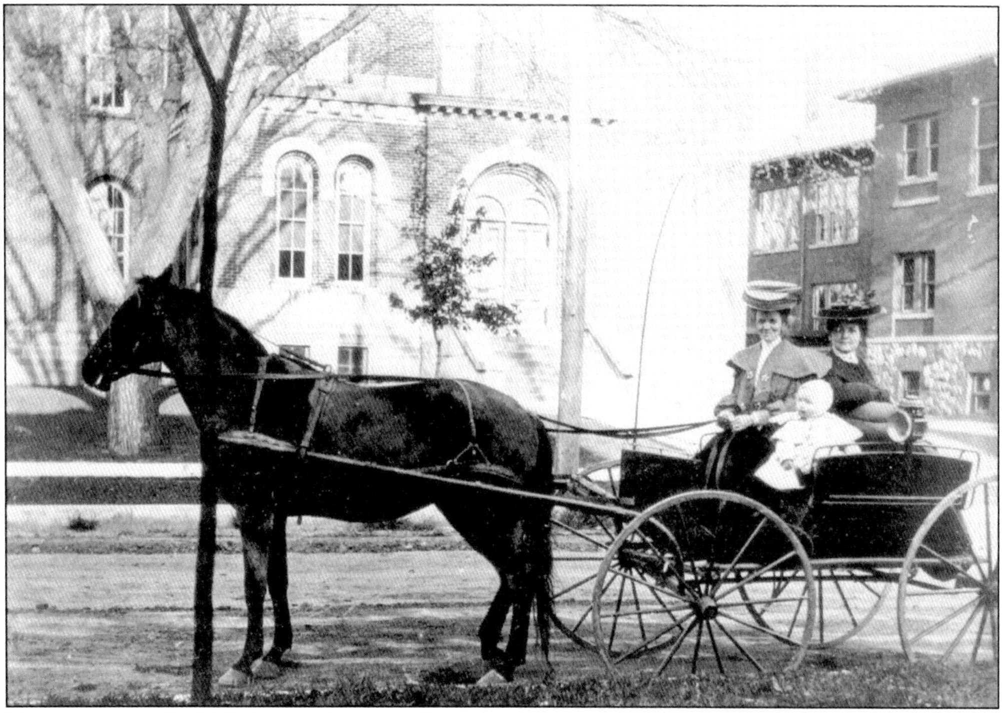

Two women with old-fashioned bonnets (but very stylish in their day) take a ride in a horse-drawn buggy with a young child.

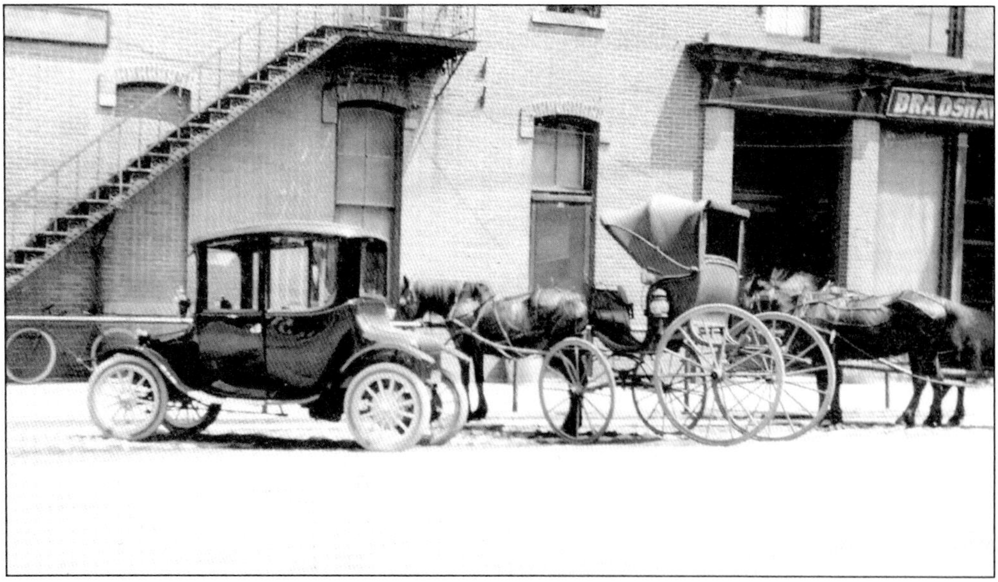

When this photograph was taken in 1920, it was appropriately labeled "Ye Ancient & Modern."

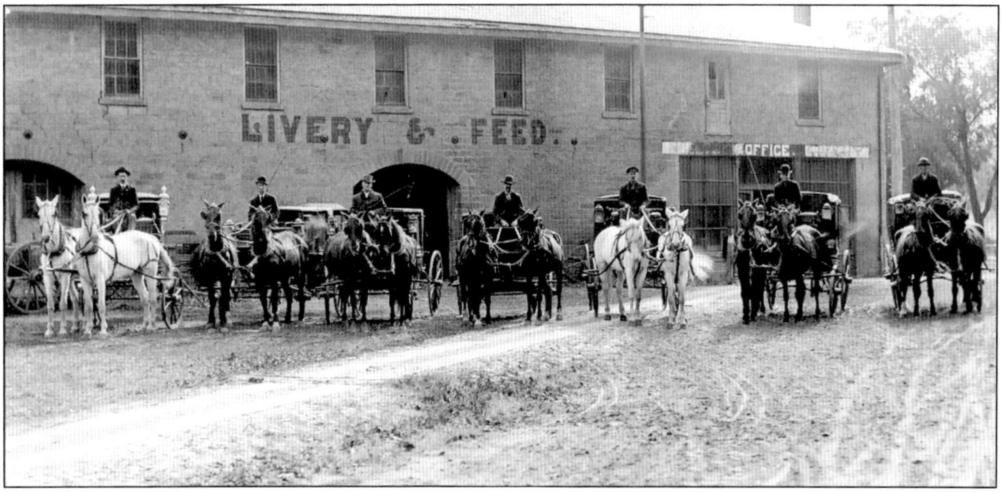

While wooden post and plank roads made traversing muddy, icy roads by horse easier, there was always the question of where to keep all these horses. Liveries were places for horses to board, either on a daily basis or for a longer period of time. Many hotels had their own liveries (as many now have parking lots or garages). William Prindle's Stone Barn shown here was both a stage depot and livery.

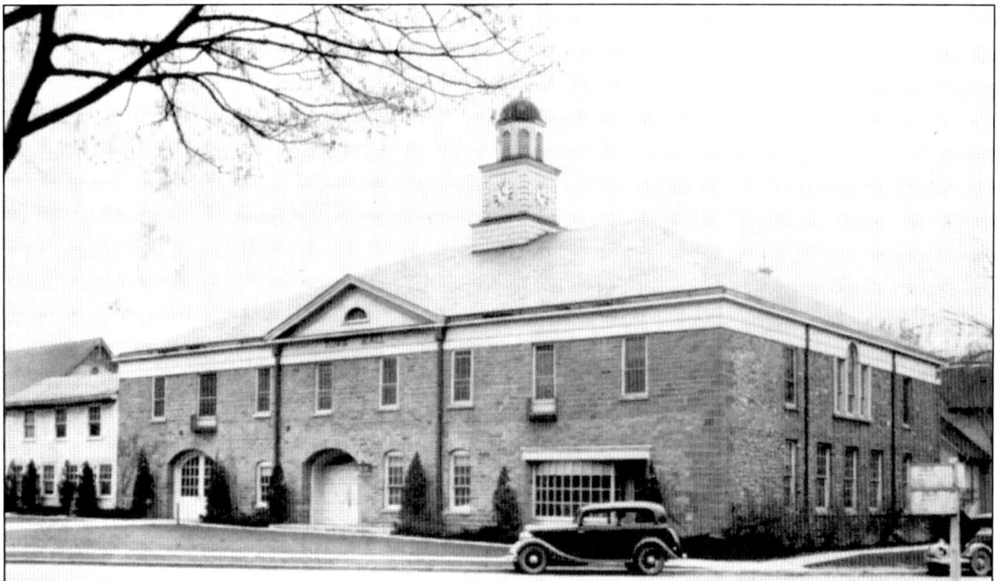

One such livery, owned by William Prindle and dating back to the 1850s, was remodeled by architect Howard F. Young in 1930 under the specifications of Mayor Harold C. Brooks and is now Marshall's town hall.

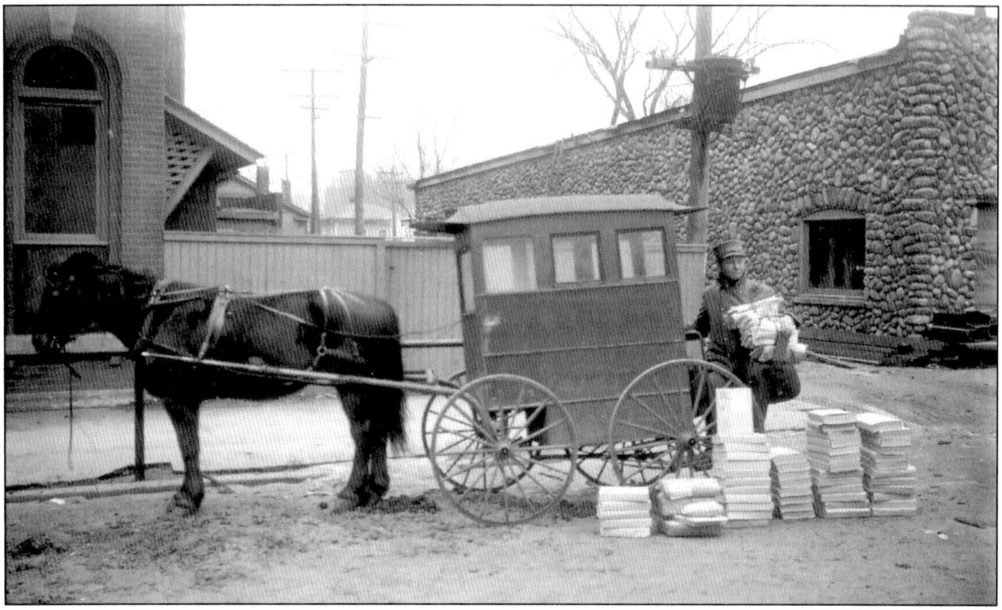

Marshall postman Pete Flynn is shown here getting ready to deliver the mail.

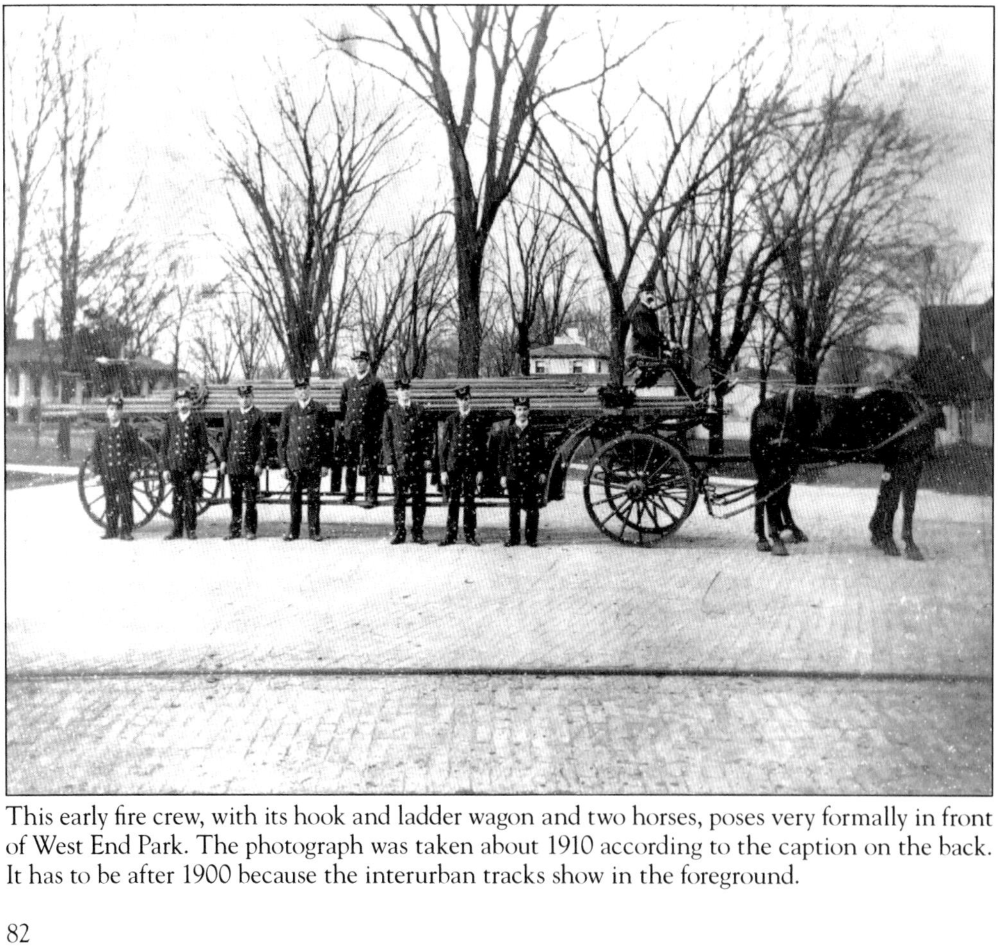

This early fire crew, with its hook and ladder wagon and two horses, poses very formally in front of West End Park. The photograph was taken about 1910 according to the caption on the back. It has to be after 1900 because the interurban tracks show in the foreground.

Horses still predominate, but this early steam fire engine shows how the transition from horsepower to other forms of power was taking place in Marshall. Notice the McHugh and Devereaux shoe store across the street (105 West Michigan Avenue) advertises boots. People needed them for these muddy streets.

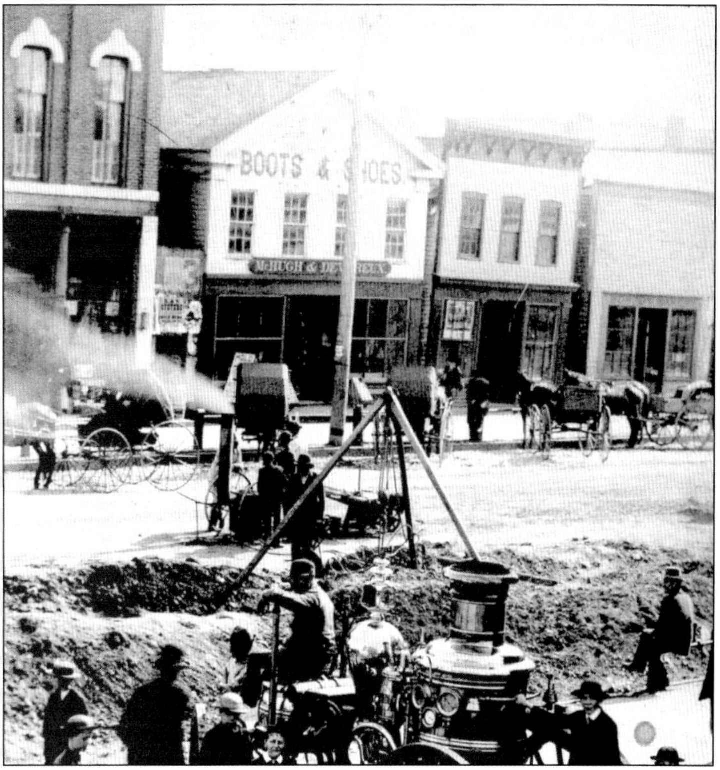

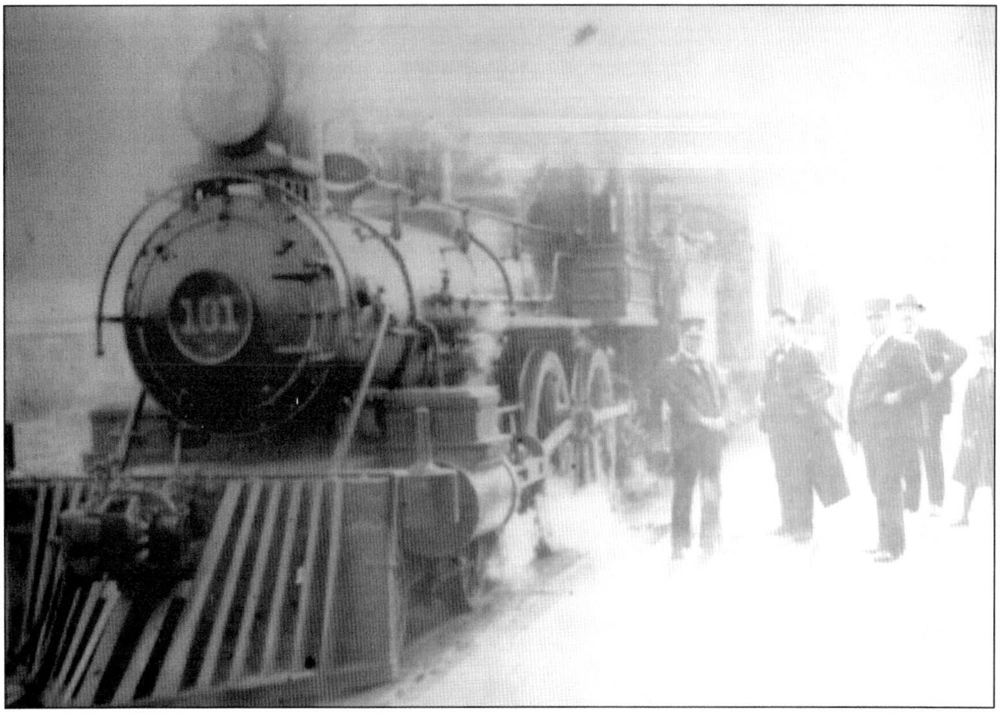

A Detroit, Toledo and Milwaukee engine, built in Marshall, waits at the station in Toledo, Ohio, in this photograph dated 1900.

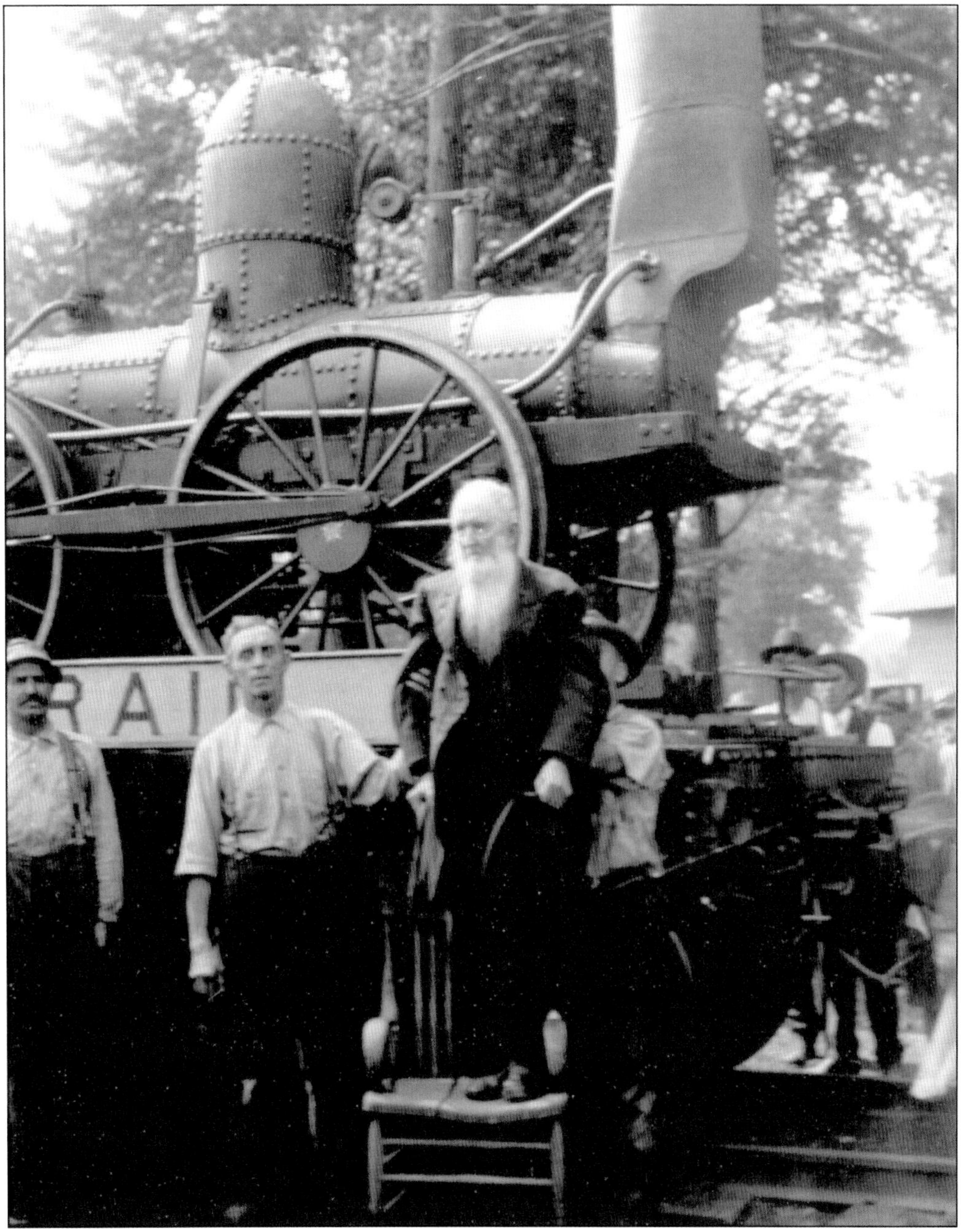

John T. Vernor, one of Marshall's leading citizens, was born in Albany, New York, and moved to Detroit in 1844 and then to Marshall. Vernor died at age 97 and at the time was the last survivor of those who had ridden on the first train on the New York Central line from Albany to Schenectady. This photograph shows Vernor on August 26, 1921, standing next to the *DeWitt Clinton* engine.

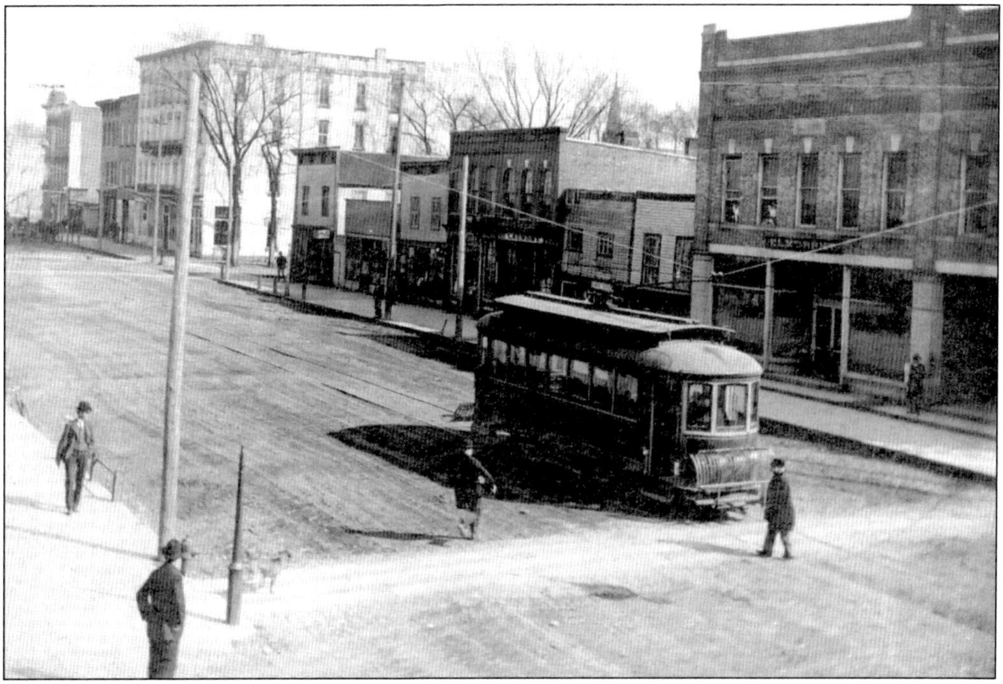

The interurban ran from Detroit to Chicago from 1900 to 1929. It was an electric trolley and made it possible to leave Marshall early in the morning and spend the day in either of those cities, returning in the evening in time for bed.

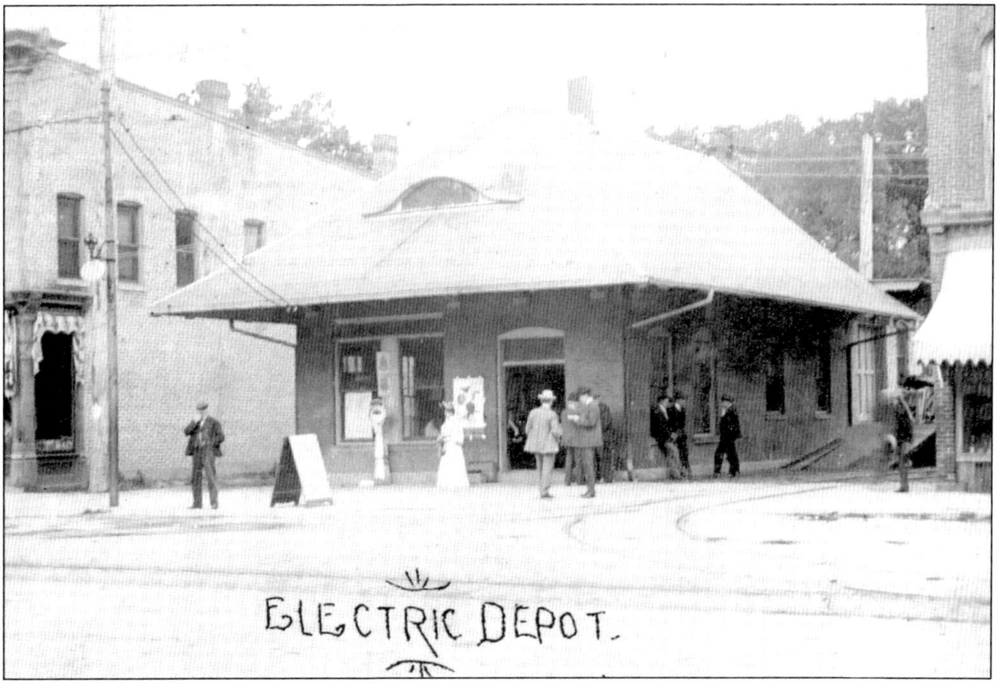

The depot for the interurban on West State Street (now Michigan Avenue) has many people waiting for the trolley. Whether they were traveling as far as the 10 miles to Albion or the 179 miles to Chicago, it was a fast, clean, and efficient way to move across lower Michigan.

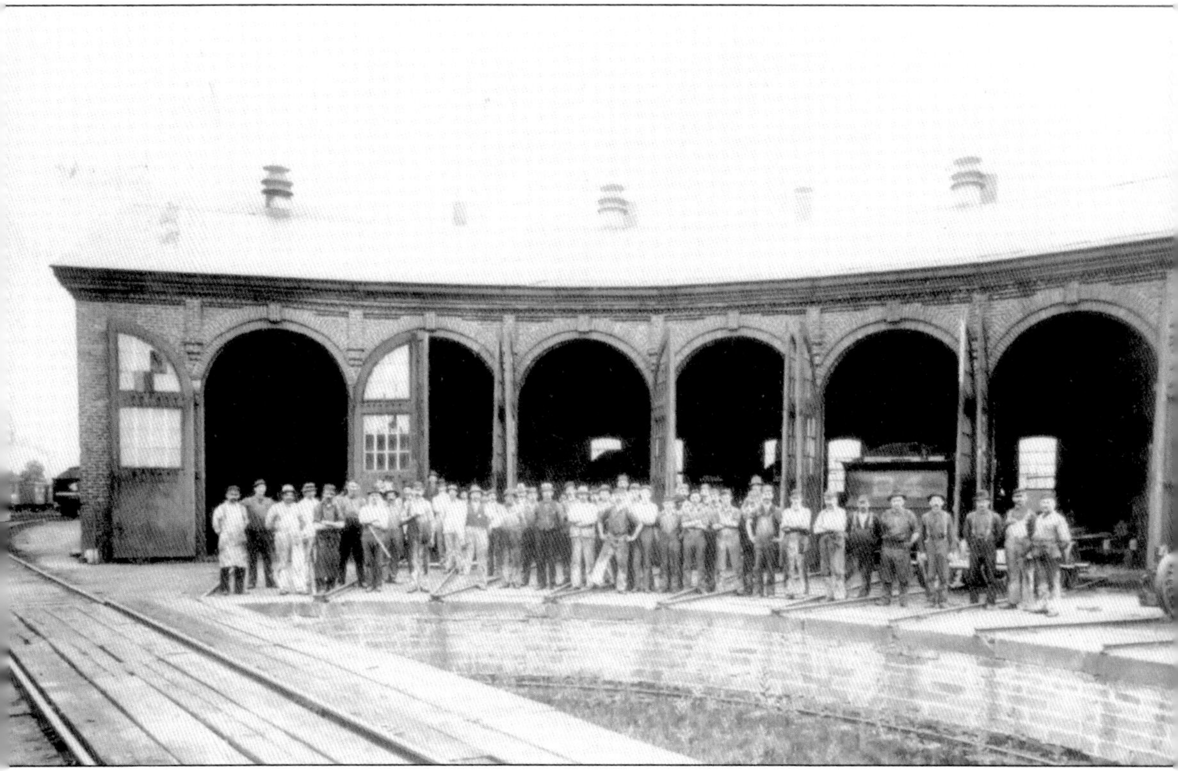

This photograph shows the Michigan Central Railroad's roundhouse (also known as an engine stable). In front is the turntable for switching locomotives. The 107-mile railroad trip east to Detroit cost $3.20 by the end of the 1850s, according to local historian Mabel Cooper Skjelver, and $5.20 to Chicago, which is 179 miles west. The roundhouse shown in this photograph is now located in Greenfield Village, part of the Henry Ford Museum in Dearborn.

Martin Ryan, whose parents emigrated from Ireland in 1867, started working for the railroad after graduating high school. He held many positions, including telegraph operator and ticket agent. He retired in 1939 after decades of service.

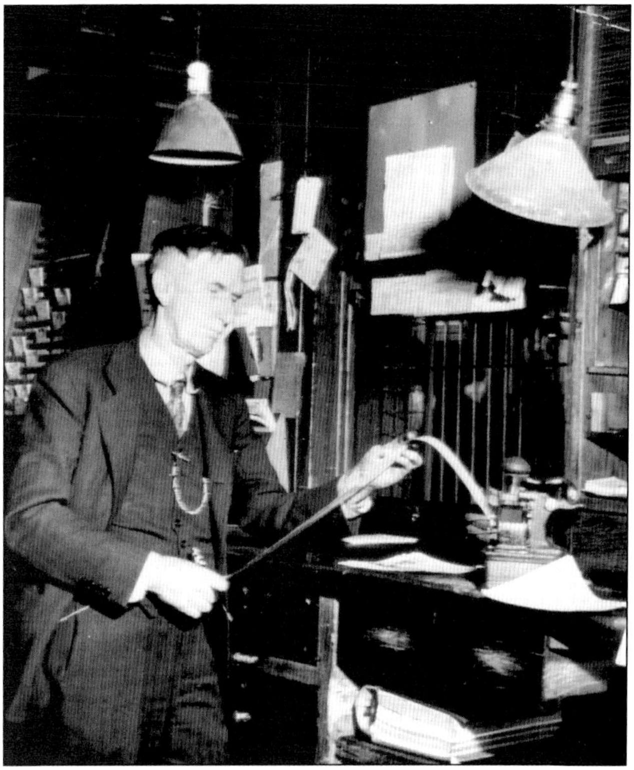

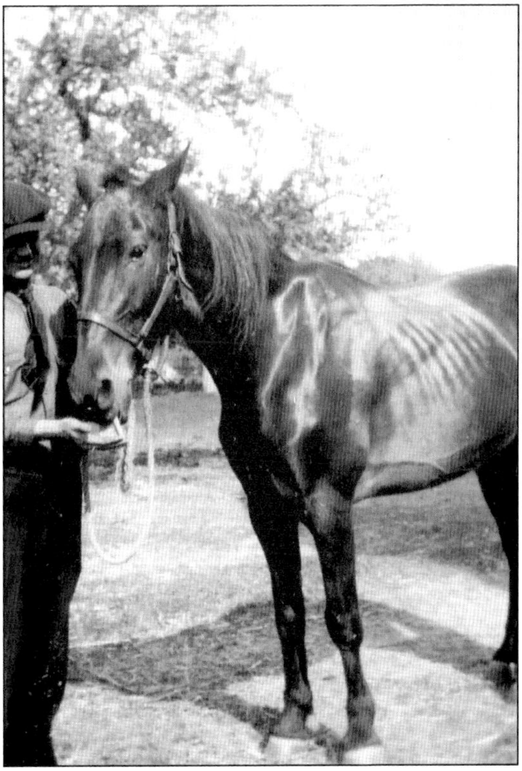

Gibson Glen, a longtime Marshall agent for the Railway Express, is shown here with his horse Freddie.

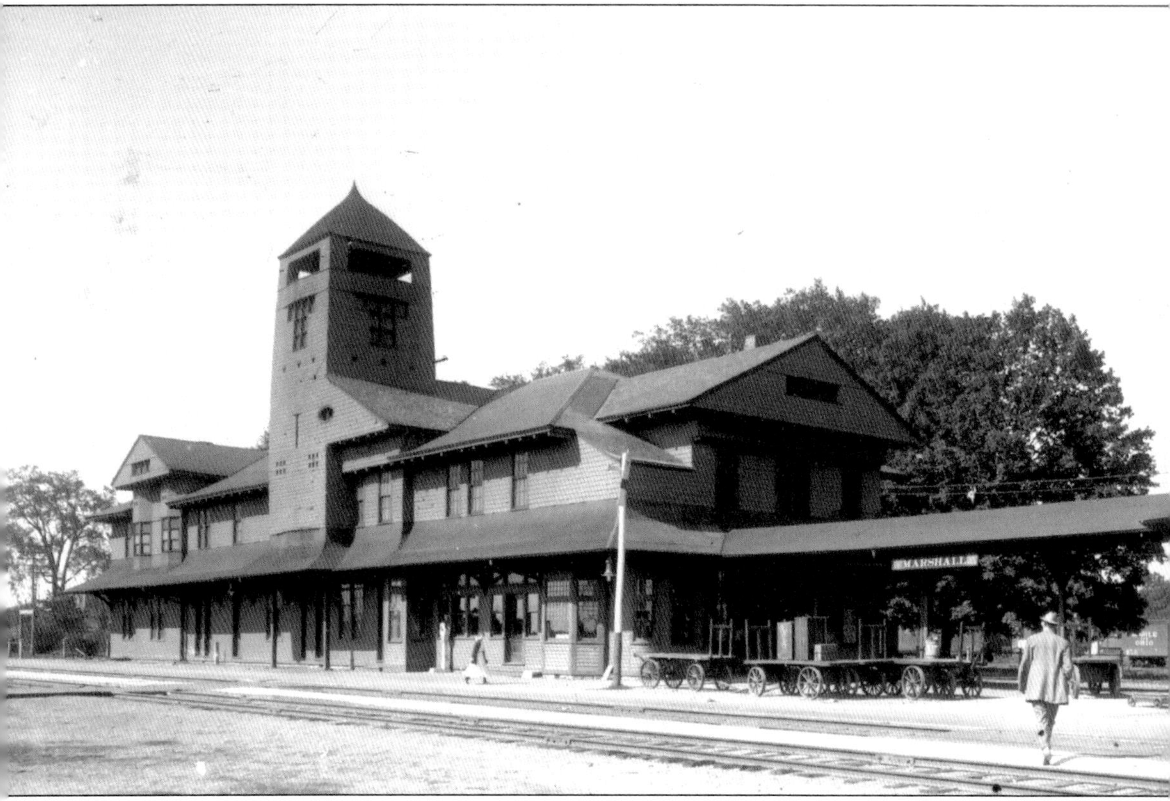

The Michigan Central Railroad depot is shown at the end of the 19th century after being moved across the tracks and remodeled. When completed in 1865, the depot, which cost $28,000, was the first edifice in Marshall to have gaslights and steam heat.

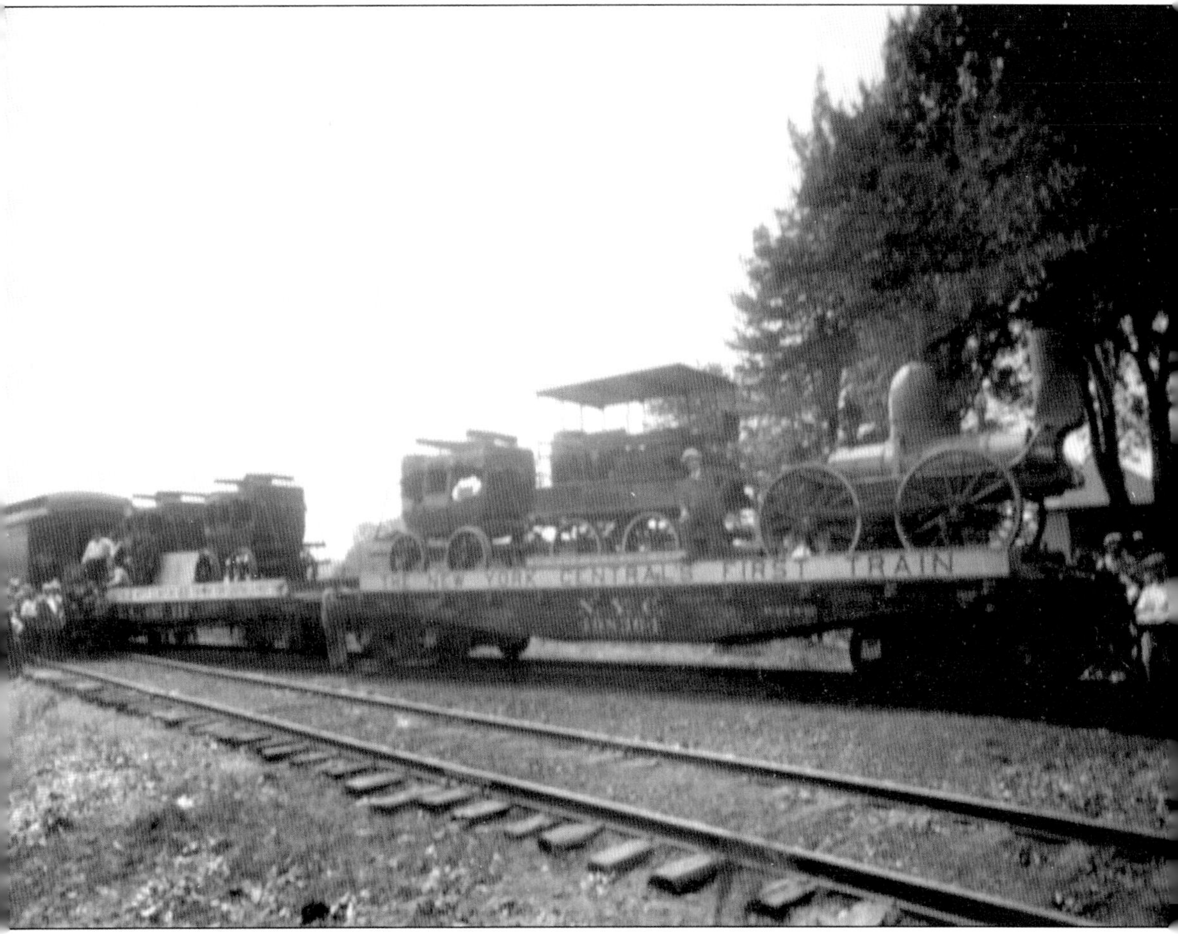

In 1921, the first engine Michigan Central Railroad had ever purchased was brought to Marshall and placed on a siding for a week so that people could see what railroad engines looked like in the old days.

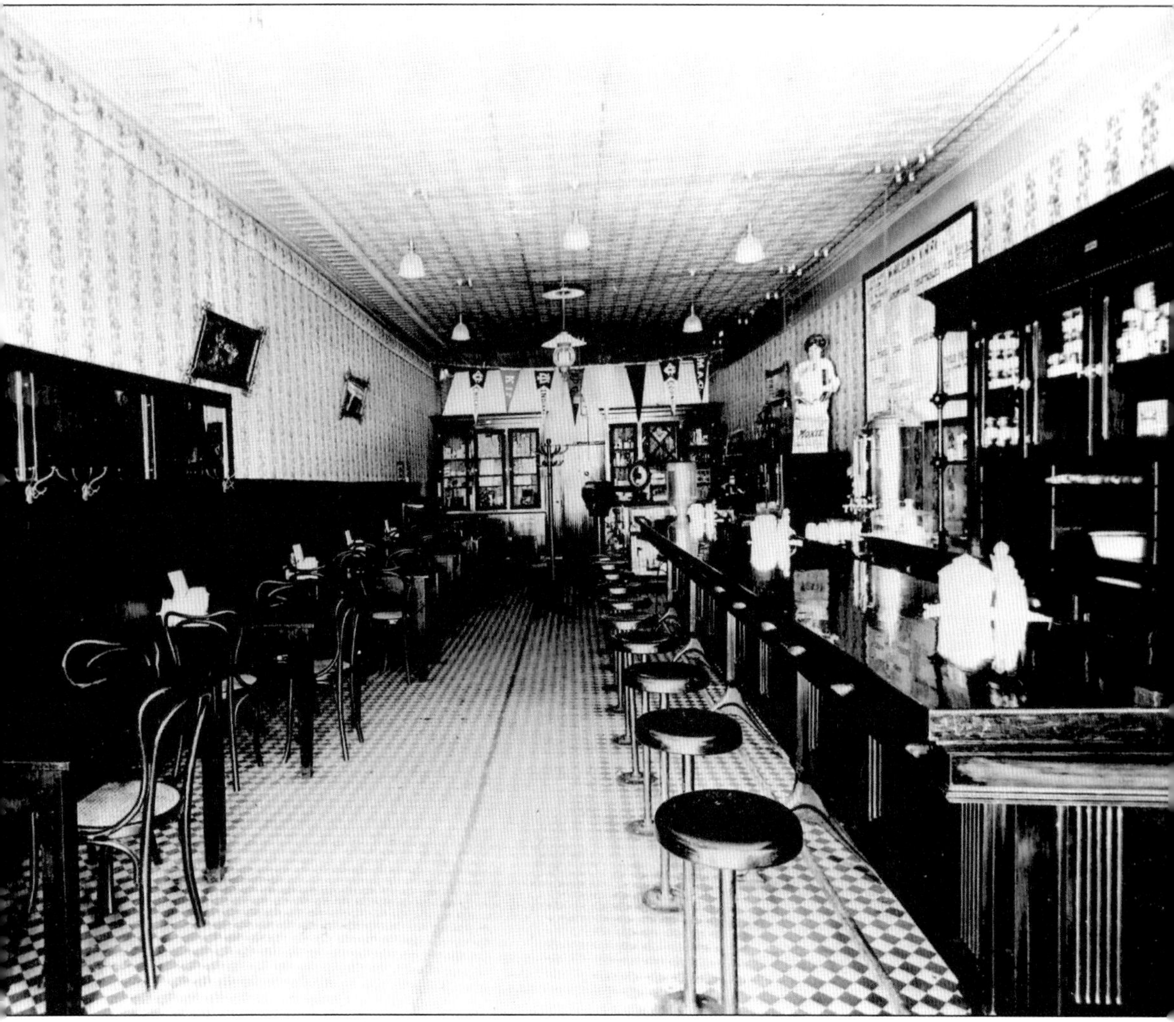

Whether traveling by rail or car, people need to eat. And Schuler's, a longtime Marshall restaurant that opened in 1909, has always been a popular stop.

Seven

CITY OF HOSPITALITY

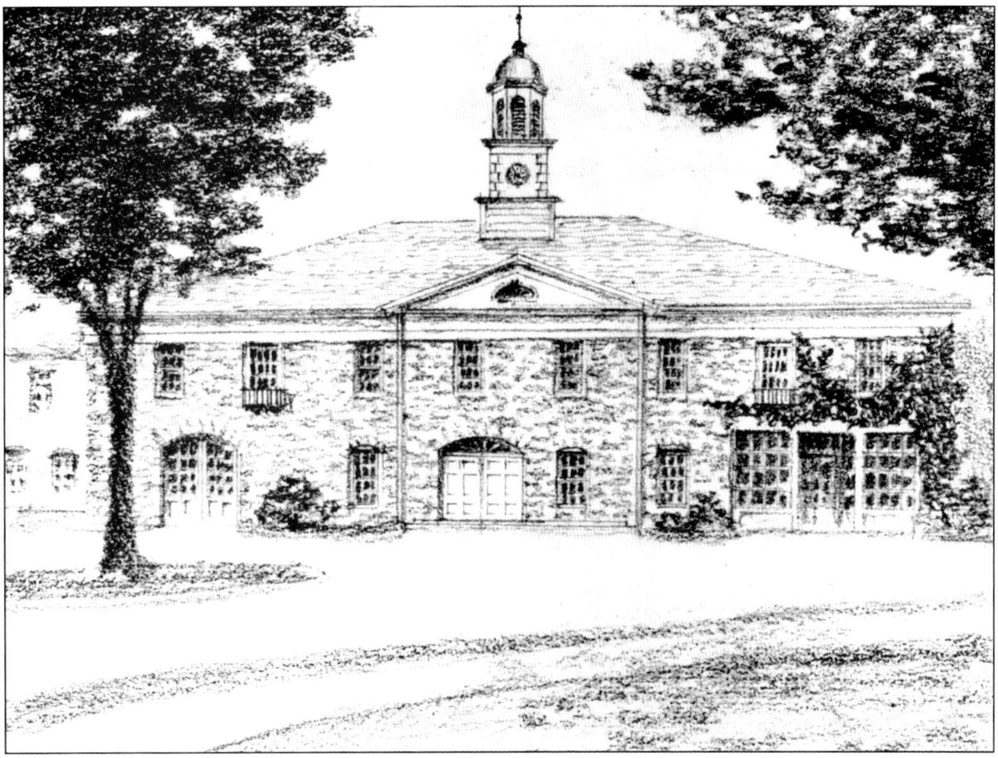

In 1927, Harold C. Brooks asked Howard F. Young to submit a plan for the redesign of the tire store and car repair shop located on the old courthouse circle. This is Young's drawing of his plan for the new town hall, fire station, and police station. His plan called for gutting the interior of the old barn and building an entire new structure inside it using iron I-beam construction and then poured concrete inside that.

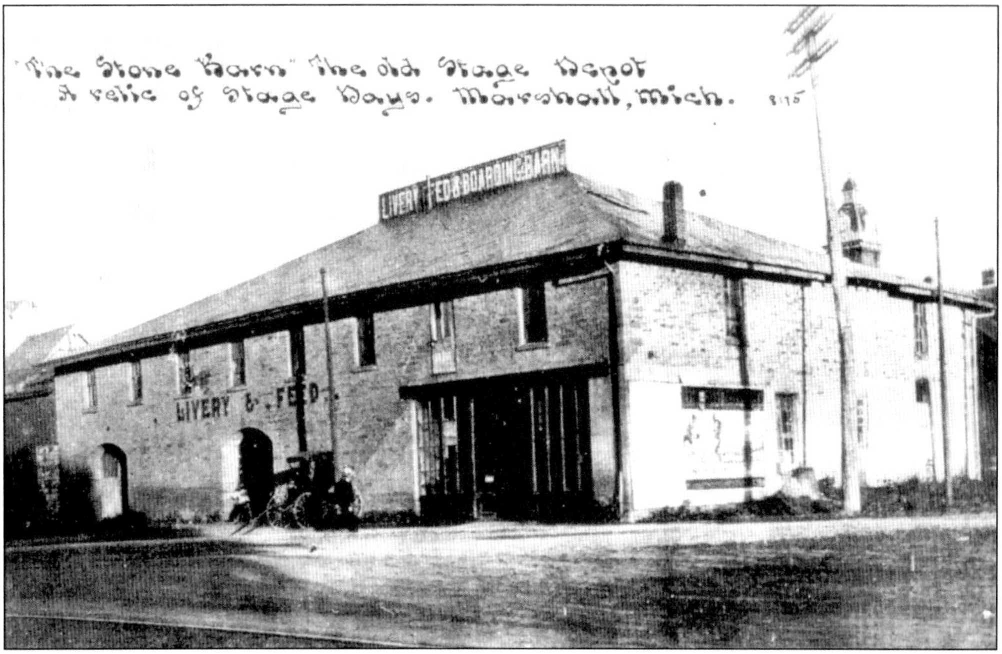

Originally built in 1857, the Prindle Livery Stable was used as a stagecoach stop and was also the Marshall stop on the Underground Railroad during the 1840s and 1850s. It was the drop-off and pick-up point after the local citizens were certain all was clear. Many other houses and barns throughout the community were used by the operators of the Underground. One can see the clock tower on the old county building in the background.

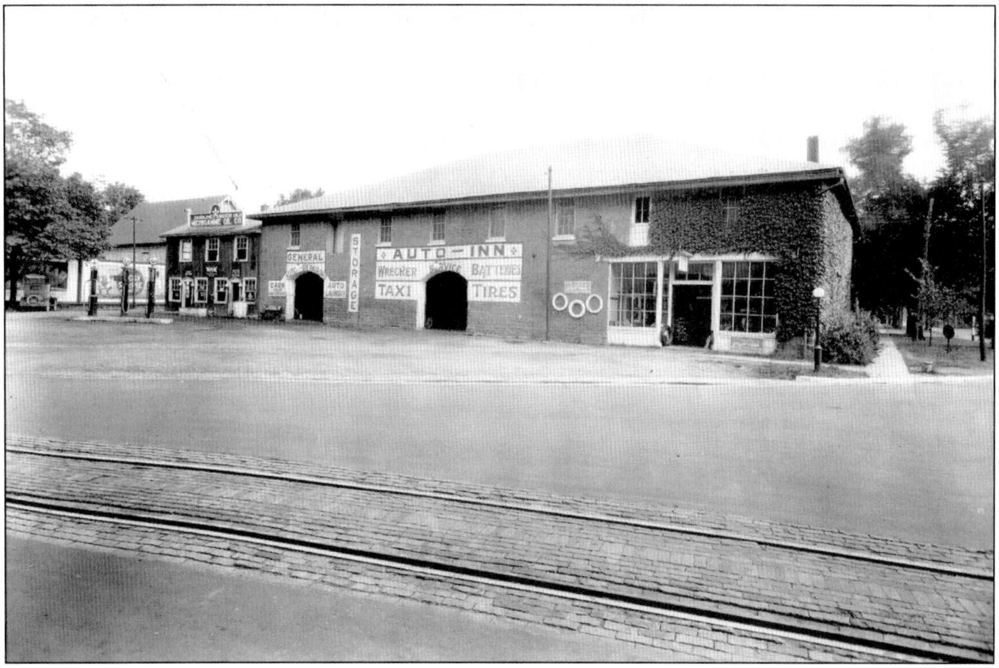

By the late 1920s, the old livery barn had become a tire store and car repair shop with a roller-skating rink upstairs.

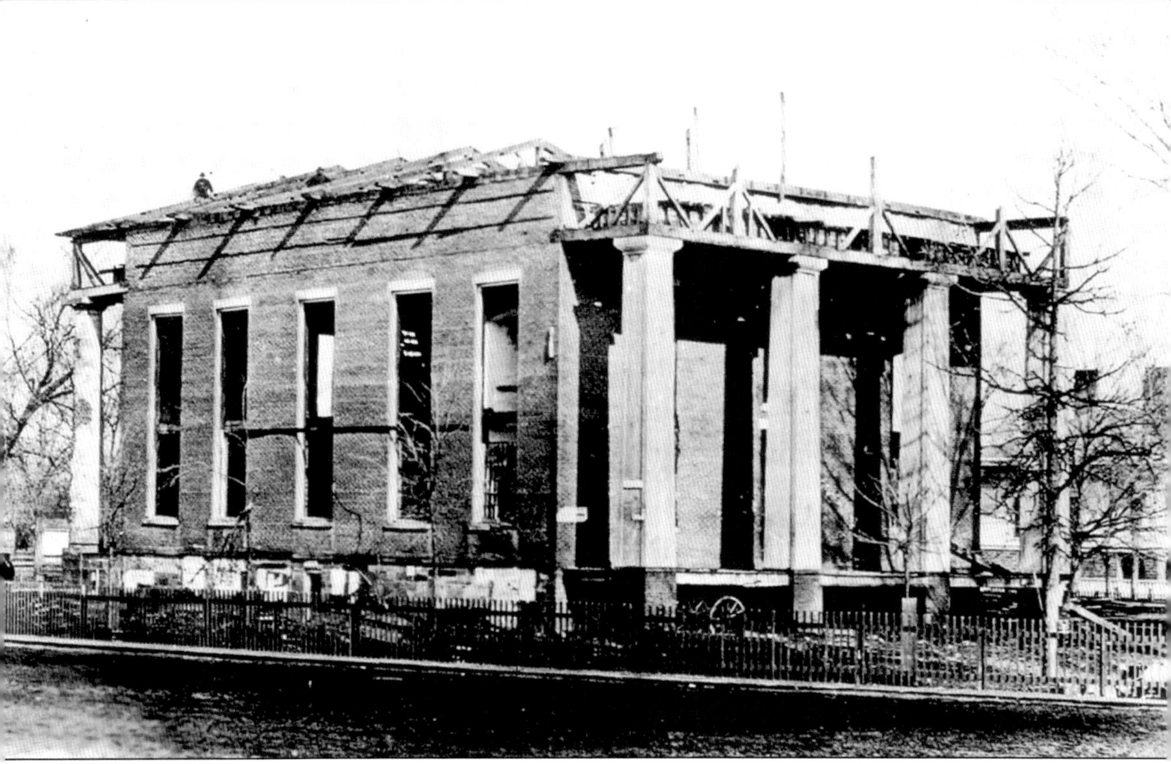

Marshall was founded in 1830 and first settled in the spring of 1831. It was determined to be the county seat of Calhoun County. Marshall was named for chief justice of the United States Supreme Court five years before John Marshall died. He hailed from Virginia, and the county was named for John Calhoun, who was from South Carolina. It is interesting that a small abolitionist community like Marshall could be named for a southerner and a county seat named for another. This view shows the original courthouse, built in 1837, when Marshall's population was about 1,000. By 1871, the building was deemed derelict and beyond repair. Thus, this only known remaining photograph shows it in a state of demolition.

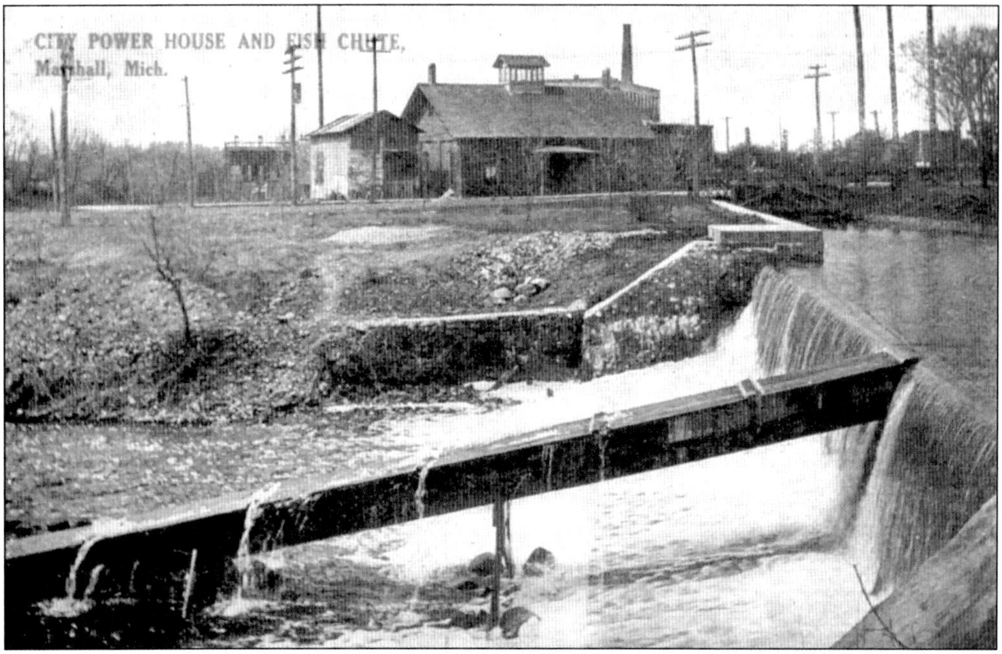

The Marshall Municipal Power Plant on South Marshall Avenue and the Kalamazoo River is the second-oldest electric power plant in the United States. The oldest is in Marquette. The fish chute in the foreground of this picture no longer exists, but the rest of this picture looks pretty much the same in 2007 as it did when this photograph was taken back in the 1930s.

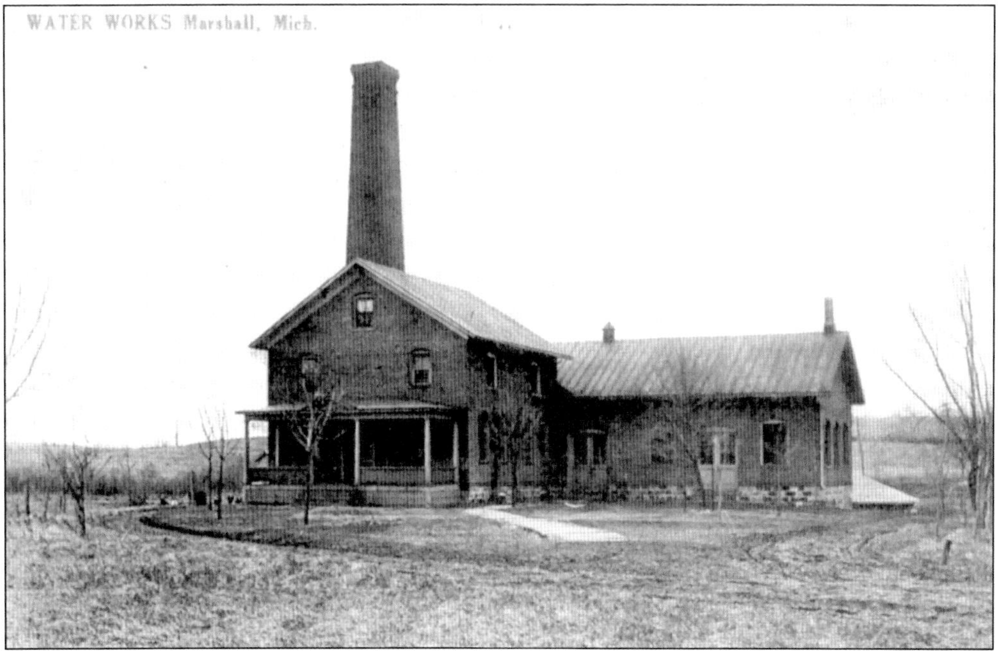

The waterworks building has not changed much either. It is located on the east side of Marshall on Rice Creek. The City of Marshall still provides electricity, water, and sewerage to its citizens in a timely and clean fashion.

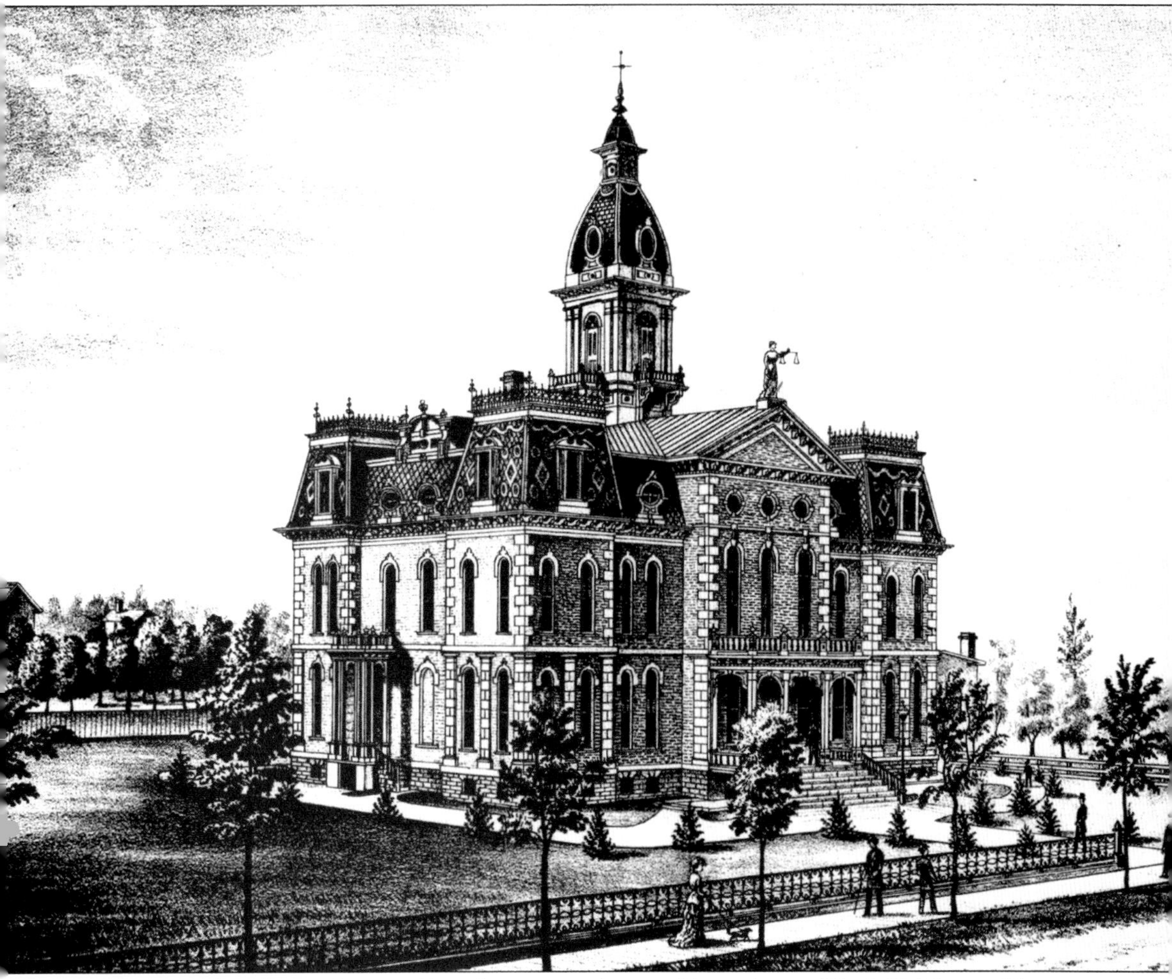

The second Calhoun County Courthouse was designed by architect Elijah E. Myers of Detroit. Myers also designed the Michigan State Capitol in Lansing. He went on to design the state capitols of Colorado, Texas, and Utah. He also successfully sued the State of Indiana for stealing some of the designs he submitted for the new building in Indianapolis.

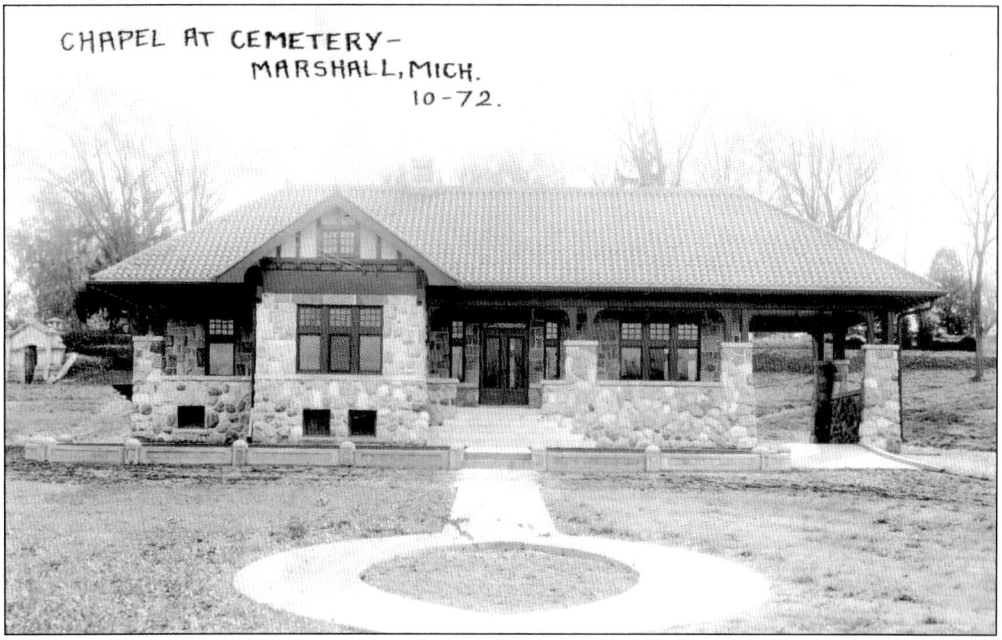

The chapel at Oakridge Cemetery was designed by the architectural firm of Spier and Rohn of Detroit. It its early days, shortly after 1900, many funeral services were held in this chapel before the deceased was taken on up the hill to be buried.

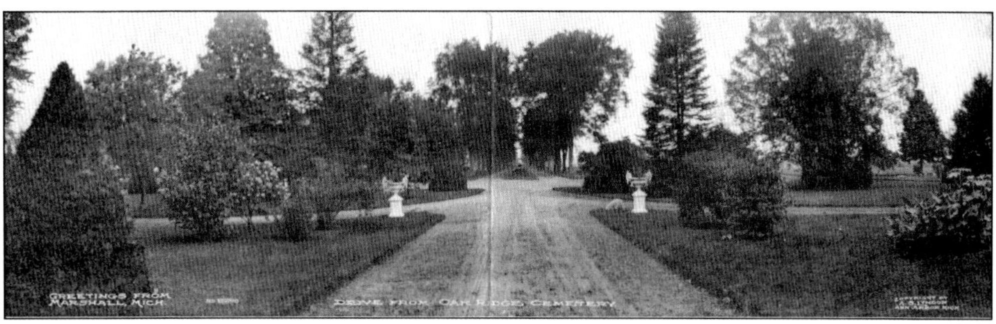

This rare double postcard shows an early view of Oakridge Cemetery in Marshall. It is the second-oldest cemetery in Michigan, only dating after one in Detroit. The wide double avenue leads to the back of the cemetery, which is the oldest portion. There are numerous congressmen, ambassadors, supreme court justices, and local dignitaries buried here, not to mention the composer of "The Sweetheart of Sigma Chi."

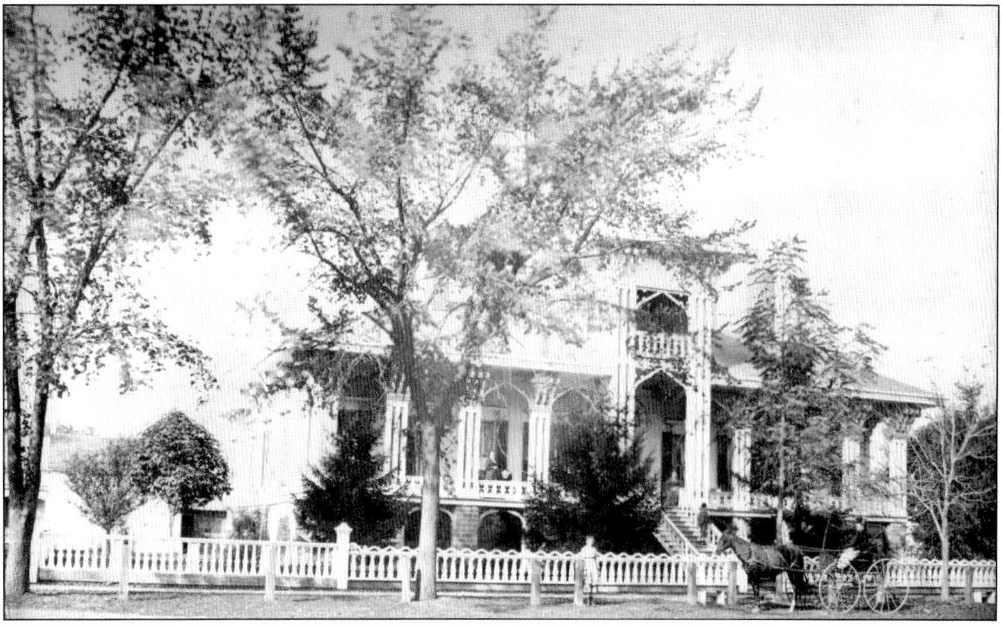

The Honolulu House Museum only had four private owners. This photograph was taken during the time Mayor Cap Wagner owned it, and the people in the photograph are the members of the Wagner family. The wonderful white wooden fence was long gone before anyone today can remember. The house is run as a house museum by the Marshall Historical Society and is open daily from May through October.

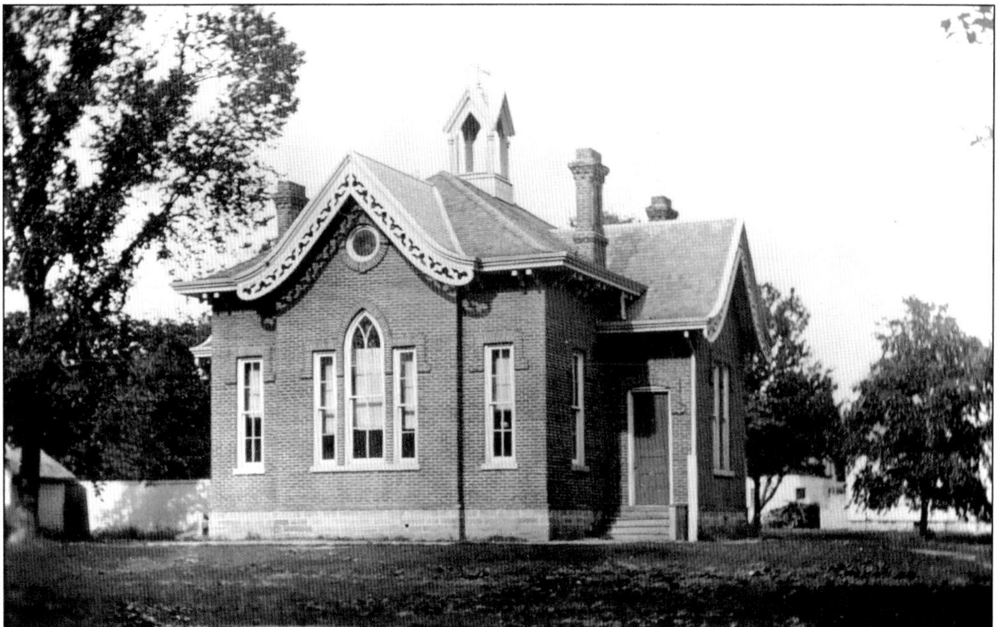

Capitol Hill School is one of the three schools built in 1860 by Sheldon Smith of Detroit for $8,000. It is a children's museum today with an early-1900s classroom on one side and a museum with toys, books, and puppets on the other. The school is operated by the Marshall Historical Society and is open for the home tour and by appointment the rest of the year.

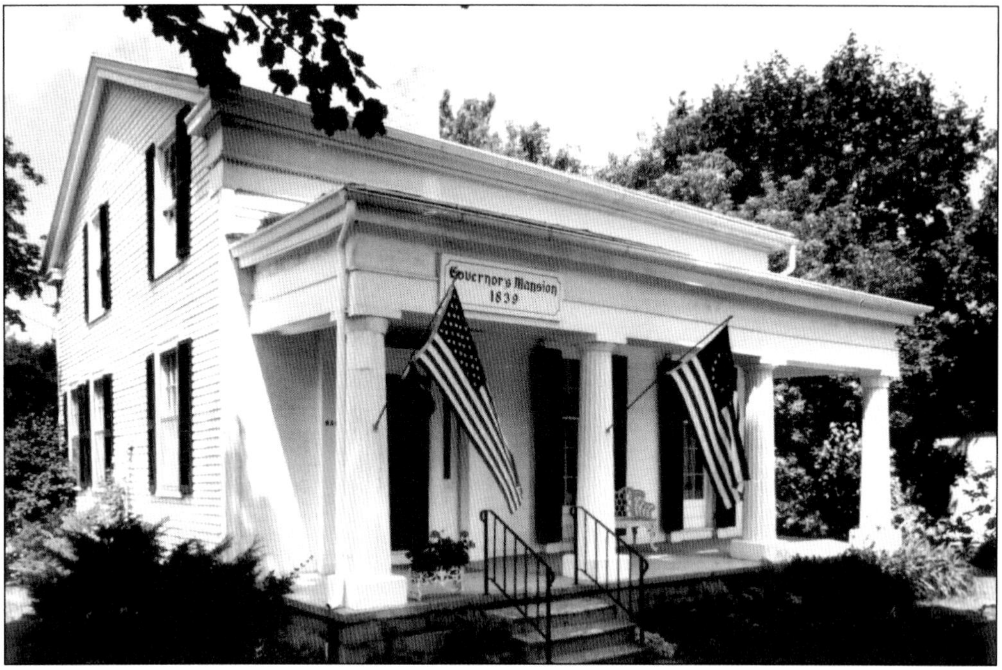

James Wright Gordon moved up from the position of lieutenant governor to governor of Michigan in 1841 when Gov. William Woodbridge moved on to become a U.S. senator. Gordon built this small Greek Revival house on South Marshall Avenue in 1839. He built it expressly to be the governor's mansion for the new state of Michigan. Isaac Loomis is the purported architect of this modest home.

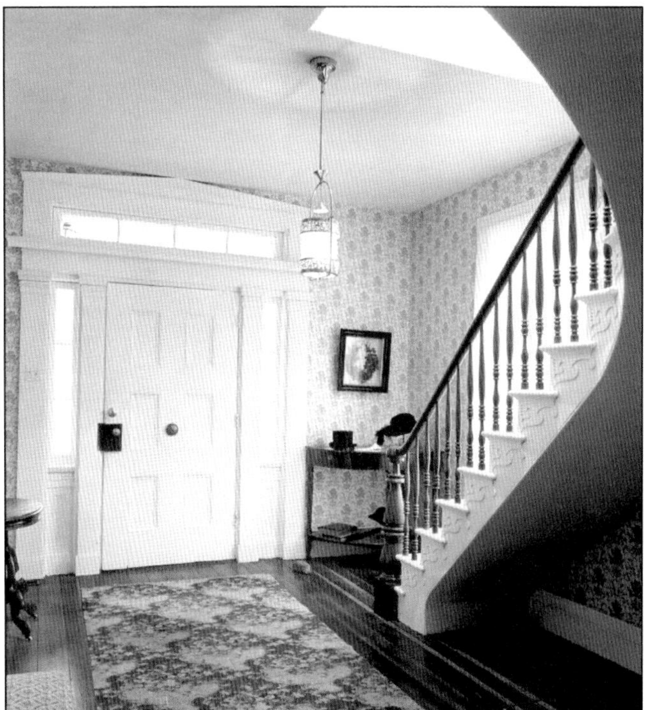

This mid-20th-century view of the entryway of the governor's mansion shows the gracious curved stairway to the second-floor bedrooms. The large original lock is very visible, as is the hair wreath to the right of the door. These wreaths were made by the friends of the lady of the household for her to bring west. This house now belongs to the Mary Marshall chapter of the DAR.

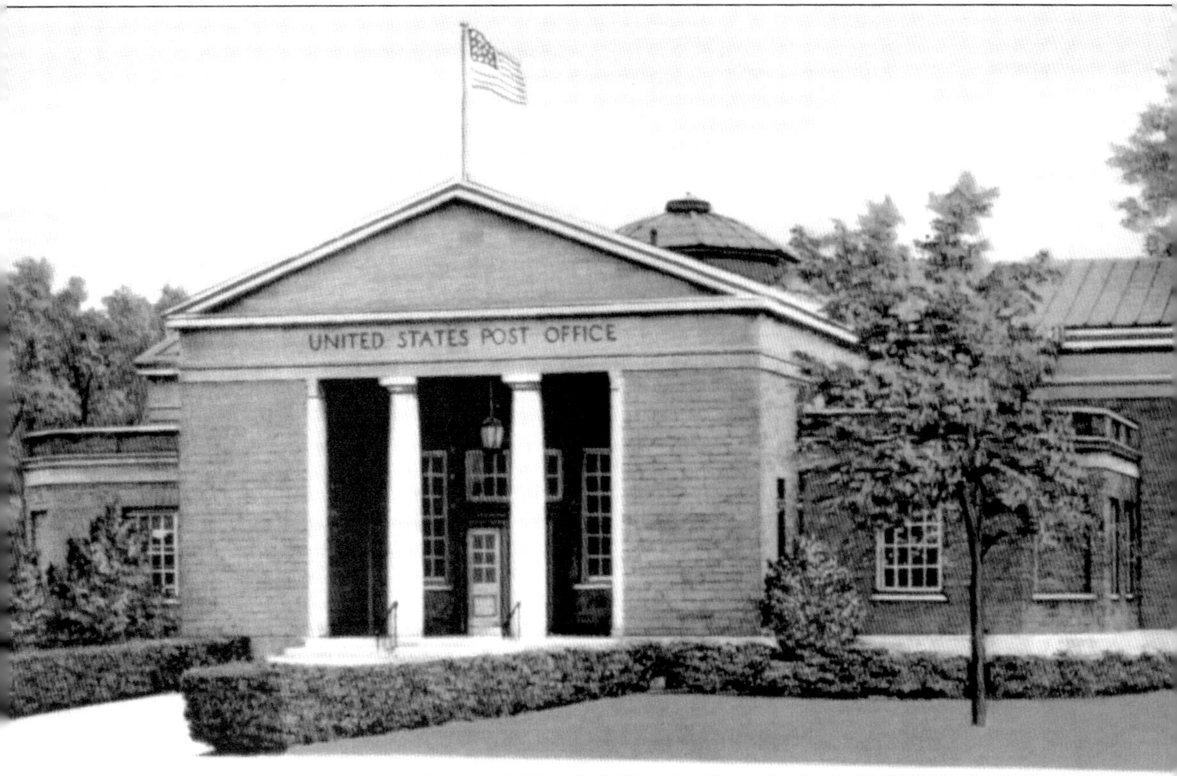

Marshall's 1930 post office was designed in Marshall sandstone by Howard F. Young. He used the classical revival style at H. C. Brooks's request. Brooks made a deal with the U.S. Postal Service that if he could have design review he would pay for the materials while the postal service would create Depression-era jobs by paying for the labor. Former postmaster Michael Schragg started a postal museum in the basement of the building many years ago. It has grown to be the second largest in the country, after the Smithsonian National Postal Museum.

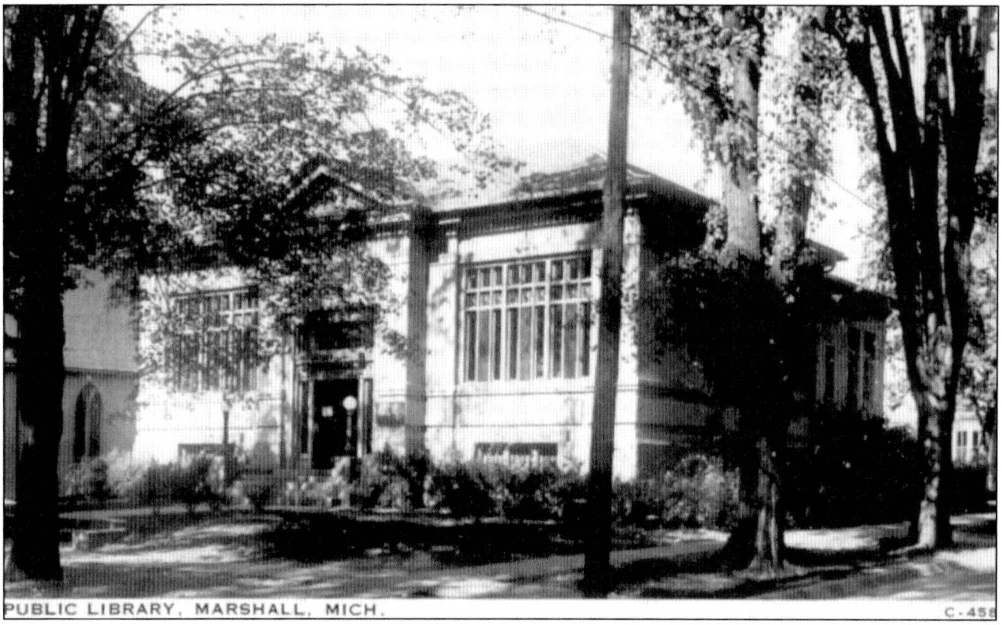

Built in the craftsman style, Marshall's library was unusual because it was not a Carnegie library. This building was Marshall's second public library building. The Marshall Ladies' Literary Society raised the funds to build this structure in 1915. The group of ladies met weekly to read together. This was the public library in Marshall for more than 90 years. It is now the library for the American Museum of Magic.

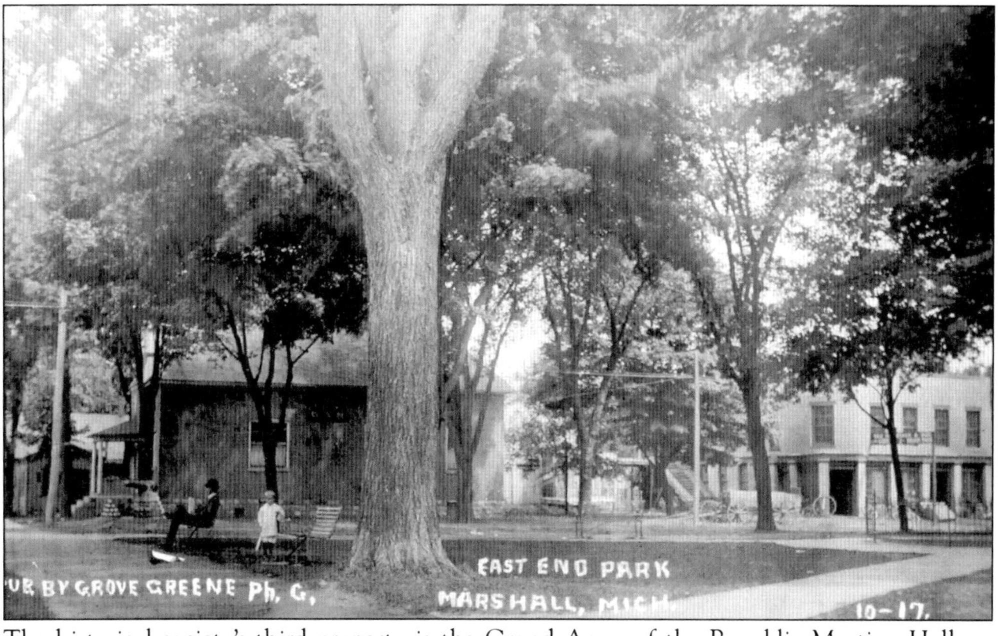

The historical society's third property is the Grand Army of the Republic Meeting Hall on East State Street. After the Civil War, the returning soldiers all over the country formed an organization of veterans of the Union forces. A few groups were large enough to build meeting halls, and one of those was in Marshall. It is still used as a meeting place for the Sons of Union Veterans.

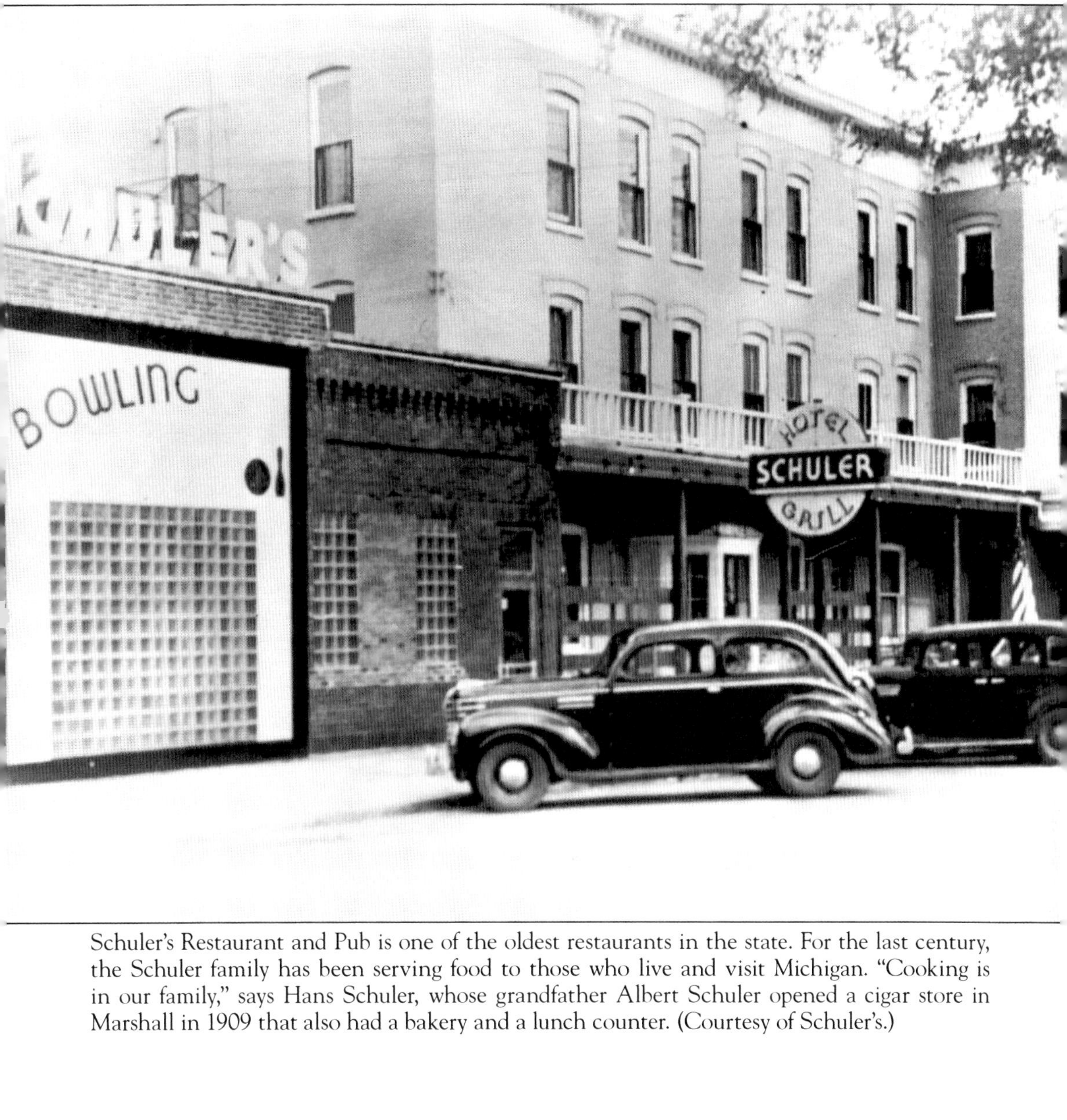

Schuler's Restaurant and Pub is one of the oldest restaurants in the state. For the last century, the Schuler family has been serving food to those who live and visit Michigan. "Cooking is in our family," says Hans Schuler, whose grandfather Albert Schuler opened a cigar store in Marshall in 1909 that also had a bakery and a lunch counter. (Courtesy of Schuler's.)

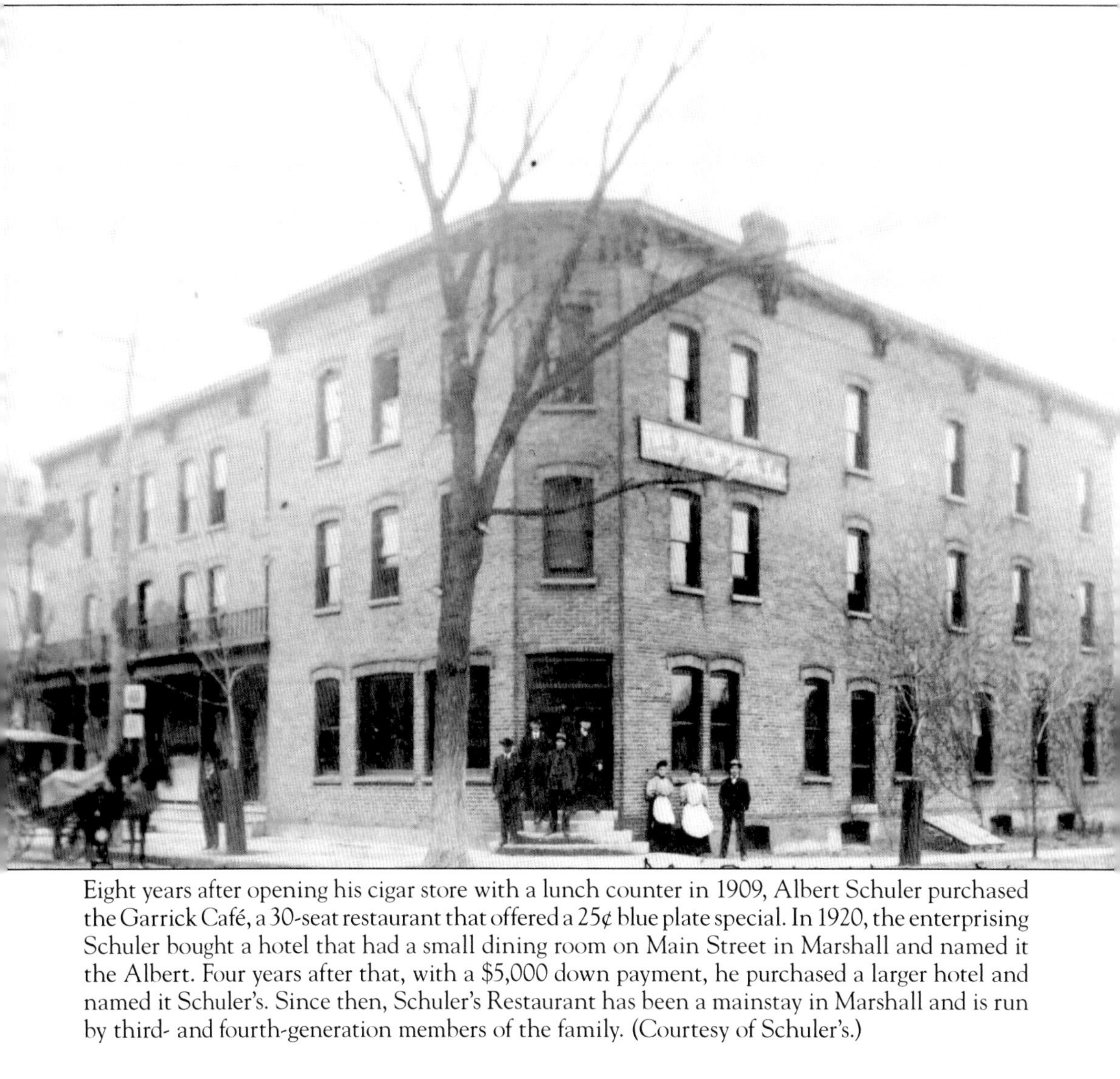

Eight years after opening his cigar store with a lunch counter in 1909, Albert Schuler purchased the Garrick Café, a 30-seat restaurant that offered a 25¢ blue plate special. In 1920, the enterprising Schuler bought a hotel that had a small dining room on Main Street in Marshall and named it the Albert. Four years after that, with a $5,000 down payment, he purchased a larger hotel and named it Schuler's. Since then, Schuler's Restaurant has been a mainstay in Marshall and is run by third- and fourth-generation members of the family. (Courtesy of Schuler's.)

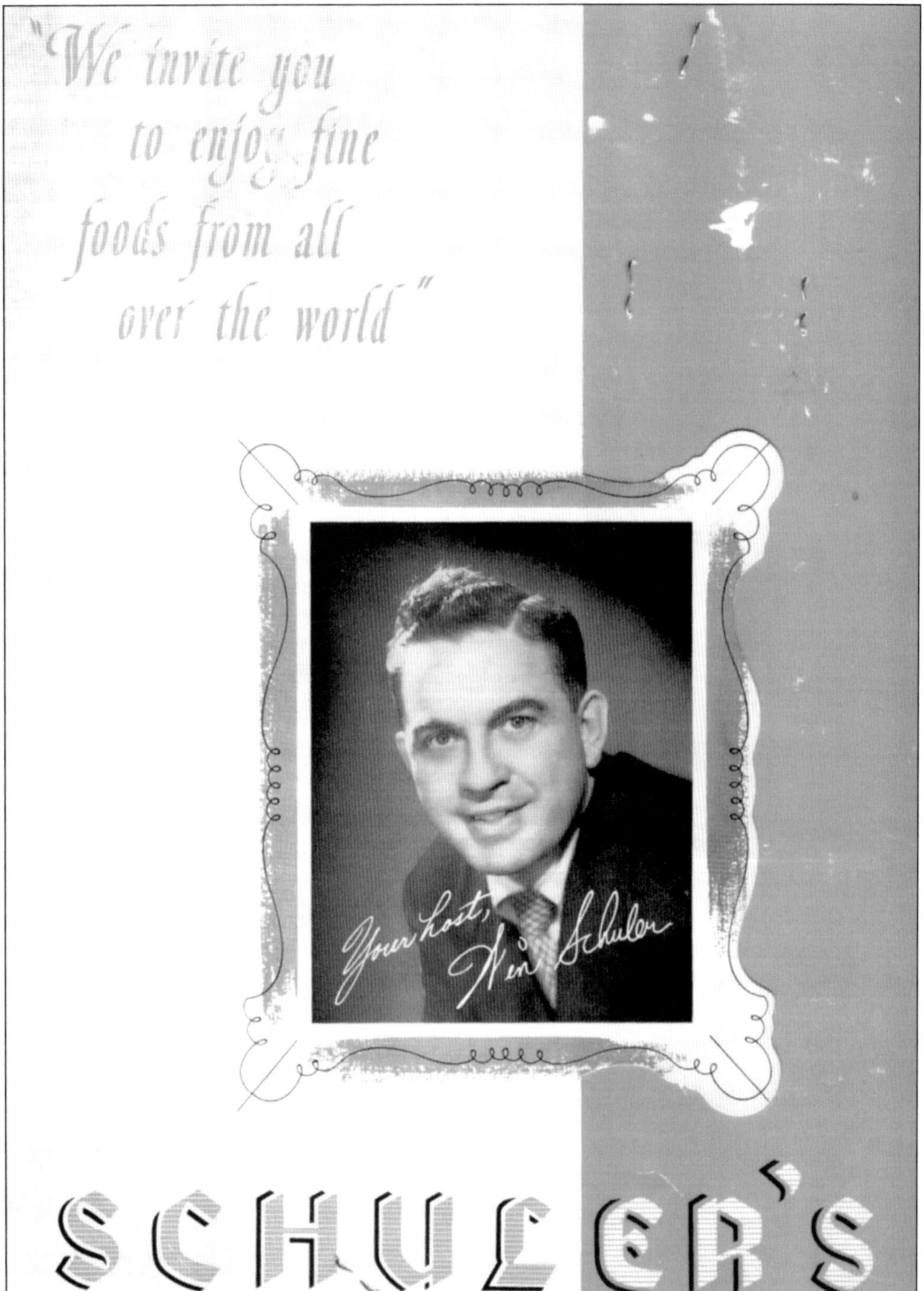

Here is an old menu from Schuler's, a fourth-generation family-owned restaurant that is one of the oldest operating restaurants in the state. The menu shows that diners could order broiled African rock lobster tails with drawn butter for $2.35, steak for two for $7.25, and soft-shell crabs from the Chesapeake Bay for $2.25. (Courtesy of Schuler's.)

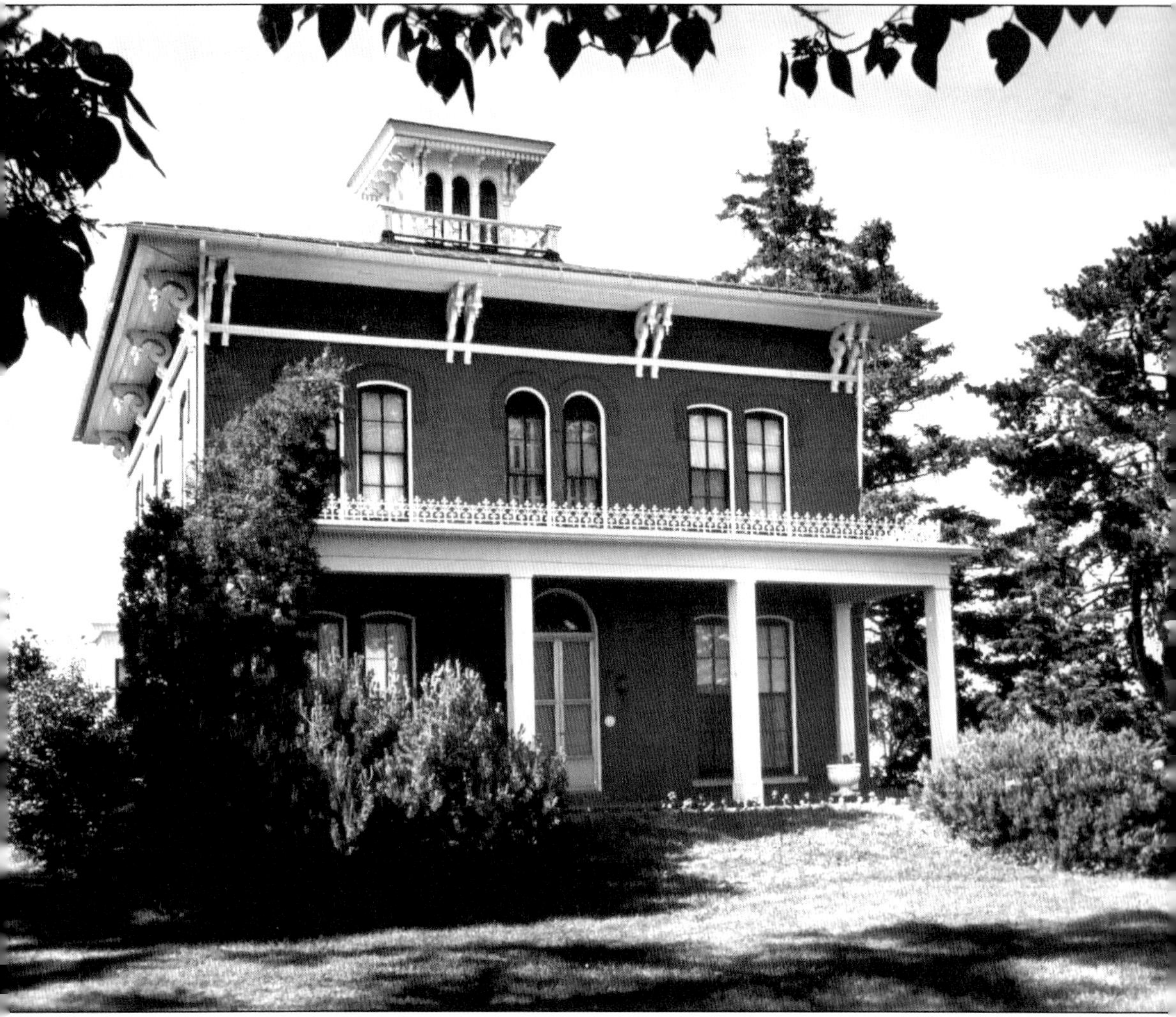

The Butler family built this in 1860 to try to keep up with Mrs. Edward Butler's sister, Mrs. Chauncey Brewer. It sits on land once owned by author James Fenimore Cooper. By the 1990s, W. D. Boyce purchased the property. Boyce was famous for having been lost in a London fog. A young man led him to his destination, and when Boyce tried to tip the boy, it was refused with the lad saying he was one of Lord Baden-Powell's Boy Scouts and this was his good deed for the day. Boyce returned to Chicago with a trunkload of literature and founded the Boy Scouts of America. While he owned this property as his summer residence, he installed a bowling alley in the basement of the barn and had a golf course on the grounds. It is now Rose Hill, a bed-and-breakfast inn with a swimming pool and tennis court.

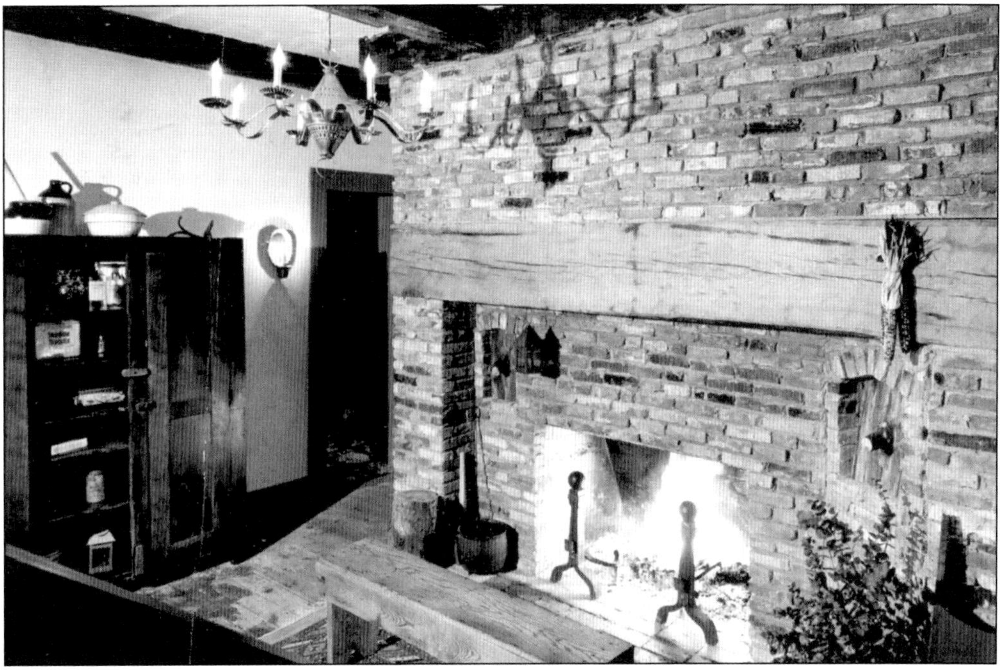

The National House Inn, on Marshall's picturesque Fountain Circle, is the oldest operating hotel in Michigan and is both a state historical site and on the National Register of Historical Places. The inn was built in 1835 by Col. Andrew Mann using wood from the Ketchum sawmill and bricks molded and fired on-site to build what is the oldest brick building in Calhoun County. (Courtesy of the National House Inn.)

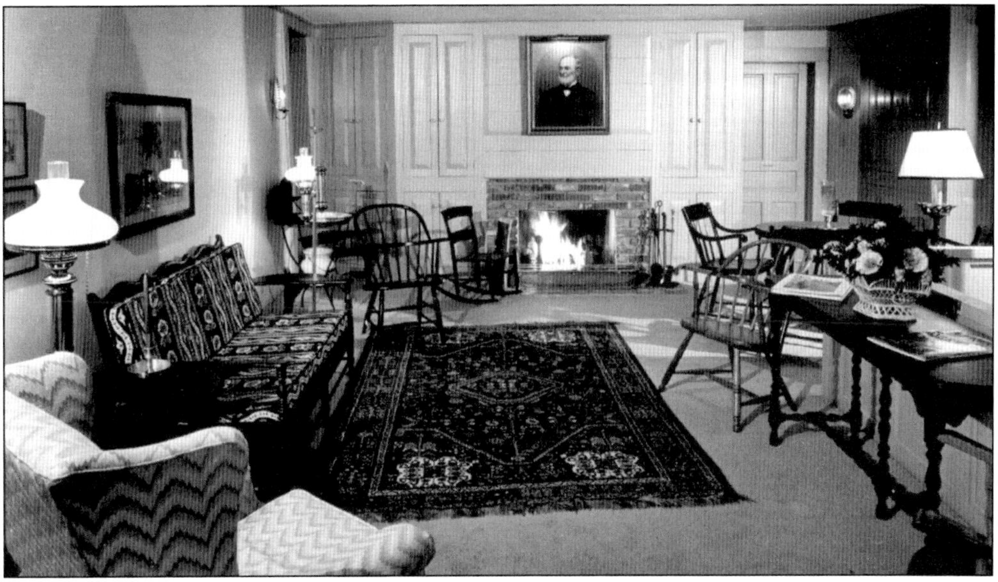

The National House Inn was situated two dusty (or muddy depending on the weather) days and nights by stagecoach from Detroit on the way to Chicago, so it was a convenient stopping place for weary travelers. From its beginnings as a stagecoach stop, the inn shifted gears with the advent of the Michigan Central Railroad in 1844, becoming, for the next 30 years, a railroad hotel. (Courtesy of the National House Inn.)

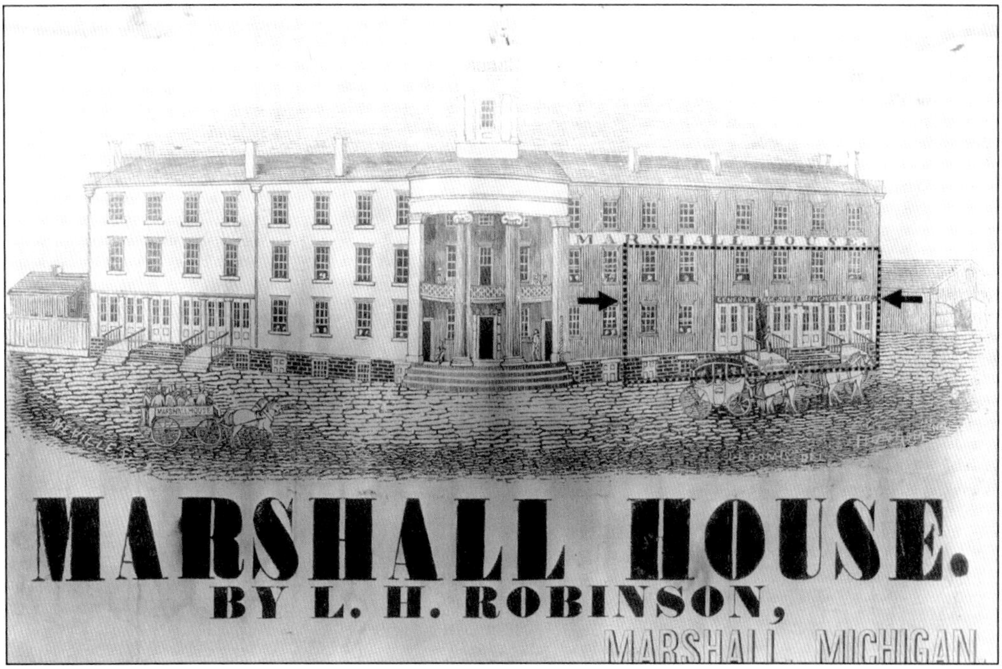

The Marshall House, in a handbill dated 1849, was considered not only one of the largest but one of the best hotels outside Detroit. It was a major stop for the stagecoach lines. The building later became the Perrin Collegiate Institute, a boarding and day school for young women, and then later the Court Funeral Home.

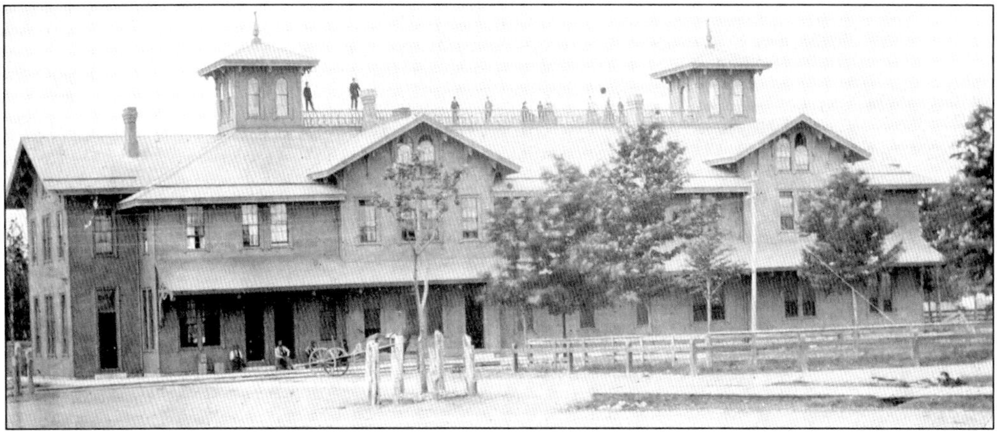

The restaurant at the Michigan Central Railroad depot became known as the Forbes House. Under the management of A. V. Pantlind (whose son opened the famous Pantlind Hotel in Grand Rapids, now the Amway Grand), the restaurant was known for its chicken pie a la bourgeoise. Other menu items included cottelle de veal in tomato sauce and English plum pudding with brandy sauce. It closed in 1892.

Eight

INDUSTRY

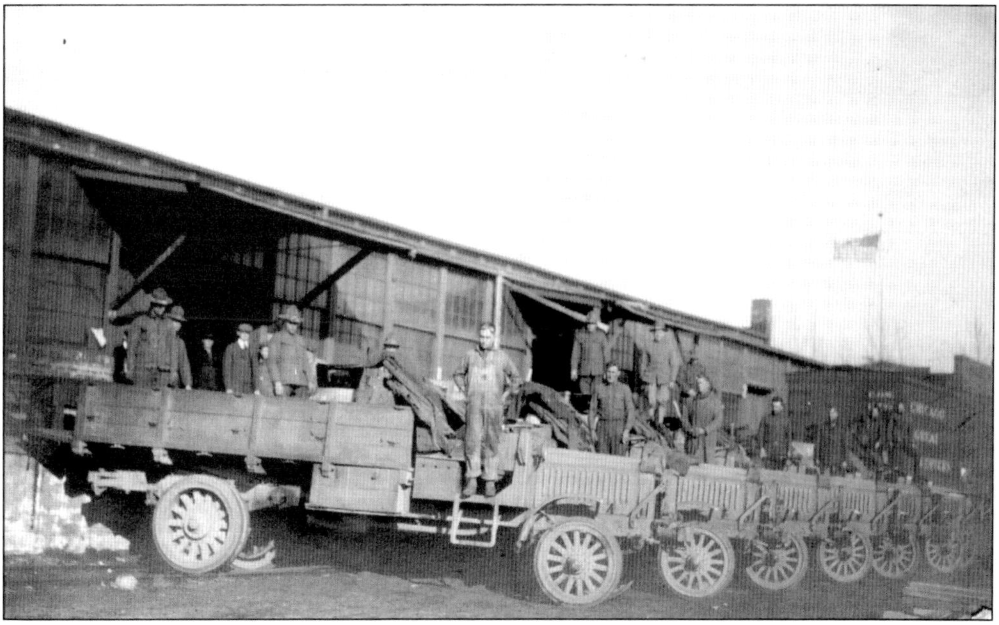

Dobbins Furnace Company was happy to donate storage space for the World War I war effort. The reverse of this photograph says, "Custer trucks at Dobbins Furnace Co. loading up for camp. Taken last week by Dr. Rowland." Fort Custer is just about 20 miles away on the far side of Battle Creek.

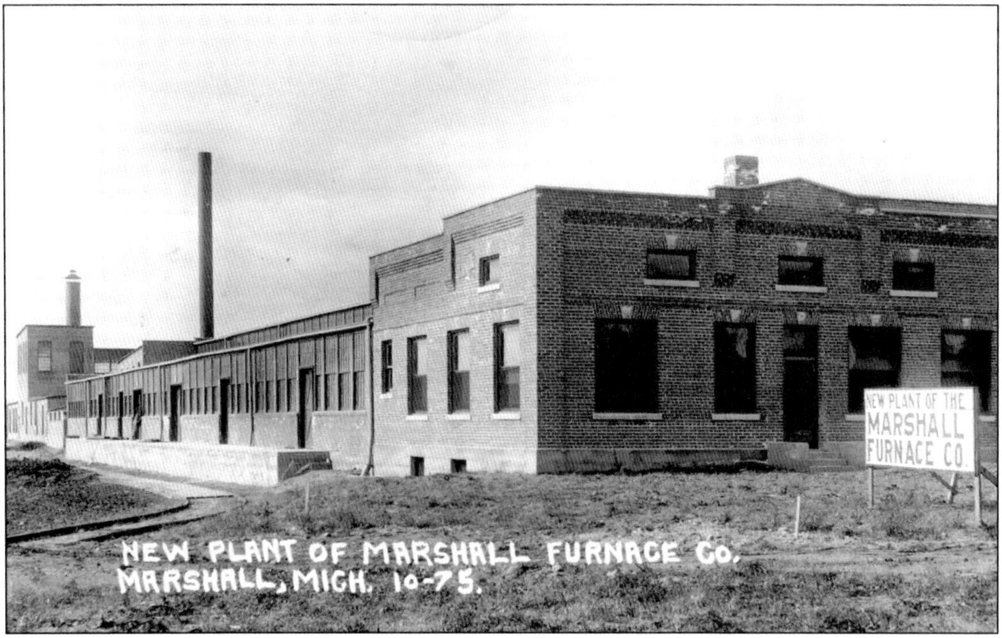

Marshall Furnace Company built this new plant on West Hanover Street back in the early 20th century. It was sold to Wilcox-Rich when it was enticed here from Battle Creek and Saginaw by a group of local investors.

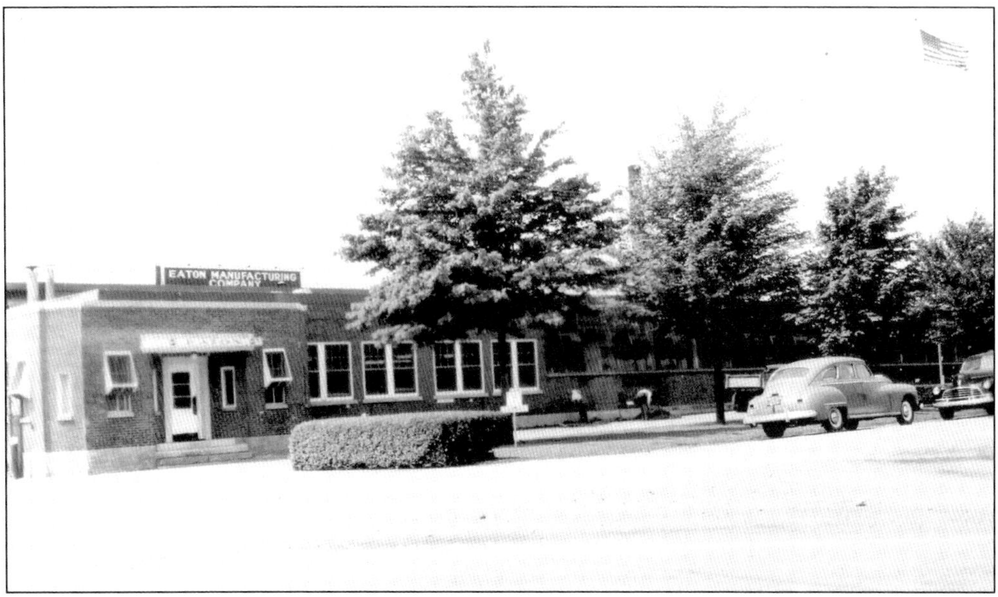

Marshall Furnace sold its new building to Wilcox-Rich. Eventually Eaton bought it out and moved the headquarters for one of its divisions into this facility in the late 1920s. It manufactured truck and automobile components here until 2006. Eaton was Marshall's largest employer for over 80 years.

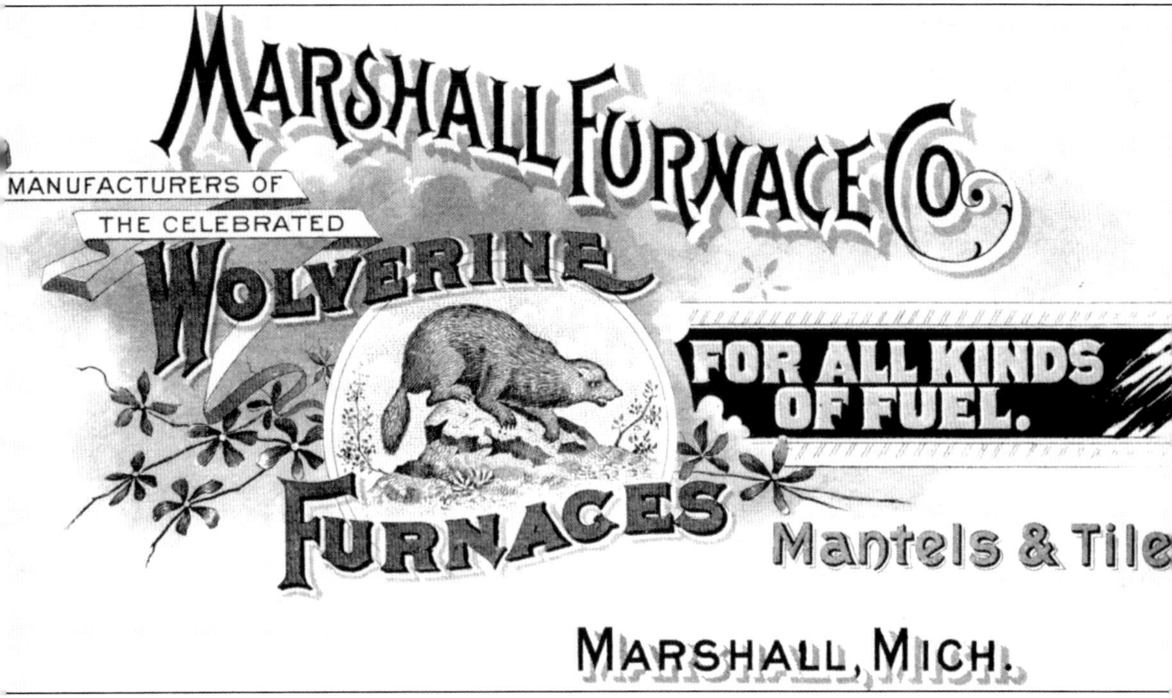

The wonderful texture and design of 19th-century advertising cards shows that they were real works of art. How can anything make a furnace look so rich and elegant as this card suggests?

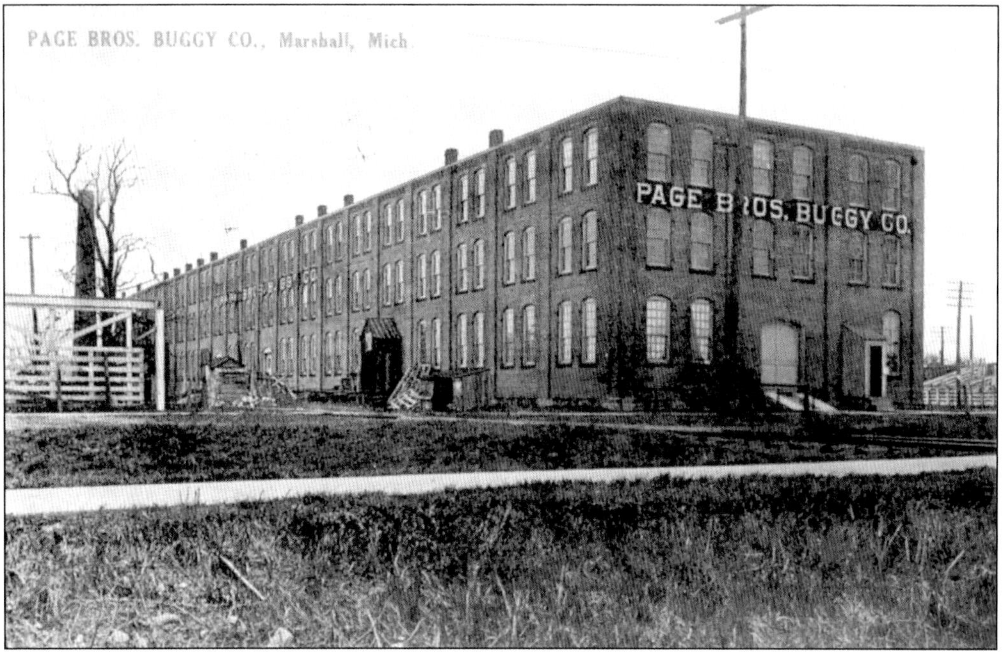

The Page Brothers Buggy Works on South Kalamazoo Avenue made all sorts of vehicles before the gasoline engine ruined its business. The building was used for manufacturing well into the last of the 20th century.

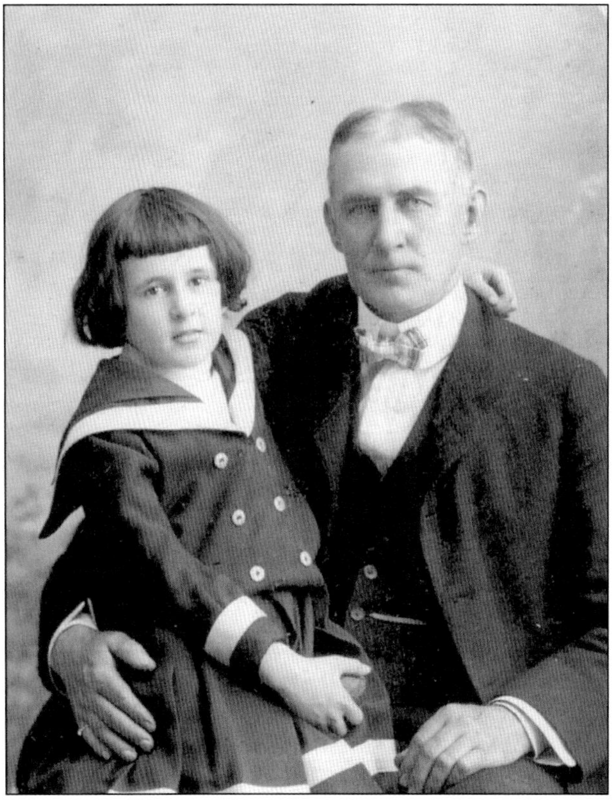

Lute and Narcissa Page pose for a daddy-daughter photograph. Is there any wonder why the employees made such adorable small carriages and sleighs for the Page children? There are two of these on display at the Capitol Hill School Children's Museum.

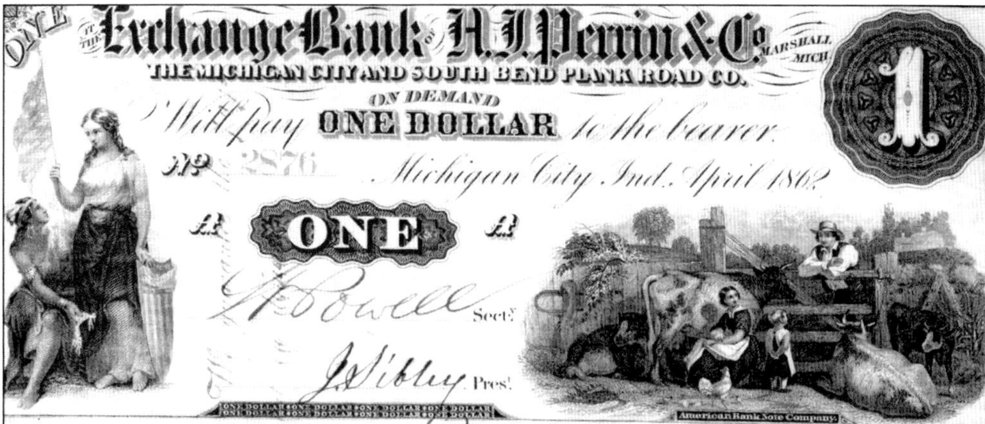

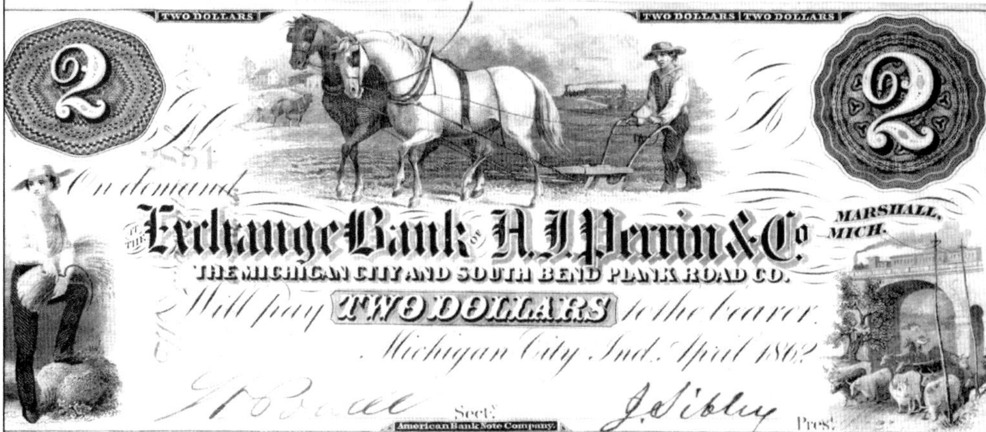

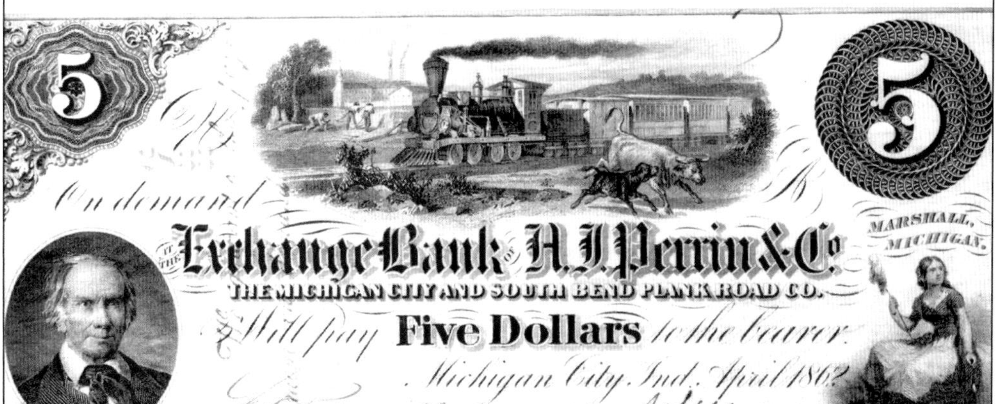

The largest industrialist in Marshall's history also had his own bank called the Exchange Bank of H. J. Perrin and Company. The bank was located on the northwest corner of Hamilton Street and Michigan Avenue. The safe is still in use in the shop there today. Horace J. Perrin acquired the water rights along the Kalamazoo River. He owned the old Ketchum mill on the river. He built a distillery, a flour mill, a foundry, and machine shops in the area that is still referred to as Perrinville. Just east of his industrial empire, he built a very large home, which burned in 1972. Perrin was undoubtedly the richest man in Marshall in the 19th century.

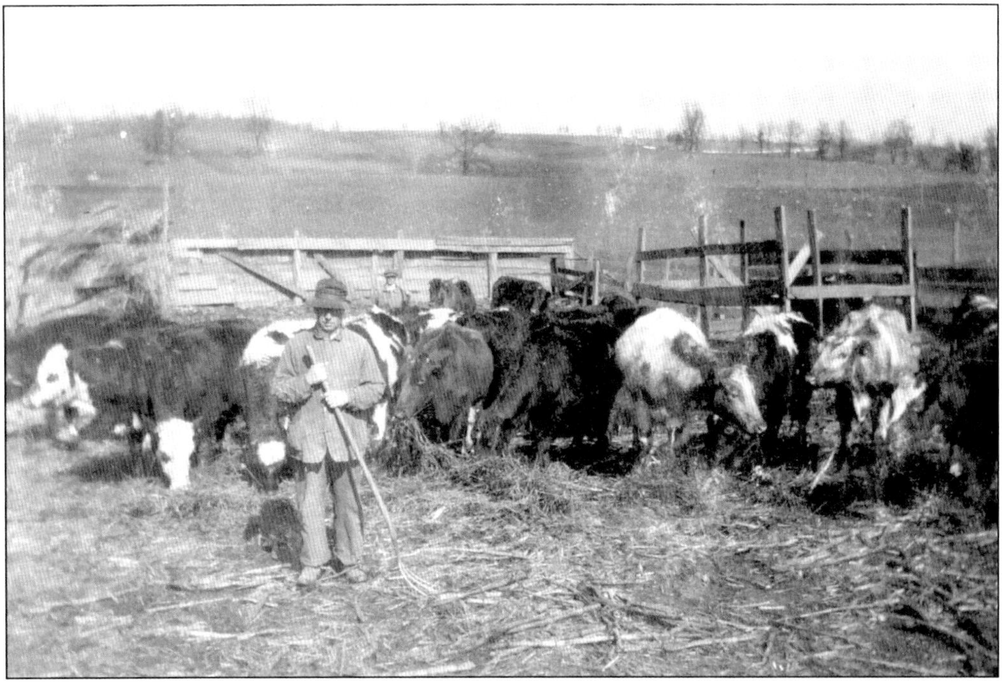

Although Marshall was settled to be a business and political center, it had an agrarian industry as well because of its rural location. This business really grew when it was discovered how good the soil was. It is now the largest corn-producing county in the state. George Tingay was a very successful farmer on Seventeen Mile Road north of town. His cattle would not be quite so happy today since his farm is now subdivided into very large home sites.

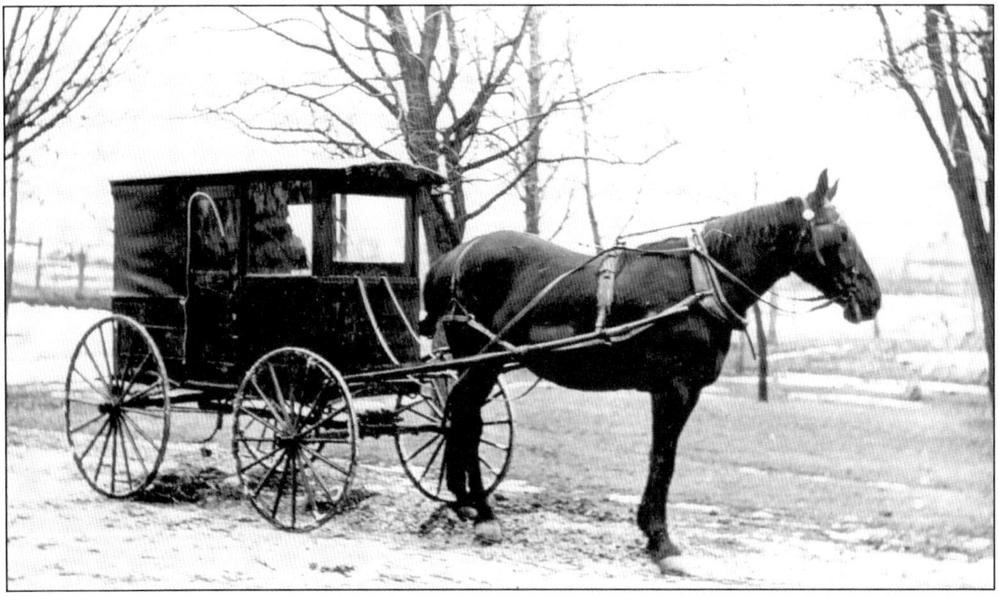

Ken Leach and his horse braved mud, ice, and snow in this small buggy to deliver the milk to Marshall area residents. Without refrigeration in the home, everyone really needed fresh milk on a daily basis.

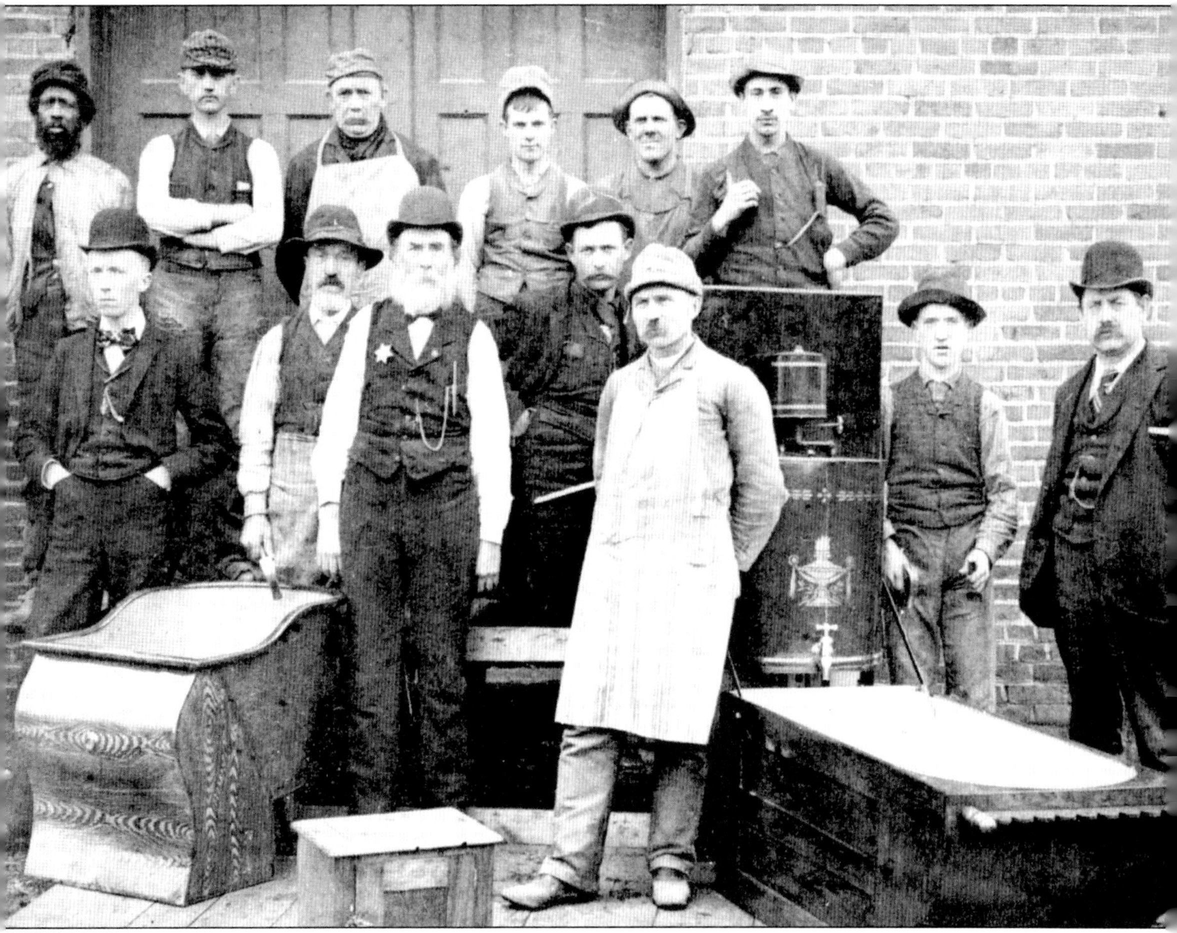

From the middle part of the 19th century until about 1920, bathrooms did not exist in the average American home. The Marshall Folding Bathtub Company had a solution to counteract the annual "whether you needed it or not" bath. It manufactured several answers to the problem. From the large fold-down unit on the right to the tiny sitz bath on the left, it had a bathtub that would fit in any room of the house. For those without the gas hot water tank, the dining room was usually the most popular room in the house for the weekly Saturday night bath, of course with only a small amount of hot water the entire family had to share it. Father got the first bath, mother came second. Then for the children, it was in the order of birth. By the sixth child's turn, the water was often dirtier than the child! This company today makes frozen food counters for grocery stores in Marietta, Georgia.

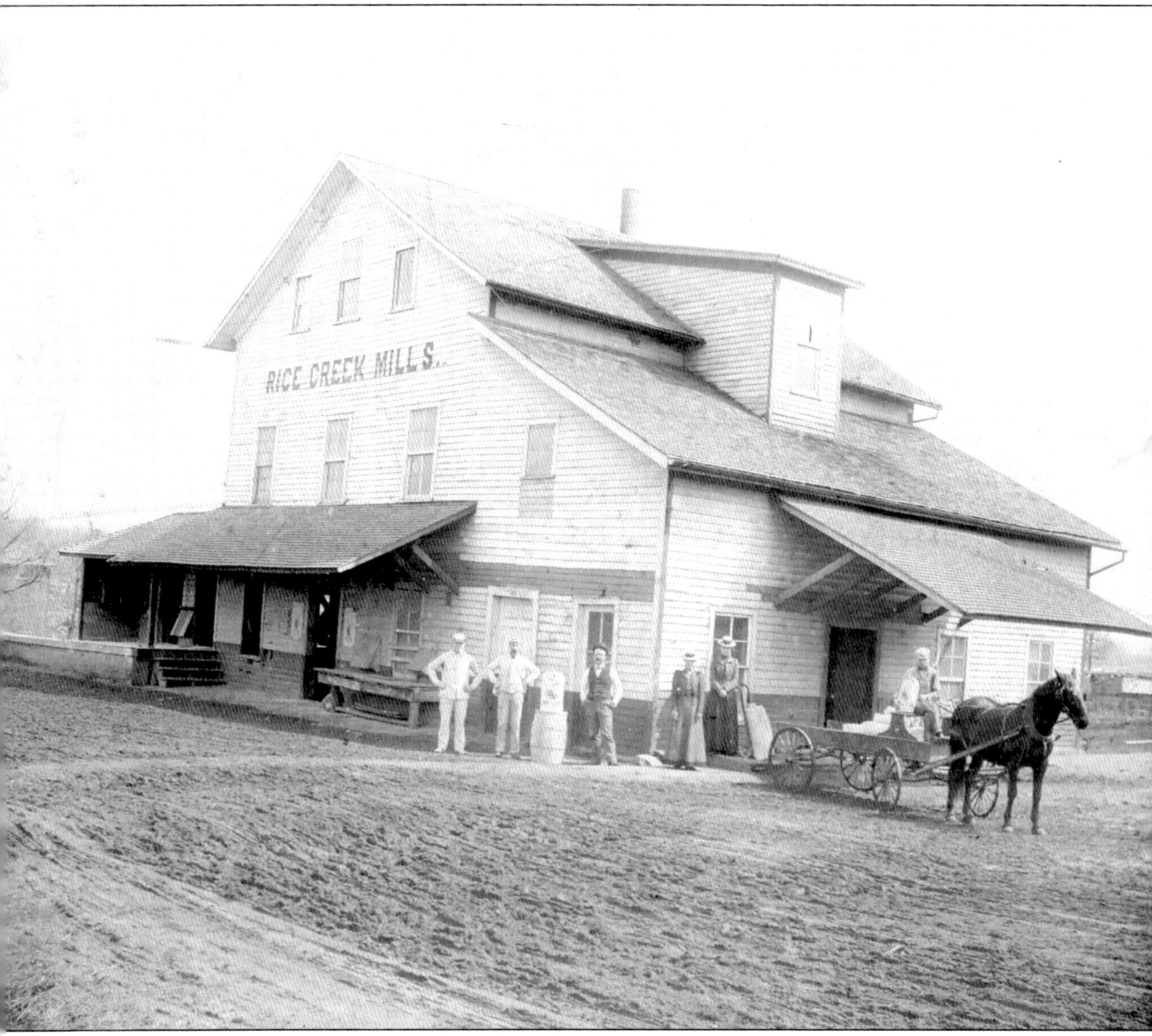

Milling was one of the first industries in Marshall and continued until the 1950s. This flour mill was one of 10 or more located on Rice Creek. After they were all demolished, Marshall's major city park was developed on the site by two couples, the Rotary Club, and 4-H.

Nine

CELEBRATE THE CENTENNIAL

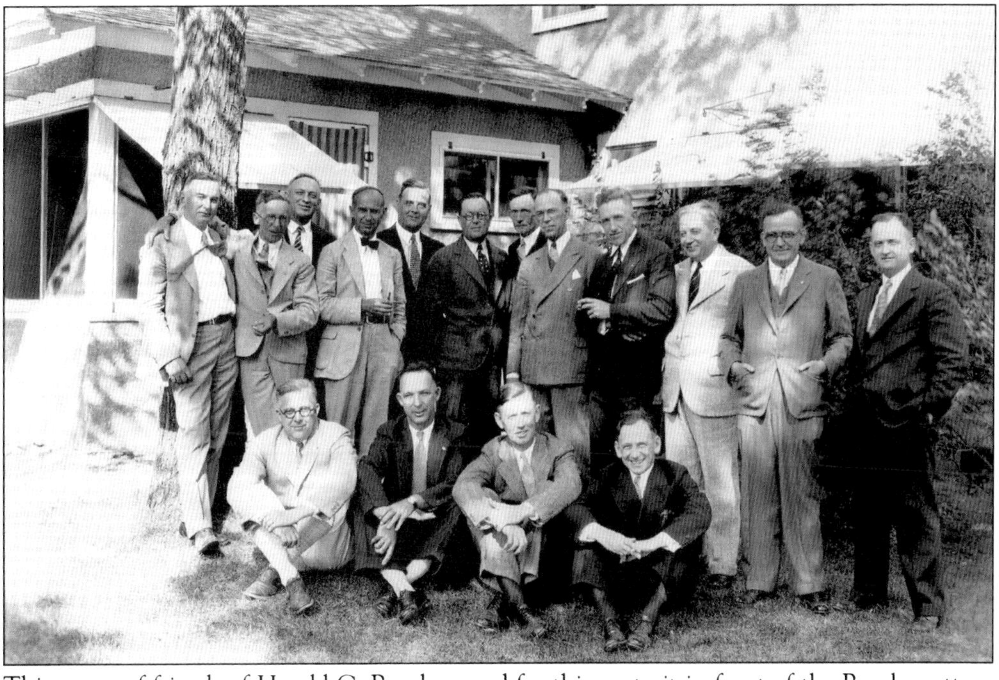

This group of friends of Harold C. Brooks posed for this portrait in front of the Brooks cottage at Lyon Lake in July 1930. From left to right are (first row) Richard Weyler, Evanston, Illinois; Allan Seymour, Ann Arbor; Harold M. Davis, Evanston, Illinois; and Harold C. Brooks, Marshall; (second row) Joseph C. Duell, Marshall; Charles W. Dobbins, Phoenix, Arizona.; Frank W. Moses, Marshall; Clyde C. Cortright, Marshall; Glenn E. Grant, Marshall; Willard Wright, San Francisco; A. Tracey Vary, Whittemore; James S. Cox, Chicago; Robert D. McNames, Battle Creek; Murray C. Bentley, Marshall; Russell B. Merrill, Detroit; and Ord Rhodes, Detroit.

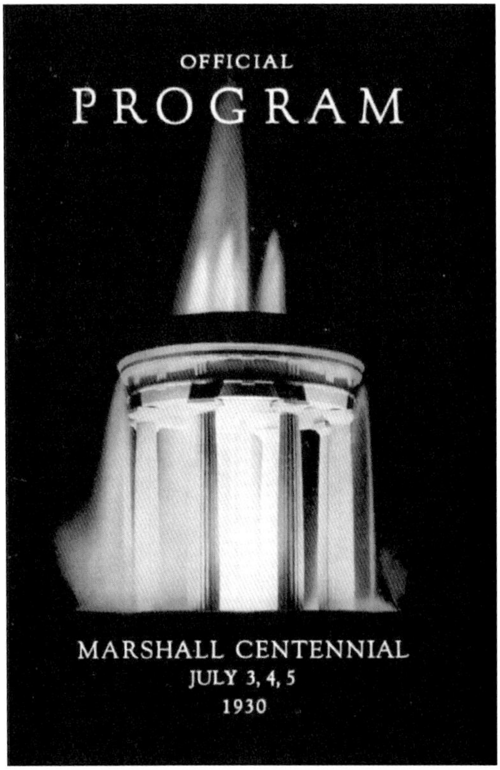

There was a three-day celebration put together by Mayor H. C. Brooks, and everyone in attendance was given a program to keep track of all the events. The fountain on the cover of the program was H. C. Brooks's gift to the city in honor of the birthday.

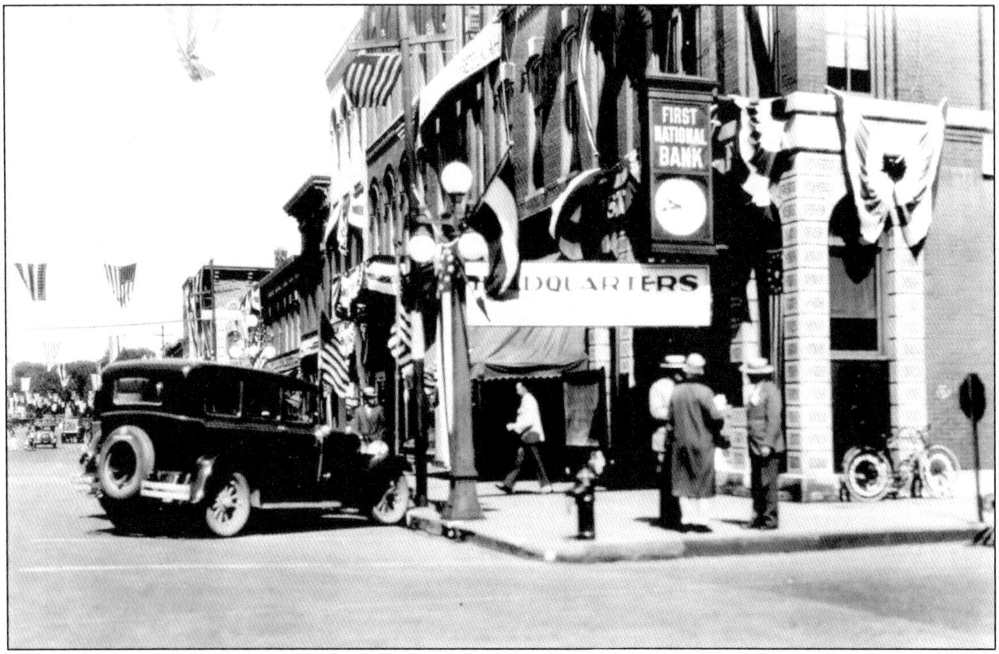

To coordinate all the events going on during the centennial celebration in July 1930, the First National Bank was designated the headquarters. Anyone could register there and pick up his or her program, proclamation, or information on what and where things were happening. There were also free rides to wherever in Marshall a homecomer wanted to visit.

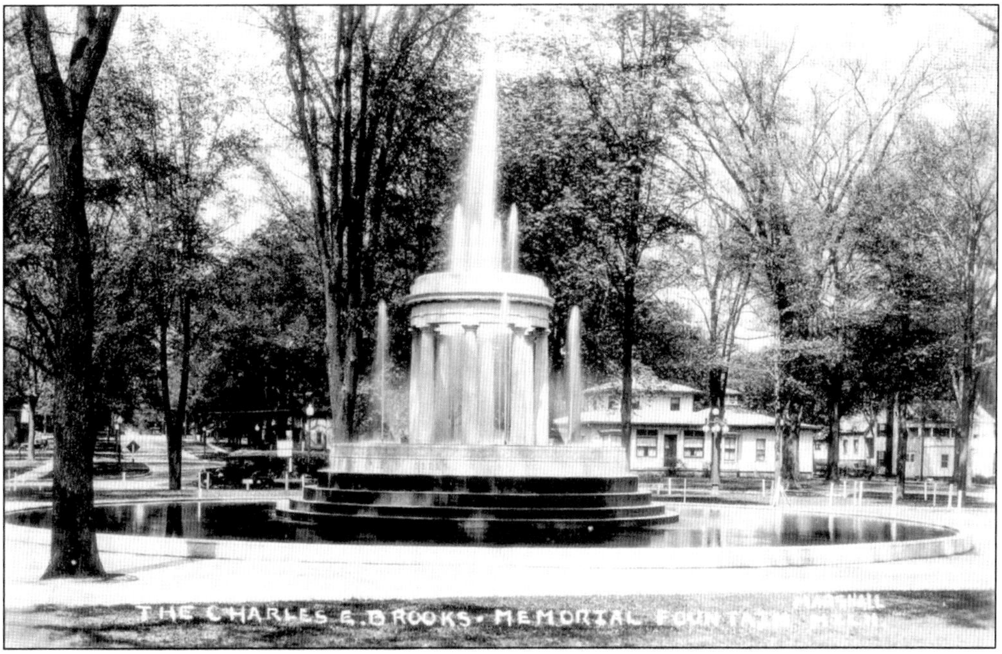

In celebration of Marshall's centennial in 1930, H. C. Brooks and his family gave the community of Marshall a new fountain in the middle of West End Park. It was named in honor of the mayor's father, Charles E. Brooks. It has been the focal point and logo for the city since that time. It is maintained by grants from several local foundations and the city coffers.

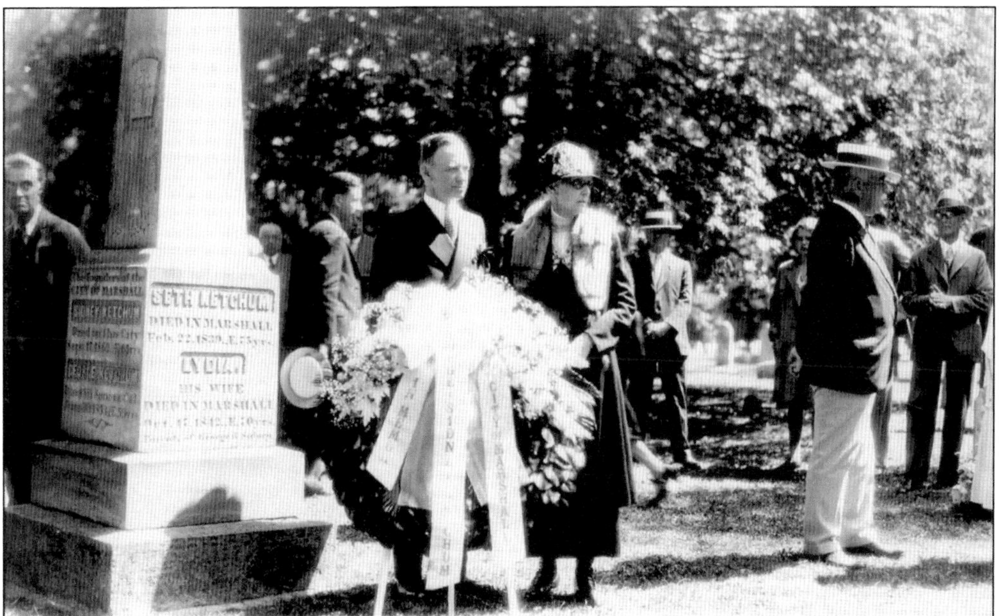

H. C. and Gladys Brooks place a large floral tribute at the marker for the Ketchum family at Oakridge Cemetery. This was part of the kickoff for Marshall's centennial celebration in July 1930. Sidney Ketchum was the founder of Marshall, and his brother George Ketchum was the first settler in April 1831.

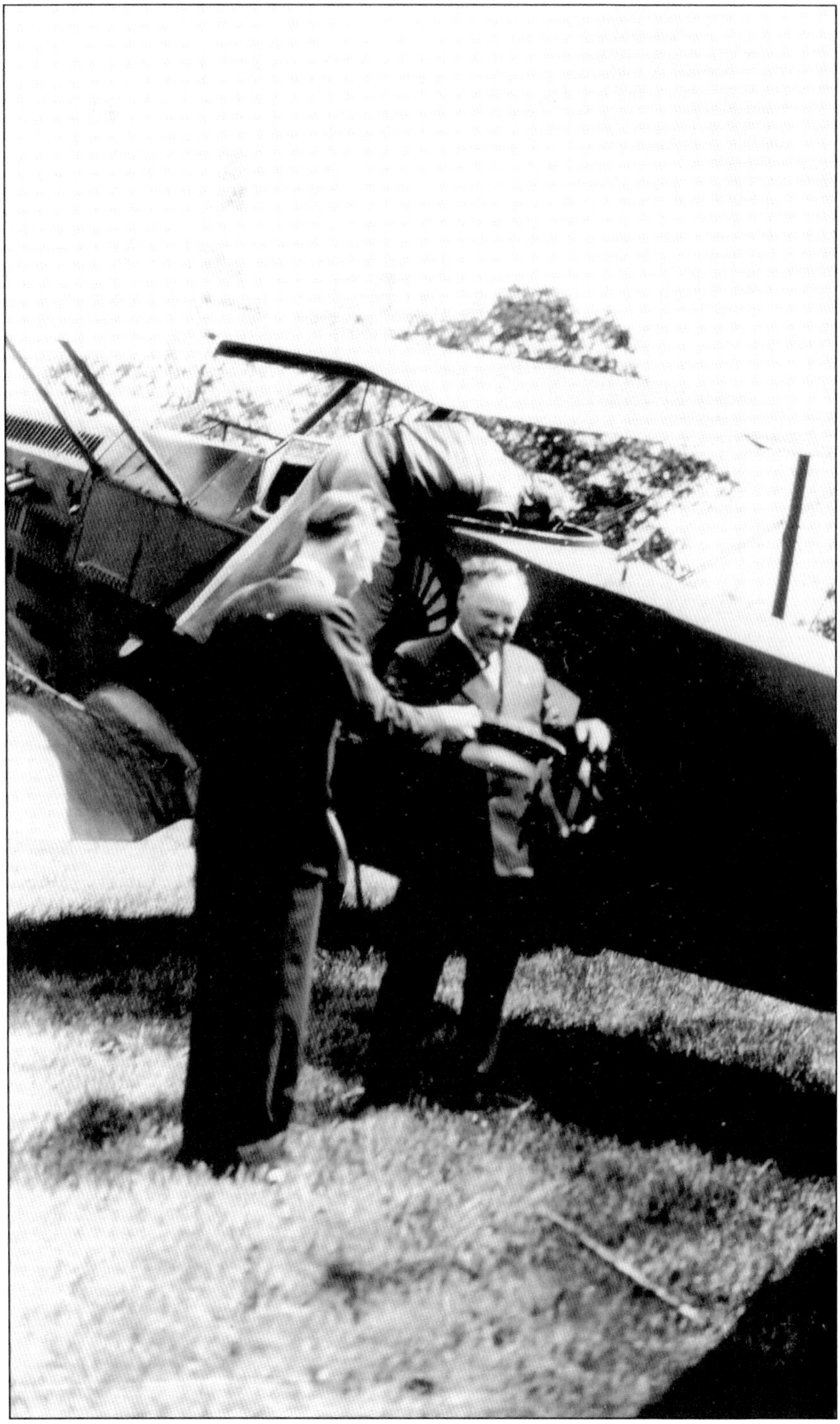

Gov. Fred Green arrived in Marshall for the centennial celebration in 1930 in this plane. Once he had removed his white coverall and leather flying helmet, Mayor H. C. Brooks presented him with his hat. From airplane to horse and buggy, they then took a carriage downtown to view the parade.

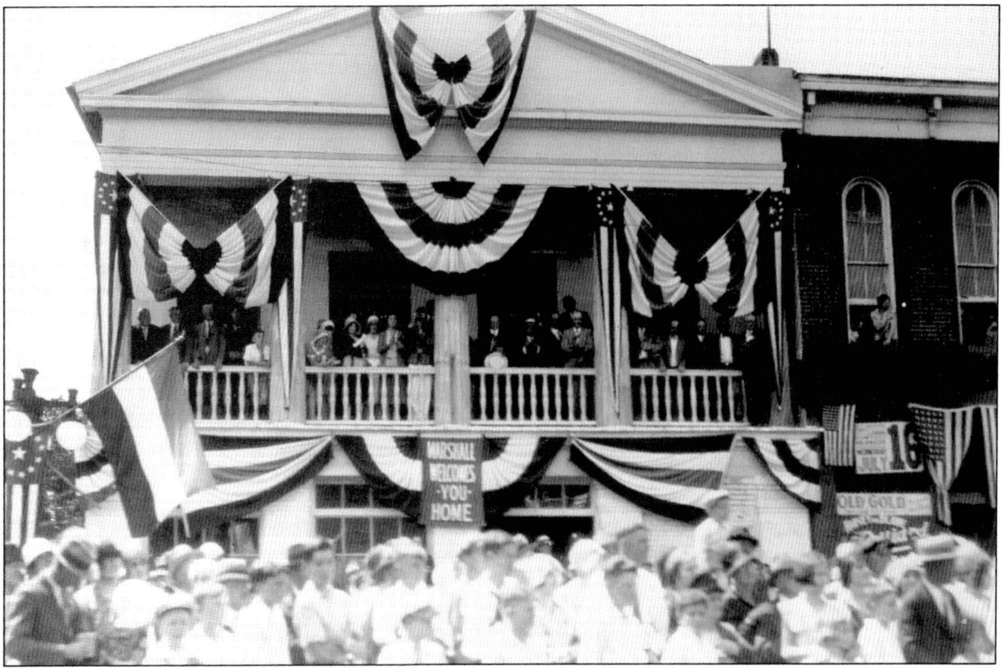

Mayor Brooks bought the old Mechanics Hall and had it restored on the exterior so that he and Governor Green could have a good reviewing stand for the centennial parade. The building is one of only three Greek Revivals in town featuring five columns. His son Buddy Brooks is standing next to the second column in his Culver Military Academy uniform. His assignment all weekend was to take movies of all the events.

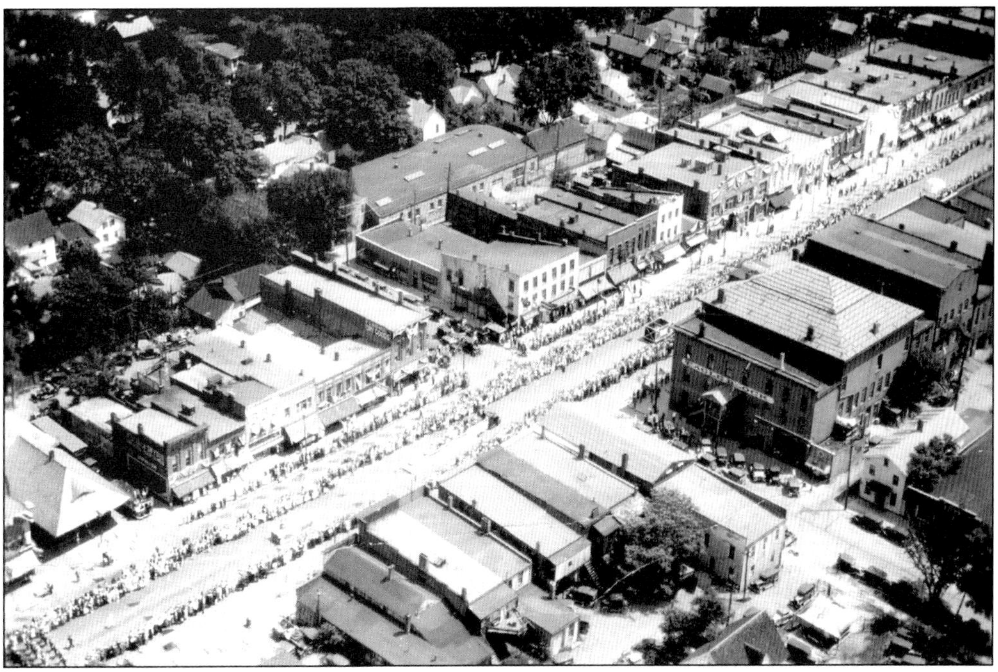

Thousands of people lined the streets to watch the big parade to celebrate the 100th birthday of the founding of Marshall. Many even stood in the middle of the avenue to get a better view.

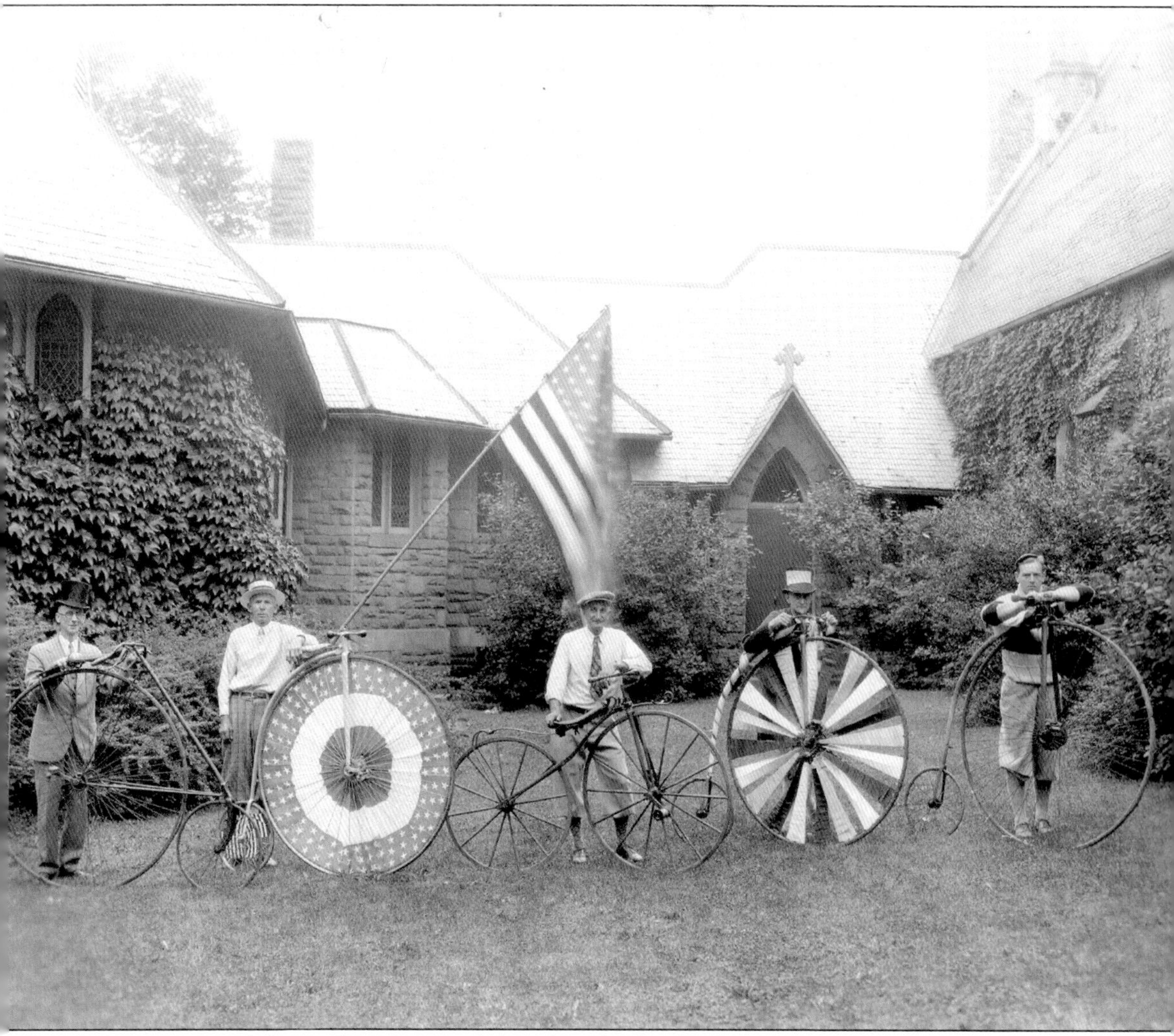

The Century Club members decorated their bicycles for the parade. Here they pose on the front lawn of Trinity Parish Hall. They include Ernest Vernor, Joseph Tusker, Bert Thompson, Lew Thompson, and Charlie Gauss.

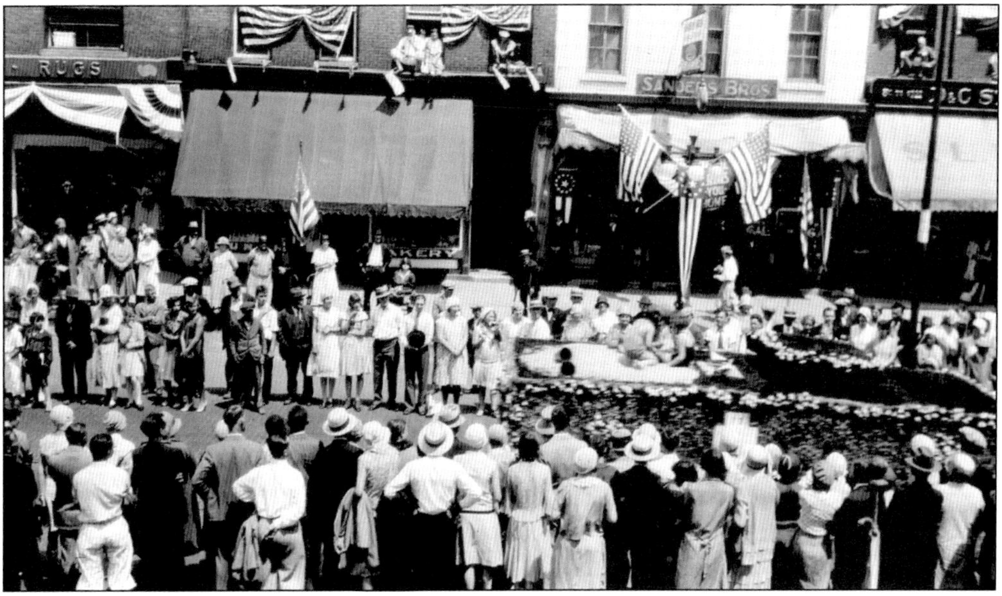

The parade at the time of the centennial in 1930 drew people from all over the country as Mayor H. C. Brooks invited everyone he could find who had ever lived in Marshall. This particular float was a favorite of his since one of the little girls playing in the sand is his younger daughter, Emily. In order to keep them digging in the sand rather than waving at the spectators, he buried a roll of loose pennies. They could each keep whatever they found.

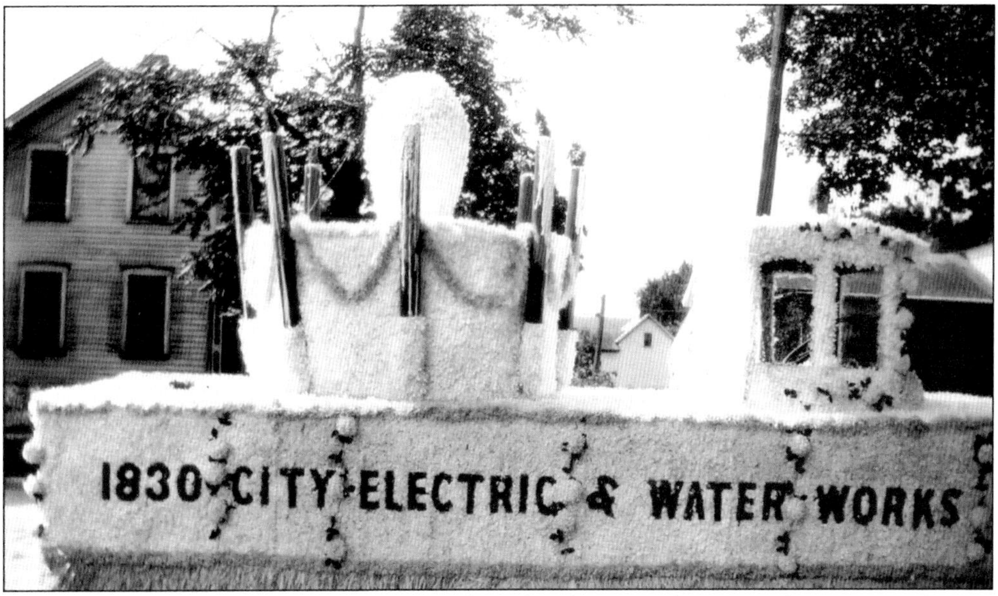

The city employees joined in with this float from the electric and water works. Just to make sure they had the brightest candle, they put an electric lightbulb on the cake.

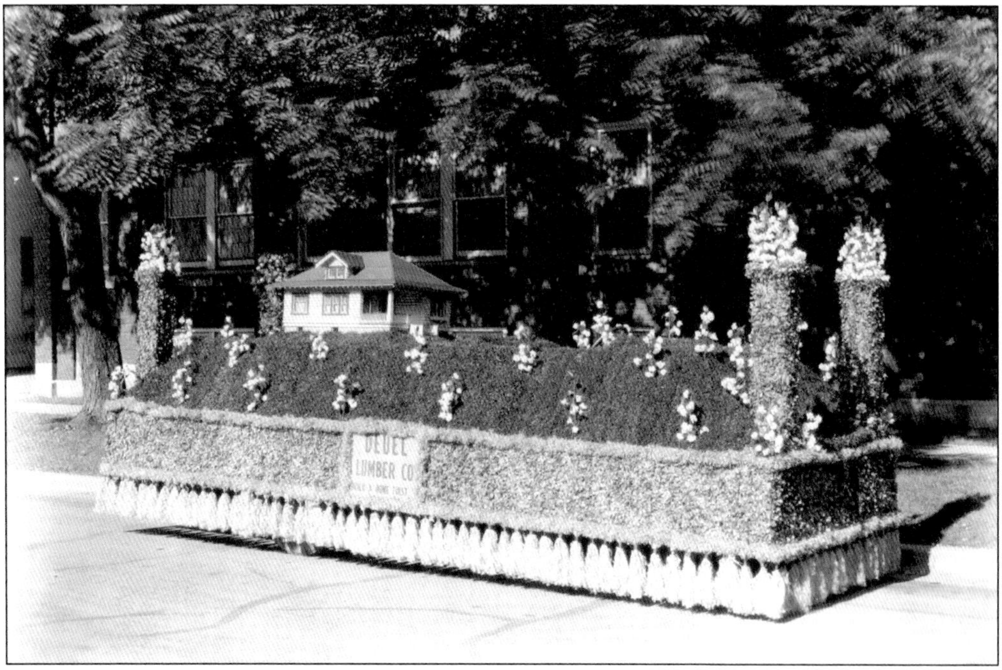

Deuel Lumber Company created this elaborate float to show what wonderful bungalows could be built using its products. The lumber company was located where the parking structure for Oaklawn Hospital now stands.

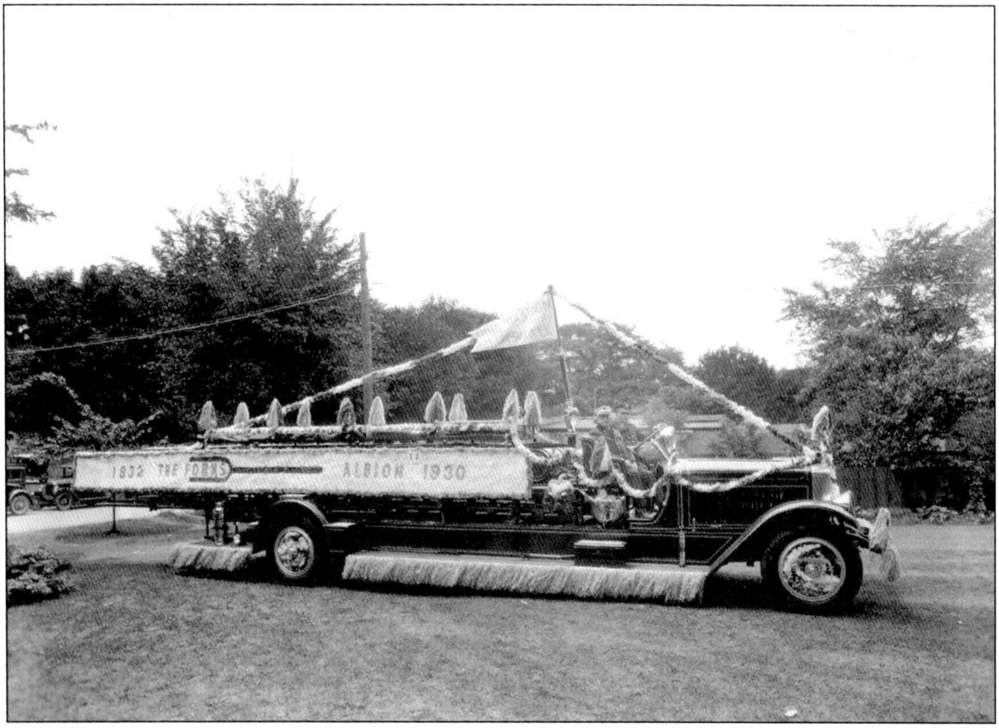

Neighboring city Albion joined the parade by sending its ladder truck festooned with birthday wishes. Marshall and Albion were great rivals on the athletic field in those days.

Ten

Trials and Triumphs

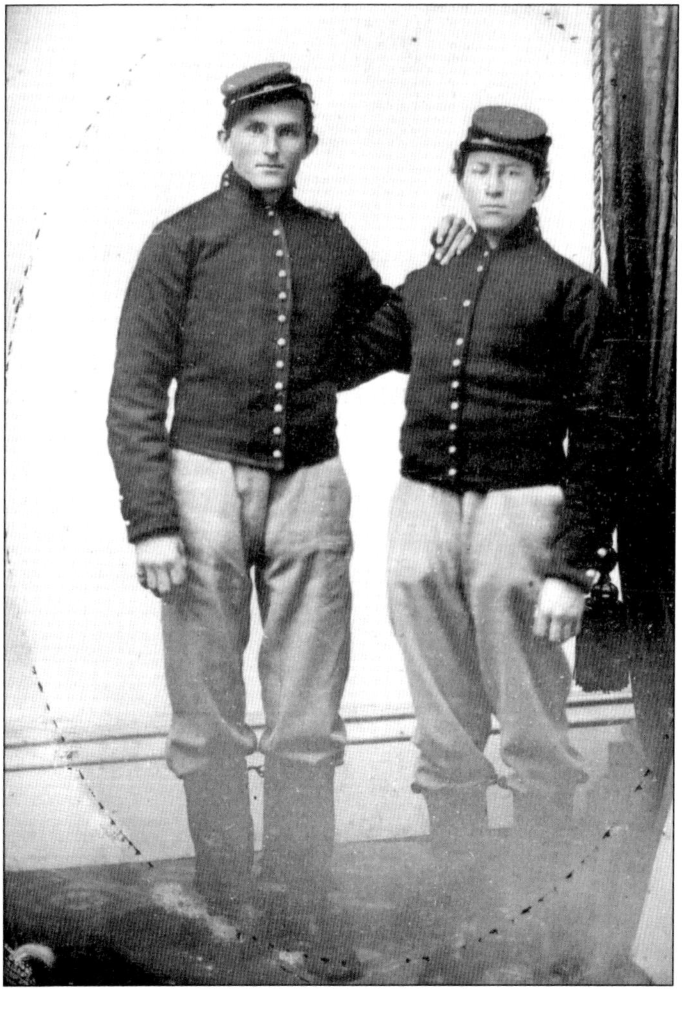

Marshall lost several of its citizens during the Civil War. One was Calvin Colegrove, a color sergeant who was killed in July 1861 at the first Battle of Bull Run. Colegrove was a member of the first volunteer company from Marshall, 1st Michigan Infantry Company I. These volunteers were greeted by Pres. Abraham Lincoln when they arrived in Washington and were declared the "first from the West."

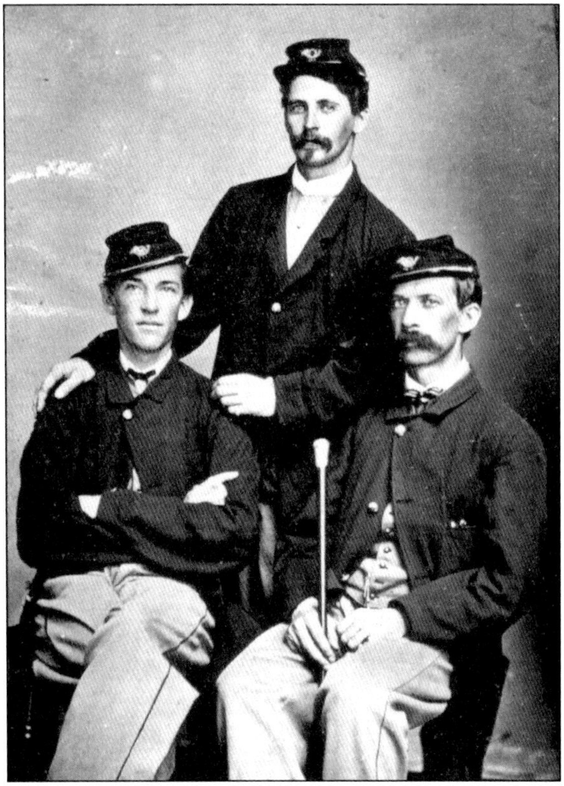

According to Grand Army of the Republic documents, George Woodruff, a West Point graduate, saw much action during the first two years of the war. He was ultimately killed on the third day of the Battle of Gettysburg. He commanded a U.S. artillery battery and was shot from his horse while leading his men in repulsing the famous charge of Confederate general George Pickett. His father, Judge George Woodruff, went to Gettysburg and brought his son's body home, where he is buried in Marshall's Oakridge Cemetery.

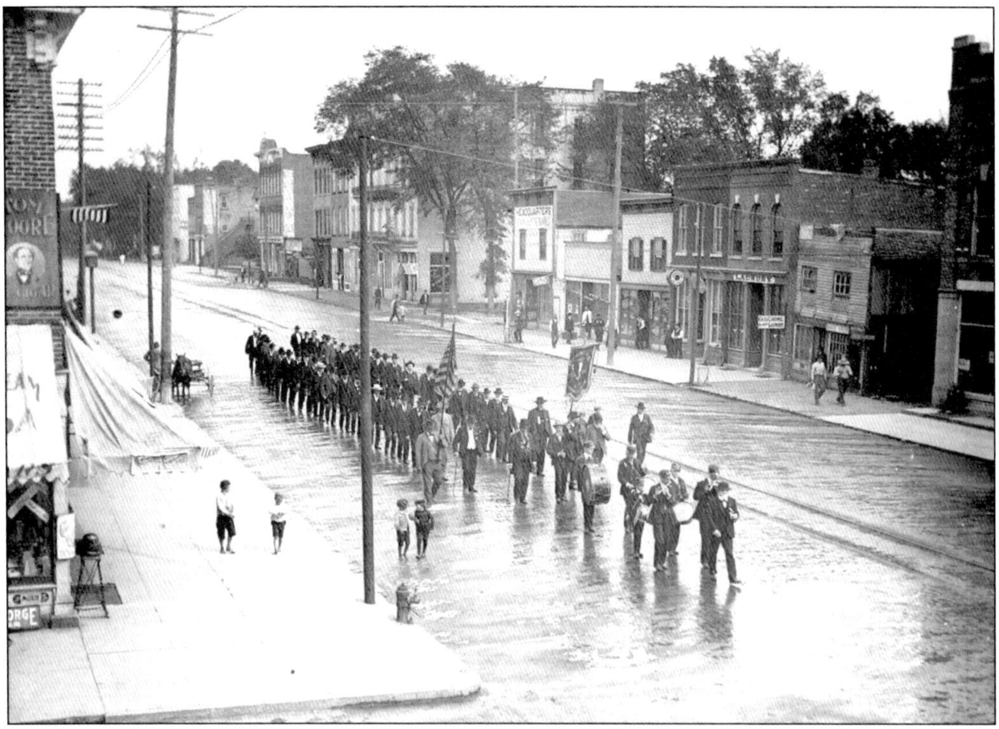

A drum and bugle corps marches down Michigan Avenue in Marshall.

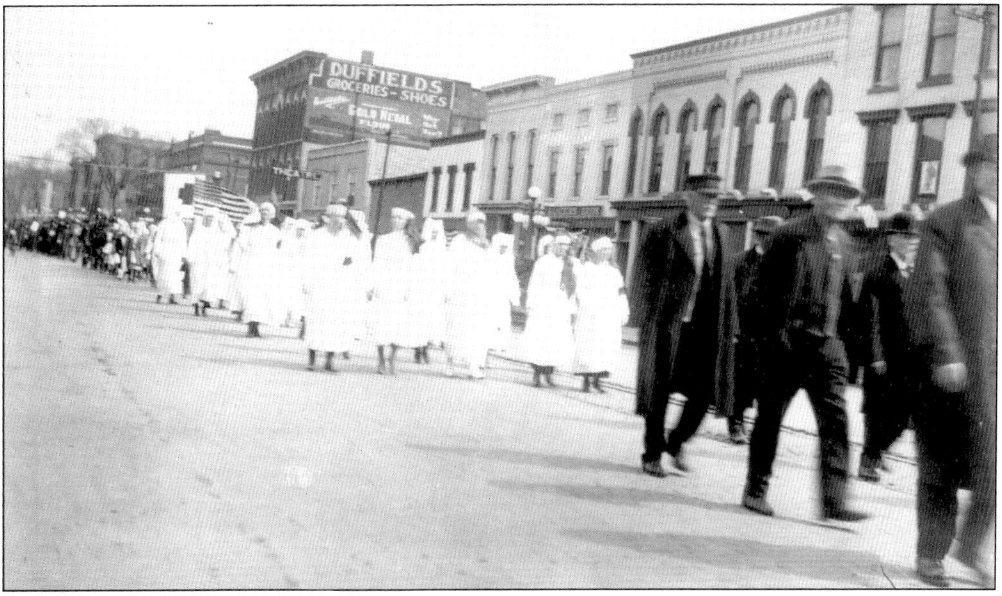

Dressing nurses are on parade in 1918.

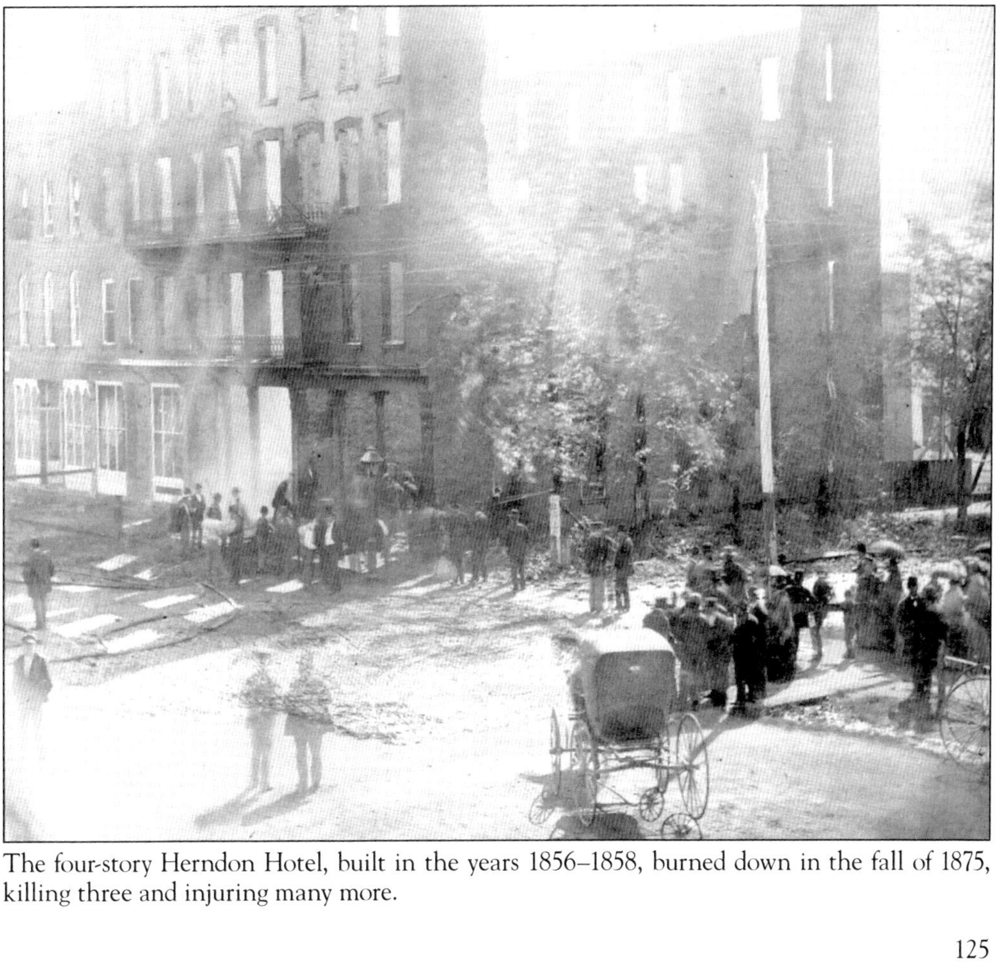

The four-story Herndon Hotel, built in the years 1856–1858, burned down in the fall of 1875, killing three and injuring many more.

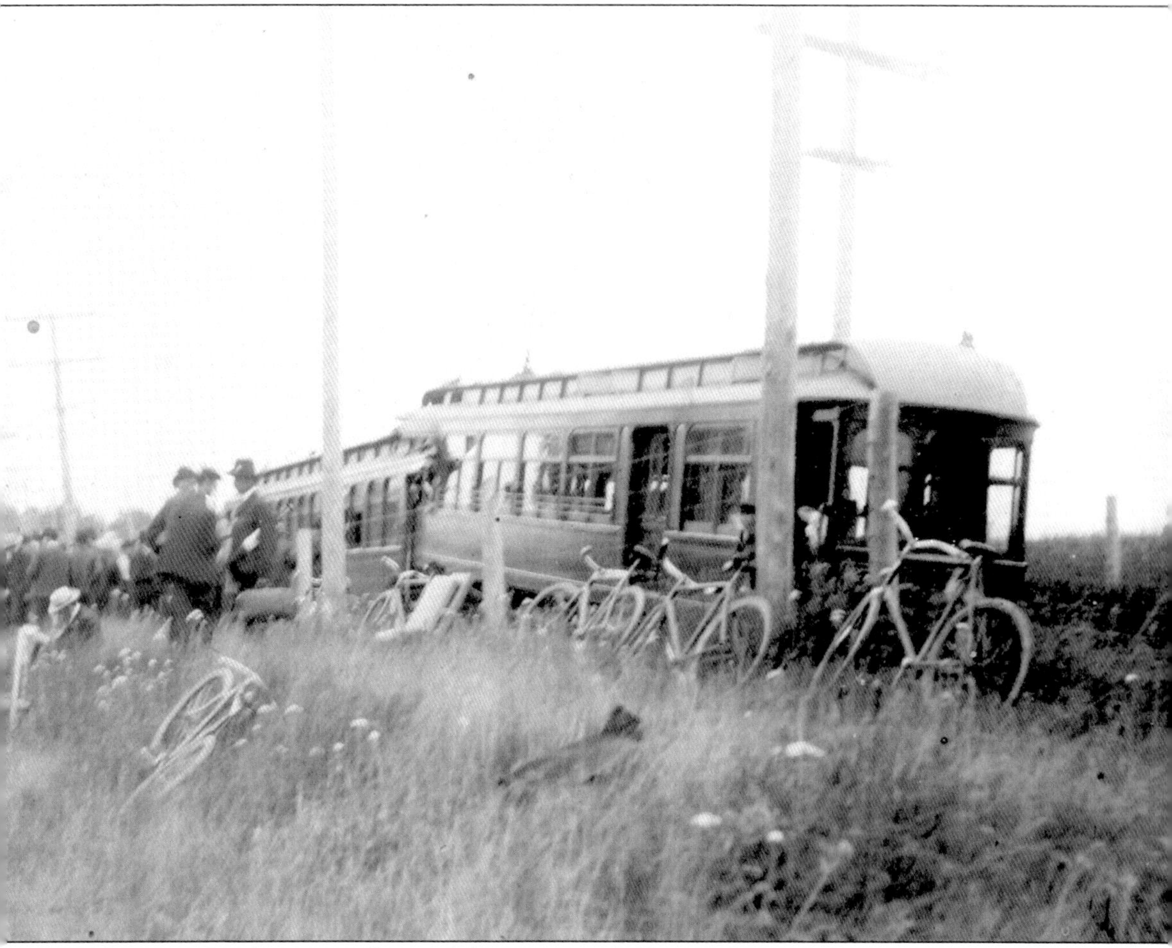

The interurban has come off its track between Marshall and Albion. Railroad accidents were not common, but with so many trains and interurbans running, accidents were bound to happen.

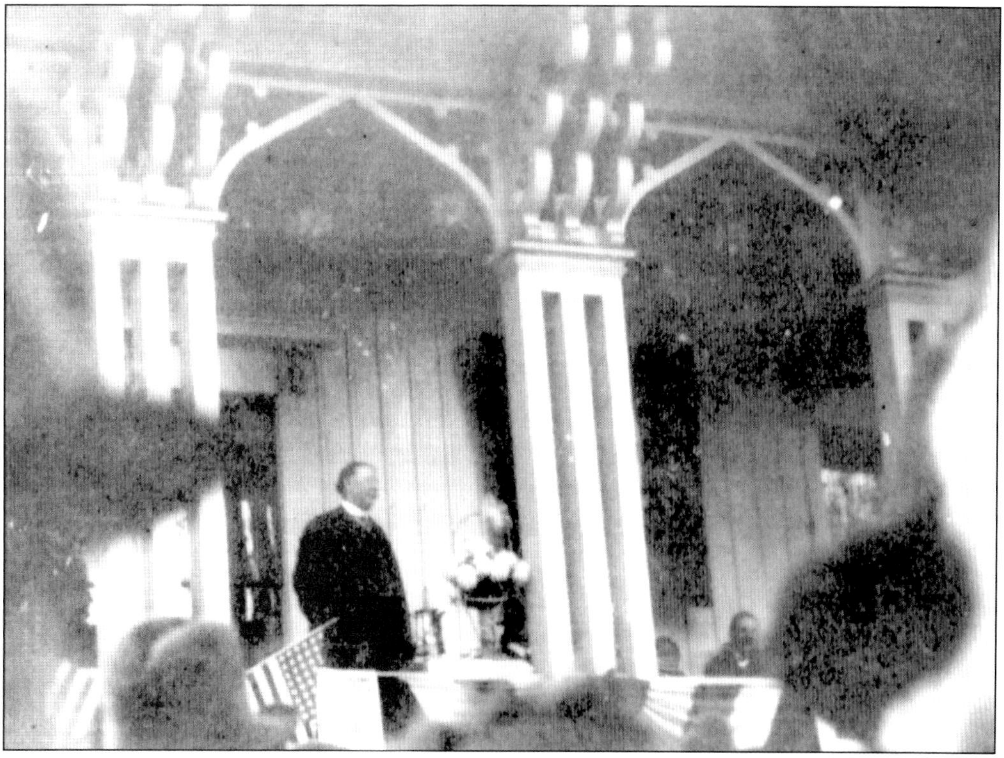

Marshall may be a small-sized city compared to many, but it was big and important enough for Pres. William H. Taft to schedule a campaign stop here. Here the president stands on the porch of the Honolulu House, one of the premier homes in Marshall.

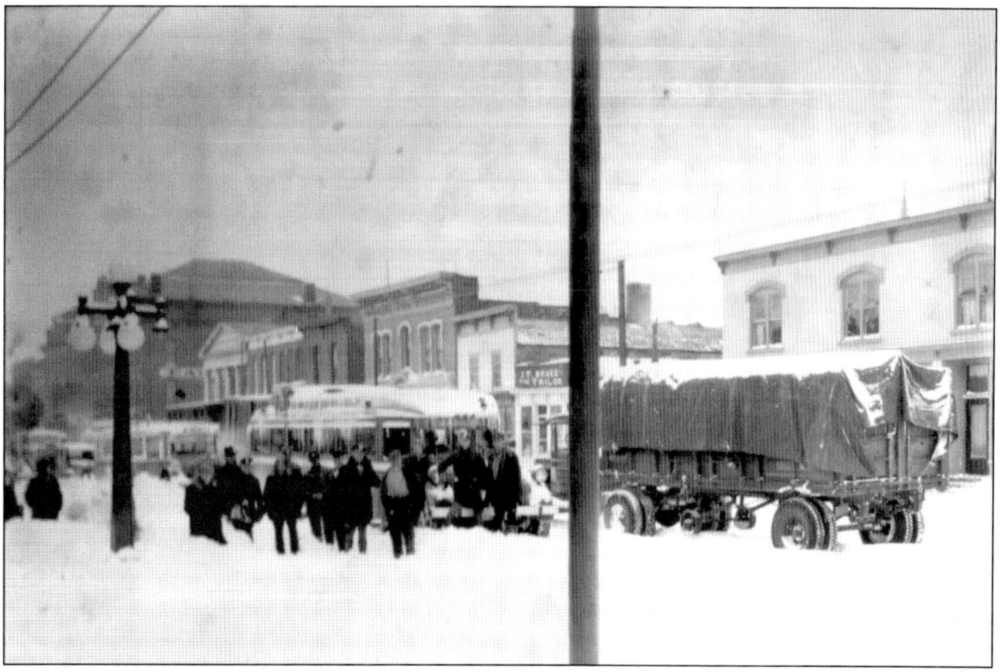

A heavy snow fell on Marshall on December 18, 1929, making the streets nearly impassable.